BROADBAND
BRINGING HOME THE BITS

Committee on Broadband Last Mile Technology

Computer Science and Telecommunications Board

Division on Engineering and Physical Sciences

National Research Council

NATIONAL ACADEMY PRESS
Washington, D.C.

NATIONAL ACADEMY PRESS 2101 Constitution Avenue, NW Washington, DC 20418

NOTICE: The project that is the subject of this report was approved by the Governing Board of the National Research Council, whose members are drawn from the councils of the National Academy of Sciences, the National Academy of Engineering, and the Institute of Medicine. The members of the committee responsible for the report were chosen for their special competences and with regard for appropriate balance.

The majority of the support for this project was provided by the Defense Advanced Research Projects Agency under contract No. N00174-99-C-0052 and the National Science Foundation under grant No. ANI-9908155. Additional support was provided by the Association for Computing Machinery's Special Interest Group on Data Communication, Hewlett-Packard, Intel Corporation, Interval Research Corporation, WorldCom, Sun Microsystems, Texas Instruments, and Qwest. Any opinions, findings, conclusions, or recommendations expressed in this material are those of the authors and do not necessarily reflect the views of the sponsors.

International Standard Book Number 0-309-08273-0

Additional copies of this report are available from:

National Academy Press
2101 Constitution Ave., N.W.
Box 285
Washington, DC 20418
800-624-6242
202-334-3313 (in the Washington metropolitan area)
http://www.nap.edu

THE NATIONAL ACADEMIES

National Academy of Sciences
National Academy of Engineering
Institute of Medicine
National Research Council

The **National Academy of Sciences** is a private, nonprofit, self-perpetuating society of distinguished scholars engaged in scientific and engineering research, dedicated to the furtherance of science and technology and to their use for the general welfare. Upon the authority of the charter granted to it by the Congress in 1863, the Academy has a mandate that requires it to advise the federal government on scientific and technical matters. Dr. Bruce M. Alberts is president of the National Academy of Sciences.

The **National Academy of Engineering** was established in 1964, under the charter of the National Academy of Sciences, as a parallel organization of outstanding engineers. It is autonomous in its administration and in the selection of its members, sharing with the National Academy of Sciences the responsibility for advising the federal government. The National Academy of Engineering also sponsors engineering programs aimed at meeting national needs, encourages education and research, and recognizes the superior achievements of engineers. Dr. Wm. A. Wulf is president of the National Academy of Engineering.

The **Institute of Medicine** was established in 1970 by the National Academy of Sciences to secure the services of eminent members of appropriate professions in the examination of policy matters pertaining to the health of the public. The Institute acts under the responsibility given to the National Academy of Sciences by its congressional charter to be an adviser to the federal government and, upon its own initiative, to identify issues of medical care, research, and education. Dr. Kenneth I. Shine is president of the Institute of Medicine.

The **National Research Council** was organized by the National Academy of Sciences in 1916 to associate the broad community of science and technology with the Academy's purposes of furthering knowledge and advising the federal government. Functioning in accordance with general policies determined by the Academy, the Council has become the principal operating agency of both the National Academy of Sciences and the National Academy of Engineering in providing services to the government, the public, and the scientific and engineering communities. The Council is administered jointly by both Academies and the Institute of Medicine. Dr. Bruce M. Alberts and Dr. Wm. A. Wulf are chairman and vice chairman, respectively, of the National Research Council.

Preface

Since its inception, the Computer Science and Telecommunications Board (CSTB) has examined how the nation's networked infrastructure has been evolving. At the close of the past decade, the popular appeal of the Internet was evident and growing, and with it the range and richness of the uses to which the Internet might be put. The vision of a popular Internet leads inevitably to thoughts about how people use it in their homes—and then to the arresting observation that most people get the best possible access to the Internet from outside their homes, if they can get it at all. That observation led CSTB to frame an assessment of broadband technologies in what the telecommunications industry has traditionally called the last mile—the link to homes (and small offices). This project complements prior CSTB studies of the core of the network—the backbone, the architecture, broad categories of applications, and specific categories of networking technology—in its concern to (literally) bring networking home.

The key questions about broadband technology in the last mile are deceptively simple. First, what is feasible, technically and economically? But feasibility is a nuanced quality: it is in the eye of the beholder, and beholders differ considerably in terms of their assumptions and preferences. Those same conditions confound answering the second key question: how can public policy foster dissemination of broadband in the last mile? Many industries are involved in supplying broadband technology, and their existence and strategies are already shaped by public policy. And many outside those industries, trying to figure out what is going on, have their own views of what policy is or should be. Moreover, recent industry trends, from mergers to business failures, feed speculation of all kinds—except for an expectation that broadband deployment will accelerate. Thus, to have any claim to completeness, an assessment of broadband in the last mile must combine consideration of technology, economics, and law and policy.

Accordingly, CSTB convened a committee of 14 people with expertise in the following areas: the different kinds of technology that could be used in the last mile; the economics, law, and policy of the telecommunications and networked content industries; and trends in the home and local use of various kinds of networks and their applications.[1] The committee combined people with academic, other nonprofit, and commercial experience, and it embraced both supply- and demand-oriented perspectives. The committee met five times in plenary session and received extensive input through briefings, a workshop, and solicited white papers. In addition, it had two plenary conference calls and made extensive use of e-mail and a private Web site for electronic exchange and deliberation.

The committee thanks the many people who helped to make this report possible, although of course the responsibility for the final result is its own.

A number of individuals provided valuable information through briefings to committee meetings. Aubrey Bush and Rodger Ziemer of the National Science Foundation (NSF) presented the charge to the committee. Dale Hatfield, then chief of the Federal Communications Commission (FCC) Office of Engineering and Technology, and John Berresford, FCC antitrust attorney, presented the range of telecommunications policy concerns from a regulator's perspective. Jeffrey Chester, executive director, Center for Media Education; Eugene Kimmelman, co-director, Consumers Union; and Mark Cooper, director of research, Consumer Federation of America, discussed concerns emerging from consumer advocates. Andrew Sharpless, then senior vice president of interactive media at Discovery Communications, described the perspective of an online content provider; David Kettler, then executive director and vice president of science and technology with Bellsouth, and C. Lincoln ("Link") Hoewing, assistant vice president, Internet and Technology, Verizon, presented incumbent telephone company perspectives; William St. Arnaud, CANARIE, Inc., described the Canadian experience and the larger opportunities in local investment in deploying optical fiber; Milo Medin, chief technology officer and senior vice president of engineering, Excite@Home Network, discussed the cable industry's approach to Internet service and broad-

---

[1]David Butler, who had recently retired from AOL at the time the study started, resigned from the committee for personal reasons in 2000.

band deployment; Jorge Reina Schement, professor of telecommunications and co-director of the Institute for Information Policy, Pennsylvania State University, provided context for considering universal service issues by describing the big picture of communications and information consumption across different population segments; Ted Darcie, director, AT&T Labs Research, analyzed the merits of different broadband technologies and explained AT&T's thinking about its choices; Douglas Sicker, FCC Office of Engineering and Technology, discussed perspectives on DSL and HFC technologies; James Hannan, vice president of network technology, Sprint Broadband Wireless, discussed wireless broadband; James Stratigos, vice president and general manager of EchoStar Data Networks, discussed satellite broadband; Kevin Lu, executive director of the Integrated Access and Operations Department, Telcordia, discussed fiber in the last mile; George Abe, venture partner, Palomar Ventures, characterized venture capitalists' view of investment opportunities; Thomas G. Krattenmaker, senior counsel at Mintz Levin, outlined challenges in thinking about regulatory options; Glenn Woroch, a University of California at Berkeley economist, presented an economic model of asymmetric regulation of the broadband race; Andrew Cohill, director of the Virginia Tech Communications Network Services and director of the Blacksburg Electronic Village, outlined concepts for a comprehensive municipal fiber plan; Richard Esposto, director of market activation, Western Integrated Networks, discussed conditions and options confronting local government, drawing on his immediately previous work of many years with the Sacramento cable commission; Joseph Van Eaton, principal partner with Miller & Van Eaton, discussed local franchises and licensing; and Richard Civille, Washington director for the Center for Civic Networking, discussed economic development and aggregating demand for rural telecommunications. Some of these individuals and a number of other people provided white papers to the committee (these are available online at <http://www.cstb.org> and are listed in Appendix C).

This project owes its existence to the support of its sponsors, in this instance an unusually large and diverse group, reflecting combined public and private interest in the topic. The majority of funds came from government or nonprofit sources: the National Science Foundation, the Defense Advanced Research Projects Agency, and the Special Interest Group on Data Communication of the Association for Computing Machinery. Small contributions—from Hewlett-Packard, Intel Corporation, Interval Research Corporation, WorldCom, Sun Microsystems, Texas Instruments, and Qwest—were developed by members of the Computer Science and Telecommunications Board, who recognized that without those resources the project could not be undertaken. In view of the politics of broadband, it is important to note and emphasize that as is typical of CSTB projects, the sponsors enabled but did not influence the outcome of the project. From among these, the consistent encouragement of NSF's Aubrey Bush and members of CSTB are especially noted.

CSTB committees are often assembled with experts from very different backgrounds, and this committee was certainly no exception. It is to the credit of our distinguished members that they constantly derived strength from the diversity in their team and realized an end result characterized by a substantial, and in some ways unexpected, degree of consensus. My thanks to each and every member of the team for their diligence and commitment. On behalf of the team and myself, I extend special thanks to David Clark, who played a major role in launching this study and served as its "virtual co-chair," contributing to and inspiring the work of the committee on many occasions. The CSTB staff, by now well known for its standards of broad excellence, performed once again with supreme distinction. Thanks to D.C. Drake for facilitating our work in every way possible and to Marjory Blumenthal for relentlessly challenging the committee to be comprehensive as well as creative, and finally, many thanks to Jon Eisenberg for his role in anchoring the report of the committee and for representing its work with remarkable timeliness and sophistication.

Nikil Jayant, *Chair*
Committee on Broadband Last Mile Technology

Acknowledgment of Reviewers

This report has been reviewed in draft form by individuals chosen for their diverse perspectives and technical expertise, in accordance with procedures approved by the NRC's Report Review Committee. The purpose of this independent review is to provide candid and critical comments that will assist the institution in making its published report as sound as possible and to ensure that the report meets institutional standards for objectivity, evidence, and responsiveness to the study charge. The review comments and draft manuscript remain confidential to protect the integrity of the deliberative process. We wish to thank the following individuals for their review of this report:

Robert Broderson, University of California at Berkeley,
Eugene Cacciamani, Hughes Network Systems,
Vincent Chan, Massachusetts Institute of Technology,
Andrew Cohill, Blacksburg Electronic Village and Virginia
    Polytechnic Institute,
David Kettler, H.I.G. Capital,
Tom Krattenmaker, Mintz, Levin, Cohn, Ferris, Glovsky and Popeo,
    P.C.,
Milo Medin, Excite@Home,
Sharon L. Nelson, University of Washington Law School,
Andrew Odlyzko, University of Minnesota,
Paul W. Shumate, IEEE Lasers and Electro-Optics Society,
Marvin Sirbu, Carnegie Mellon University, and
David Waterman, Indiana University.

Although the reviewers listed above have provided many constructive comments and suggestions, they were not asked to endorse the conclusions or recommendations, nor did they see the final draft of the report before its release. The review of this report was overseen by Lewis Branscomb, Harvard University (emeritus). Appointed by the National Research Council, he was responsible for making certain that an independent examination of this report was carried out in accordance with institutional procedures and that all review comments were carefully considered. Responsibility for the final content of this report rests entirely with the authoring committee and the institution.

Contents

xiii

Abstract

This report examines the technologies, economics, policies, and strategies associated with the broadband challenge (the "first mile" or "last mile" high-speed connectivity problem, depending on one's perspective) and makes recommendations aimed at fostering broadband's deployment and use. Following roughly a decade of development and experimentation and a recent period of rapid growth, first-generation broadband services, using primarily cable modems and digital subscriber line (DSL), are available in many markets. This progress is offset by recent business failures and uncertainty about the pace of future investment—factors that in part reflect slow growth in subscriptions for broadband services. Today, dial-up connections over the public telephone network remain the dominant way homes and small businesses connect to the Internet or other online services. Broadband, though, not only provides higher-performance options for connecting to familiar Internet and other online services, but its capacity and "always-on" nature also enable new network-based activities. Together, these capabilities promise significant social and economic benefits. The Computer Science and Telecommunications Board initiated this study in an effort to understand the hows and whys of broadband deployment and use.

The Committee on Broadband Last Mile Technology found that broadband should be defined in a dynamic and multidimensional fashion, and it offers two complementary approaches to characterizing what constitutes broadband service: (1) local access link performance should not be the limiting factor in a user's capability for running today's applications, and (2) broadband services should provide sufficient perfor-

1

mance—and wide enough penetration of services reaching that performance level—to encourage the development of new applications. These definitions reflect the central "chicken-and-egg" conundrum: an application will not be made available unless a sufficient number of subscribers have broadband connections with performance high enough to support the application, yet service providers will not invest in higher-performance broadband until they know that there will be sufficient demand for the service. Residential broadband capabilities today, with speeds typically ranging from several hundred kilobits per second to several megabits per second downstream and several hundreds of kilobits per second upstream, support familiar applications such as Web browsing, e-mail, messaging, interactive games, and audio download and streaming. The next performance plateau, which is not widely available at present, provides downstream speeds of several tens of megabits per second, thus enabling new applications such as high-quality streaming video or rapid download of full-length audiovisual files. With the addition of comparable upstream speeds, computer-mediated multimedia communications —to enable more effective telecommuting and distance education, for example—become possible. Fiber-to-the-home (FTTH) would offer the highest performance—gigabit speeds both up- and downstream. Investment in FTTH has lagged other options because of costs and uncertainty about demand for its capabilities. Some investment currently is providing opportunities for experimenting with technology alternatives and applications and for learning about demand. At the same time, a variety of wireless options provide either cost-effective alternatives (especially for remote locations) to wireline or mobility and ubiquity that complement wireline technologies.

Development, deployment, and adoption will be an ongoing process that works through several mechanisms: incremental upgrades and reallocation of capacity in existing broadband infrastructure, improved end equipment that permits faster performance over the existing infrastructure, and installation of new infrastructure. These improvements may or may not require new technology, but all require investment premised on market demand and willingness to pay. Indeed, many factors—not simply technology—will shape the pace and distribution of broadband deployment.

While broadband is sometimes characterized in terms of a horse race between DSL and cable and between the incumbents that use these technologies, the committee believes that the long term will be technologically diverse, reflecting geographical and market variation, the maturity of and experience with different technologies, topography, and the condition of existing infrastructure. Because local conditions vary, broadband's availability will be quite uneven, especially in the earlier stages. The nature and number of competitors will vary considerably by geographical location: from areas able to attract no—or only one—incumbent terrestrial provider (likely an incumbent local exchange carrier or cable operator) to easier-to-serve, higher-demand areas likely to attract one or more facilities-based providers in addition to the incumbents. This variability and flux will be troublesome to industry, regulators, and policy makers alike, implying that provider strategy and government intervention will have to change over time as the market and services evolve.

The present policy framework for broadband, which revolves around the Telecommunications Act of 1996, is problematic and is unsuited in several respects to the new era of broadband services. Although it does not explicitly recommend revision of the act (or comment on contemporary legislative proposals), the committee anticipates such examination and is cognizant that implementation of some of its recommendations would require revisions to either legislation or implementing regulation. The committee's recommendations, outlined and condensed below (complete versions are presented in the Summary and Recommendations chapter of this report), are intended as principles to guide broadband policy over the next several years:

• *Prioritize widespread deployment and defer new regulation in the early stages.* Presupposing how broadband services and markets will evolve risks misjudgment regarding outcomes and strategies. Wider broadband availability (in the context of other recommended measures) will help stimulate new applications, which will help increase demand, which will in turn make deployment, upgrade, and new market entry more attractive. At the same time, government should enhance its monitoring of deployment, investment, use patterns, and market outcomes to provide a firmer foundation for any future action. The familiar goals of universal access to important capabilities and consumer satisfaction remain, but the knowledge of how best to achieve them in a broadband world must be developed. There is sufficient time to observe and analyze as deployment and use unfold and to defer measures that could result in a premature stall in investment.

• *Structure regulation to emphasize facilities-based competition and encourage new entrants.* The policy goal, simply put, should be to increase the extent of competition through facilities ownership (and voluntary business arrangements to open facilities) rather than through long-term reliance on mandated unbundling. It is reasonable to maintain existing rules for unbundling existing telephone copper plant facilities. But unbundling rules should be relaxed in exchange for investment in new facilities that can broaden service availability and/or increase performance—subject to appropriate mechanisms to address extensions of market power. Some locales will not see facilities-based competition, and competition in some areas will change; both situations present policy challenges. Where unbundling is warranted, particularly with respect to new facilities, logical layer unbundling—unbundling at a higher service-level of communication, as in cable open access—should be preferred in the long run to physical unbundling because it promises technical advantages and administrative ease.

• *Take active steps to promote deployment and facilities-based competition, including at the local level.* The degree of competition and prevalence of technology options will vary by region, state, and municipality. Federal rules should continue to bound the range of outcomes, but in many cases, local decision making based on local conditions and needs is appropriate. Various sorts of incentives and local arrangements, detailed in this report, can encourage broadband deployment. While a few communities have already undertaken broadband initiatives, the majority have not and could benefit from efforts to enhance local capacity. The committee recommends supporting planning grants for localities to explore options; providing cost-sharing for field trials, including local-government-sponsored initiatives; and establishing a national clearinghouse to raise awareness, provide technical assistance, and disseminate best practices for local and regional efforts to accelerate broadband deployment.

• *Support research and experimentation.* Government should support research and experimentation that would foster the emergence of new competitors; increase understanding of economic, social, and regulatory factors; and spur the development of new content and applications that would make broadband more compelling and useful and foster growth in demand and use. Many of the conditions evident today reflect current technologies, business models, and policy intervention—all of which are subject to change. Research is valuable for creating new options and lowering costs, and it should be pursued vigorously across both technical and nontechnical arenas.

Summary and Recommendations

INTRODUCTION

Broadband is a means to multiple, diverse ends encompassing family, work, and society generally. In addition to enabling entertainment and e-commerce applications, broadband can enrich the Internet's exploitation as a public space, making electronic government, education, and health care applications richer and more compelling and useful, and it can provide new modalities for communication, notably within communities or families. Broadband commands attention because it enables dramatically different patterns of use that offer the potential for significant changes in lifestyle and business.

This report from the Computer Science and Telecommunications Board's Committee on Broadband Last Mile Technology examines the technologies, policies, and strategies associated with broadband local access connectivity (often referred to as the "first mile" or "last mile" problem, depending on one's perspective) and makes recommendations aimed at fostering its deployment. The committee's findings and recommendations are confined to broadband in the United States and focus largely on broadband for residences (with some discussion of broadband for small businesses and broader connectivity issues for communities).

Broadband service to the home depends on high-speed data transmission across local access facilities—the communications links and related hardware that connect the premises and the rest of a telecommunications network, most notably between the home or small business and the set of interlinked data networks that make up the Internet. These facilities fall into two categories: (1) existing facilities built by an incumbent telephone or cable company for the purpose of delivering voice or cable TV service and (2) new facilities—such as fiber optic cable, wireless, or satellite—constructed specifically for the purpose of delivering broadband. Before broadband, dial-up connections over the public telephone network were the dominant way in which homes were connected to the Internet or other online services. The performance of these modem connections has reached a plateau defined by the bandwidth of telephone circuit switches (more than 50 kilobits per second [kbps] under optimal conditions, but possibly less depending on factors such as line, interior wiring, and modem quality), and further improvements have required new technology approaches.

At present, two access technologies that leverage existing infrastructure—digital subscriber line (DSL) and hybrid fiber coax (HFC; or cable modem)—are maturing, as evidenced by wide availability, industry standards, multiple product vendors, volume pricing, and deployment experience; others—such as terrestrial wireless and fiber-to-the-home (FTTH)—are being developed and deployed on a smaller scale. The range of technology options captures part of what makes broadband vexing—fiber promises maximum bandwidth; wireless offers pervasiveness, flexibility, and potentially faster deployment; and satellite offers nationwide coverage (albeit with some gaps and limited total capacity). Today, DSL and HFC are most prominent, shape consumer experience, and fuel much of the politics that surrounds broadband. Looking forward, as other technologies such as fiber and wireless surmount cost and other deployment barriers and become more pervasive in residential broadband, providers, consumers, and policy makers alike will face new issues.

The committee's work started in late 1999 and was completed in fall 2001, a period encompassing significant broadband deployment and both boom and bust in the telecommunications and Internet markets. Until recently, only universities and large businesses and organizations had high-speed Internet access, reflecting a favorable economic return on investment in providing service to these customers. In contrast, residences and small businesses (and smaller offices of larger organizations) have been less likely to attract investment. Also, many homes are relatively distant from neighboring homes or are connected today by hard-to-upgrade telecommunications infrastructure, and some are in remote locations—all factors that entail higher per-premises costs and inhibit deployment.

Following roughly a decade of development and experimentation, residential (and small business) broadband services have been available in selected markets for several years and more recently have become mass-market. Cable operators, incumbent local exchange carriers (ILECs), and competitive local exchange carriers offering data services (data CLECs) have been the largest players, complemented by overbuilders (using HFC, wireless, or fiber) and satellite-based providers. The past couple of years have been a period of dramatic growth in broadband deployment—by summer 2001, more than 8 percent of U.S. households were subscribers to broadband service (only a comparative handful had service in 1999). Mid-2001 data also indicate that broadband-capable cable systems reach roughly 60 million households and that a substantial fraction of telephone company central offices support DSL (DSL availability for individual customers is subject to line-to-line variability). At the same time, many communities, especially smaller or more remote ones, lack broadband today, and some households in communities with general availability cannot obtain service owing to particular conditions (e.g., telephone line condition or length, or residence in a multidwelling unit without broadband).

The study period has also been marked by deployment difficulties. There have been numerous reports of poor customer service in terms of both installation delays and poor operational reliability, with charges and countercharges as to whether the data CLECs or incumbents were responsible for reported difficulties and delays in establishing DSL service. The 2001 wave of CLEC bankruptcies and shutdowns called into question the unbundling strategy contemplated in the Telecommunications Act of 1996.

If the committee had completed its work in mid-2000, it might well have done so with a rosier assessment of prospects for investment, the strength of broadband overbuilders and competitive local exchange carriers, and so forth. In formulating its recommendations, the committee was mindful of how much the situation had changed just during the course of its work and of how these changes underscore the perils of basing policy on short-term trends (either positive or negative).

Broadband deployment has been the subject of scrutiny by legislators, regulators, communities, the computing industry, and the public at large, and a number of potential barriers have been noted by these groups. Political attention has escalated along with that devoted to the Internet; like the Internet, broadband is linked to social and economic benefits. With sustained improvements in the Internet's core and in network connectivity within many businesses and other organizations, the last mile to residences and small enterprises has come to be viewed by some as a critical bottleneck. Key questions include these:

- What is broadband?
- Why do people need it?
- How much demand is there for broadband?

- How important and urgent is deployment of broadband?
- What is the likely shape of broadband deployment in the coming years?
- Is the pace of deployment reasonable and adequate, or are there failures that necessitate intervention?
- How will broadband deployment be paid for?
- How might the present policy regime for broadband be made more effective?

The multifaceted and dynamic future anticipated by the committee in the findings and recommendations below will be troublesome to regulators and policy makers. This future implies that different forms of intervention will be required in different geographical regions; that intervention should change over time as players enter and leave the market and as the working definition of broadband changes (which could change the number of real options); and that problems will arise, given the typical slow pace of the policy-making process. Finally, the ebb and flow of competition will inevitably lead to claims and recriminations of predatory pricing, obstructionist incumbents, partial regulation, and so on. The remainder of this summary presents the committee's key findings and recommendations with respect to these vexing questions.

While implementing some of the committee's recommendations would require changes to the Telecommunications Act of 1996, many would not. Viewing the act's provisions as only one of a number of factors shaping broadband deployment, the committee believes that revision of the act or associated regulation is not critical at present, but that changes in light of the realities of broadband will become increasingly important over time. At the same time, the committee has not shied away from making recommendations simply because they would be inconsistent with the provisions of the present act. Further, the committee anticipates that in view of the public spotlight enjoyed by broadband, there will be multiple efforts to change the act itself as well as to undertake more evolutionary changes within the act's framework. Rather than comment on the merits of any particular pending legislation (the committee is explicitly not doing this), the committee offers its recommendations as guidelines, as broadband policy evolves over the next several years.

FINDINGS

Finding 1. Broadband Is a Convergent Platform Capable of Supporting a Multitude of Applications and Services.

Although the term "broadband" can be used to refer to other services, such as digital television, that are not necessarily carried using Internet technology, the main focus of this report—and the issue of most interest to service providers, consumers, and policy makers alike—is broadband Internet connectivity. Although broadband is often associated with particular facilities or transmission technologies used for its implementation, it is a more general concept. With convergence, everything—video, audio, text, and so forth—has become a digital stream that can be transported across the Internet. Taken together with the Internet's layered design, this phenomenon makes broadband Internet a platform that is capable of supporting many different types of applications—the familiar e-mail, World Wide Web, games, audio, and video; new applications not yet in widespread use; and applications yet to be invented. The Internet's design also permits broadband Internet to be run over many different types of communications links—DSL, HFC, fiber, wireless, and so forth. At present, however, such services as television and telephony are different products employing distinct facilities.

The convergent nature of broadband will permit, if not foster, industry convergence and consolidation across traditional industry lines—cable television and telephone service are viewed today as separate markets, but the distinction will make less sense over time. Convergence is a potential enabler of competition: with multiple broadband providers that compete in terms of performance and services, users can switch providers to find the most attractive combination of price and performance. A stove-piped policy environment—in which different rules apply to broadband services depending on whether they are provided using cable, public telephone network, wireless, or other technologies—will come under increasing pressure. Technology trends suggest another mismatch between present policy and the nature of broadband services. To obtain greater performance, access networks will likely converge on similar architectures in which fiber reaches close to premises, and high-speed coax, upgraded DSL, or wireless links connect to the premises themselves. Another option is for fiber to be run all the way to the premises. In either case, treating different "flavors" of broadband under disparate regulatory regimes becomes more problematic.

While the similarities are more important than the differences, there is a complicating factor: the capabilities of broadband services based on different access technologies will vary somewhat—e-mail is possible over almost any sort of link (though the experience will be better over a faster link), while high-quality video streaming demands a high minimum speed. The higher ultimate capacity and lower cost associated with providing high downstream capacity mean that the cable operators using HFC would have an easier time entering the telephone market than ILECs would have delivering high-quality video over present-generation DSL, and the latency inherent in geosynchronous satellite services makes them less suitable for telephony, videoconferencing, or games that require low transmission delays. More generally, access technologies have cost and performance trade-offs that vary across different deployment scenarios.

Finding 2. Broadband Should Be Defined in a Dynamic and Multidimensional Fashion.

Policy makers and others have struggled to come up with reasonable definitions of broadband (versus narrowband), and many groups have an interest in such definitions. Broadband definitions are important for monitoring progress in deployment at the national, state, or local level. Definitions are also an important component of specific policies, such as eligibility for tax credits or compliance of providers with build-out mandates.

Broadband development, deployment, and adoption should be viewed as an ongoing process that works through several mechanisms: incremental upgrades in the broadband infrastructure, reallocation of existing capacity to broadband, improved end equipment that permits faster performance over the existing infrastructure, and installation of new infrastructure. Today's first-generation broadband technology is not the end point in terms of performance—what is considered broadband today will not be viewed as broadband in the future, much as 300-baud modems appear inadequate compared with today's 56-kbps modems. Upgrades may or may not require the development of new technologies, but all require investment premised on market demand and willingness to pay. Much like dial-up, which went through a succession of upgrades until it reached the limits imposed by the capacity of telephone switches, broadband has launched a new cycle of incremental upgrades and opportunities for yet more new infrastructure deployment. Unlike dial-up, for which the carrier and the Internet service provider (ISP) were distinct and upgrades required only new modems at each end, broadband requires more extensive upgrades to facilities and terminal equipment.

An examination of local access technologies on the horizon, other computing and communications capabilities, and potential applications makes apparent several quantitative performance and application clusters. Today's residential broadband capabilities, which are typified by several hundred kilobits per second to several megabits per second down-stream and several hundreds of kilobits per second upstream, support such applications as Web browsing, e-mail, messaging, games, and audio download and streaming. At downstream speeds of several tens of mega-bits per second, new applications are enabled, including streaming of high-quality video, download of full-length (70- to 90-minute) audiovi-sual files in tens of minutes rather than hours, and rapid download of other large data files. Reaching this plateau would enable true television–personal computing convergence. With comparable upstream speeds, computer-mediated multimedia communications become possible, in-cluding distance education, telecommuting, and so forth. With FTTH, a new performance plateau with gigabit speeds both up- and downstream would be reached; what applications would take full advantage of this capacity remains to be seen.

This interplay between technology capabilities and application re-quirements is captured in a more general fashion by the two complemen-tary approaches to defining broadband presented below.

- *Broadband Definition 1. Local access link performance should not be the limiting factor in a user's capability for running today's applications.*

For example, today's typical Web browsing is not significantly im-proved by speeds in excess of 1 megabit per second (Mbps) because of speed-of-light limits on round-trip travel time across the Internet. In other words, upgrading a user's 1-Mbps link with one 10 times faster would not speed up the transfer of a typical Web page. To take another example: for streaming media, increasing local access performance significantly above the rate at which such content is typically streamed today would not improve the user's experience (though, per definition 2, increased capa-bilities would help spur higher-quality streams).

- *Broadband Definition 2. Broadband services should provide sufficient performance—and wide enough penetration of services reaching that performance level—to encourage the development of new applications.*

Capacity improvement and application innovation are tightly coupled in a "chicken-and-egg" fashion: an application will not be made available until a critical fraction of subscribers receives a high enough level of per-formance to support it, yet service providers will not deploy higher-per-formance broadband until there is sufficient demand for it. The perfor-mance of a broadband service should, therefore, be good enough and improve sufficiently to facilitate this cycle and not impede it. Definition 2 also implies a broadband penetration threshold effect: enough users must have a higher-performance service to create a sufficiently large market to attract application developers.

Two different notions underlie these definitions. Under definition 1, the presumption is that existing applications and capabilities of the rest of the network will be unleashed by improvements in the local access segment. The presumption of definition 2 is that application innovation will materialize if performance constraints are eased. The implications of definition 2 are familiar today—current broadband service offerings do not provide high enough performance to support applications such as high-quality video, while investment in higher performance awaits demonstration of demand and willingness to pay. The parties demanding improved performance include, along with segments of the public, applications developers and content suppliers that see the potential for new markets that they might serve (but for the availability of more bandwidth) and policy makers who project potential social and economic benefits that would result from deployment of higher-performance service.

While bandwidth is the most significant performance parameter in terms of enabling new applications, others are also important. "Always on"—a characteristic of almost all broadband services today—is important to enabling certain types of applications. It changes the way in which people experience broadband as a service. Symmetry, which refers to the relative down- and upstream bandwidths, also has implications for the types of applications that are supported. Some applications, such as Web browsing, make modest demands on the upstream channel as they require receipt of much less data than they transmit, while others, such as videoconferencing, require more symmetric bandwidth. Delay affects the performance of time-sensitive applications, notably, applications such as telephony and online games that involve real-time interactions with people.

Finding 3. Demand for Broadband Is Evident.

In the United States, some form of broadband is reportedly now available to more than half of U.S. households, and subscription rates grew rapidly during the period from 1999 to 2001. Penetration has been much higher than the average in markets where broadband has been available for several years. For example, in Portland, Maine, an early test market for Time Warner Cable, about one-quarter of households are cable modem subscribers—a mass market that illustrates the appeal of broadband well beyond a handful of early adopters. Similarly, in the current worldwide leader, Korea, where favorable conditions have already made broadband available to much of the population, broadband subscription rates are reported to be even higher: more than one-quarter of households. In the United States, numerous anecdotal reports of frustration about delays in obtaining broadband service, reliability problems, and nonavailability all support a view of a rising tide of demand and use (as well as problems). These developments indicate that broadband access is valued by a broad base of Internet users, not just a small group of technology lovers, and that broadband is viewed as an important communications service. At present, it is difficult to forecast what the ultimate total "take-rate" will be, though the 1990s penetration of personal computers (PCs) and Internet service to roughly half of U.S. households suggests growth at least up to this level.

Notably, today's demand level has been based mainly on a limited set of applications (e-mail, Web browsing, file sharing, and limited audio and video streaming). Indeed, there is a significant gap between the capabilities of current broadband services and some of the cutting-edge applications that have been touted but are not generally available to the public. Continued growth in demand for higher-speed services can be foreseen based on applications being used or tested by early adopters in enterprise and campus networks, experimental initiatives in both industry and academia, and the possibilities afforded by increasingly cheap home networks and specialized consumer electronics. With new applications, wider penetration, and broadband's use as a convergent platform for multimedia content delivery, much wider demand and use can occur.

Finding 4. Deployment as a National and Local Imperative

Today, broadband is for the most part an adjunct to home PC use and a means of faster Web browsing, and narrowband alternatives provide some measure of access to commonly used content and services. Thus, one cannot say with confidence today that broadband access in the home is critical to being a functioning member of society. But in light of robust demand and the likelihood that with growing use, new content and applications will make use of broadband capabilities, it is reasonable to project that broadband will take on increasing socioeconomic importance in the future.

There are several principal arguments for taking steps to foster broadband deployment:

- *Spillover benefits.* Because broadband can support many different types of applications and services, its full potential is unlikely to be apparent from scrutiny of any one category. When one looks at a promising individual application today, such as telework, it is easy to see that what exists—in terms of capabilities, use, or benefits—falls short of what some have forecast. But what broadband promises, because of its capacity and general-purpose nature, is the chance to try multiple applications of different types and to provide various mixes that can be valuable to different users. The economic and social benefits in the aggregate will, therefore, exceed those of one application, giving rise to spillover benefits not readily captured by any one stakeholder. For example, broadband deployed for mass entertainment can also carry noncommercial content. To the extent that broadband providers themselves are not able to fully capture the benefits of investment in performance enhancements, a broader societal interest in promoting broadband performance improvements arises from these spillover benefits. The willingness of broadband providers to invest will be less than that implied by the broader societal interest arising from these spillover effects.

• *The link between performance and applications innovation and ties to other high-technology sectors.* If broadband is to support new, rich multimedia applications, the gap between computing and deployed last mile communications performance will have to be closed. In the short term, this would translate into upgrading from today's hundreds of kilobits per second to tens of megabits per second—which all of the present generation of wireline broadband technologies can support, with appropriate investment (shorter loop lengths in the case of DSL and smaller cluster sizes and/or more spectrum dedicated to broadband in the case of HFC), and which is well within the capabilities of FTTH. Although the performance of broadband services today nearly always exceeds that available through dial-up access, the first-generation systems frequently provide only modest improvements in speed over older technology, and sustained upgrades would be needed to satisfy both broadband definitions 1 and 2.

• *Per-passing costs of initial investment.* Some infrastructure costs must be borne regardless of how many customers in a given area actually subscribe to a service. Because of the major, even dominant, role of these per-passing costs for wireline infrastructure, investment becomes, in essence, a decision contingent on a finding of collective demand. For wireless, the penalty can be somewhat but not fully offset via a strategy whereby the cluster size served by a common feed is decreased as rates of subscription and demand increase. (A similar principle also applies to wireline technologies that permit such clustering, such as HFC, but with less impact on the per-passing costs than is the case for wireless.) Also, early adopters will not be able to obtain broadband service until a service provider decides to make an investment deemed capable of attracting a broad subscriber base. As a service provided over a network, broadband stands in marked contrast with computers, which individual consumers can purchase as the need arises, and which providers produce for a market not tied to a geographic area. Similarly, an individual can upgrade to a higher-performance computer to meet individual demand, whereas broadband services will tend to have capabilities aimed at the average user.

The committee took note of the fact that other countries, recognizing these arguments and the potential societal importance of broadband, have opted for more active strategies than those of present U.S. policy or those that the committee's recommendations below would contemplate, especially at the national level. These national strategies in other countries do not match the U.S. context, in terms of political system, the historical private sector role in telecommunications, geographic diversity and population dispersion, or the nature of the existing telecommunications infrastructure. That is not to say that the goals and means of these strategies are not appropriate in their own contexts.

Finding 5. Many Factors Pace Deployment.

There is a sense in some quarters that something is "broken" with respect to broadband rollout. There are several areas of frustration: concerns over an insufficient rate of penetration of some form of broadband; associated concerns that some areas will end up being left out; concerns that the process of upgrading broadband service could stall, leaving consumers with only the performance offered by first-generation technology; concerns about business failures leaving customers with no broadband alternative; and concerns that the quality of what is being deployed will be inadequate in terms of performance, reliability, or customer service. Given the realities of the situation, what is reasonable to expect with respect to deployment?

Finding 5.1. Broadband deployment will not occur overnight.

The rapid evolution of some aspects of the Internet can lead observers to think that if something does not happen within 18 months, it will not happen. But the phenomena associated with deployment cycles measured in months have generally been in the non-capital-intensive software arena (even here, real change may lag perception), in a sector unconstrained by regulatory uncertainty. In contrast, even with a conservative estimate of $1,000 as the average cost of wiring an individual residence, the total cost of building new broadband infrastructure—such as rewiring to provide FTTH to all of the roughly 100 million U.S. households—would be $100 billion. A major portion of this figure is in construction costs that are not amenable to dramatic cost reductions. Even for cable and DSL, where delivering broadband is a matter of upgrading existing infrastructure, economics constrain the pace of deployment. Some broadband deployment will be accomplished as part of the conventional replacement and upgrade cycles associated with telephone and cable systems, but providing broadband also requires additional investment in infrastructure upgrades and broadband-specific equipment. In either new builds or incremental improvements, an accelerated pace of deployment and installation will be associated with an economic opportunity cost.

The bottom line is that broadband deployment and upgrading are gated by a complex policy and economic context, not just—or even mainly —by technology. Furthermore, it is early in the diffusion process, and too soon to judge the final outcome. Thus, today's frustrations do not necessarily justify heavy-handed intervention.

Finding 5.2. The investment rate depends critically on the perspective and time horizon of the would-be investor.

For an owner of existing facilities—the incumbent local exchange carriers and cable multiple system operators—realistic investment is incremental, builds on the installed base, and must provide return on a relatively short timescale. An incremental strategy also reflects the view that there is not sufficient demand for the added bandwidth of all-fiber replacement to justify its greater capital costs compared with those for an upgrade of existing plant.

Once a provider has a broadband-capable system, that provider will spend on upgrades only enough to continue to attract subscribers and retain existing customers by providing a sufficiently valuable service. An incumbent will also naturally weigh the benefits of investment in new services against the costs of cannibalizing from existing ones. For example, an ILEC's incentive to invest in broadband upgrades may be diminished by the prospect that the new technology may be used to provide services that compete with the ILEC's existing voice and data services. Viewing an incumbent's incentives to invest in upgrades from the perspective of the two broadband definitions provided above, it may be hard for the incumbent to justify spending so that the local access link is not the performance bottleneck, or to be in front of the demand so as to stimulate new applications. Facilities-based competition, and associated pressures to attract and retain customers, could help propel performance upgrades.

Two types of nonincumbent investor have also entered the broadband market, tapping into venture capital that seeks significant returns— and generally seeks a faster investment pace. One is the competitive local exchange carrier (CLEC), which obtains access to incumbent local exchange carrier facilities (central office colocation space and the lines running from there to each subscriber) to provide broadband using DSL. The other is the overbuilder, which enters a market by building its own, new facilities (most commonly, HFC for residential subscribers, but also terrestrial wireless or fiber). Companies may also combine these strategies. Satellite broadband providers in essence overbuild the entire country (or regions thereof through spot beams), although with the capacity to serve only a fraction of the total number of households, and with a cost structure different from that of terrestrial providers. The drying up of Internet-related venture capital that occurred in 2000-2001—and the associated failure of several CLECs—signals difficulties in sustaining deployment efforts.

In addition to providing financial incentives for private sector investment, the public sector can complement and stimulate private sector efforts by making long-term investments in infrastructure that ease market entry and foster competition among broadband providers. Such investment is most likely to occur at the state, regional, or local level, although federal support can play an important role. But decision making for such investments is not a simple matter, and, if present trends are any indication, such investments will be confined to those locales that project the greatest returns from accelerated access to broadband, possess a greater inclination for a public sector role in entrepreneurship, and are best equipped to navigate a complex set of choices.

Finding 6. The Shape of Broadband Deployment

While the long-term outcome of broadband deployment is certainly not clear, the characteristics of the technologies and related economic factors do permit the overall shape of deployment to be predicted with some confidence in the short term.

Finding 6.1. The broadband vision is rapidly evolving and is linked to the Internet and computing.

Broadband is related to several classes of telecommunications services—some stable (telephony), some somewhat stable (entertainment television), and one that is evolving rapidly (the Internet and associated developments in computing, embedded information technology, and wireless communications). Telephony and television exist in useful forms today without the need for a new generation of access technology, which suggests that the real driver of the broadband vision is the Internet and the associated computing milieu. The future form of the Internet itself is quite uncertain, with the current market downturn injecting possible uncertainty into the overall cycle of investment and the perception of overall value and utility, which suggests a need for caution when making predictions. Broadband's linkage to the Internet suggests that broadband will change more rapidly—and less predictably—than what was experienced as telephony and television developed.

Finding 6.2. Current trends appear to be able to sustain deployment over the next several years, but beyond that point the outcome is less evident.

Substantial deployment of broadband has already taken place, and both cable operators and ILECs appear to have a commitment to continue along this path (though the pace may be affected by the investment climate, consumer demand, and competitive forces). Significant cost reductions in equipment as mature broadband technologies have reached the mass market are another positive indicator. These factors suggest that infrastructure and business may be robust enough to permit widespread deployment and sustained performance improvements. However, penetration may fall short of universal access, investment in additional facilities may or may not occur, and investment in performance improvements may stall.

Finding 6.3. Broadband is not a horse race among technologies.

While popular accounts tend to focus on which technology or players are "ahead" in broadband deployment, broadband is not a horse race among technologies, with an eventual winner. The long-term outcome will be diversity in technology options, for several reasons:

• *Location matters.* The United States is very heterogeneous in many dimensions—density and dispersion of population, demographics, topography, and condition and age of infrastructure—and it is not reasonable to expect "one size to fit all." Technology diversity promotes greater ubiquity of service, as cable systems fill in where DSL cannot reach today, for example.

• *Continuing incremental investment in existing infrastructure.* Because of investor expectations for short-term return on investment, incumbents will continue to make use of existing equipment and plant and the incumbents' deployment will be based on incremental upgrades.

• *Continued exploitation of technology skills.* Companies possessing particular expertise will exploit opportunities where these skills give them an advantage. For example, designing, launching, and operating a satellite system all require know-how very different from that required to upgrade a cable or telephone system.

• *Varying levels of technology maturity.* Before wide-scale deployment, technologies must undergo an extensive development process to reduce the costs of components, installation, and management. More mature technologies will see wider deployment at the same time that less mature technologies are being developed in test markets.

Looking forward, the following trends are apparent for the various technology options:

Cable and DSL. Incremental investment building on existing technology bases will continue, together with some investment in new facilities when the right conditions exist. Particularly in denser urban and suburban areas, wireline broadband—HFC and DSL—is being utilized successfully, albeit with some growing pains. The incumbents (both ILECs and cable system operators) have considerable advantage, because wireline technologies have in common that the labor of installing the line is a significant cost component. Since there is no obvious way to decrease these costs dramatically, options that require investment in new wireline infrastructure are at a disadvantage. Also favoring the incumbents are their existing customer base and other revenue sources. There have, nonetheless, been efforts in more attractive markets to overbuild the incumbents to permit new players to enter the broadband (and associated cable TV or telephone) markets.

Fiber-to-the-Home. Given its potentially enormous capacity, format versatility, and long lifetime, FTTH is a logical technology end point (complemented by wireless where mobility is desired). Already, fiber is being driven closer to user premises as part of routine improvements to the public telephone network, cable systems, and wireless base-station feeds, and the technology evolution paths for both DSL and HFC rely on fiber optic links that reach closer and closer to the premises. For new installations, the total life-cycle costs of a fiber-based infrastructure are, generally speaking, lower than those for other wireline alternatives because of fiber's long life and because it lends itself to architectures that have no intermediate electronics (which would require periodic maintenance and/or upgrade) in the path between premises and point of presence. The advantages of FTTH are offset by two cost penalties: (1) instead of leveraging existing wireline plant, a provider incurs the cost of installing new fiber optic cables (and, depending on the architecture, splicing the cable) and (2) at present, the terminating equipment is more expensive, reflecting the cost of the optoelectronics and today's lower product volumes. The costs of terminating equipment can be expected to drop as the technology is engineered for mass deployment and production volumes increase. Because they ultimately are tied to the cost of labor, fiber installation costs are less susceptible to cost reduction, but there have been advances in splicing equipment, and a variety of techniques have been proposed to reduce fiber installation costs in particular situations (including creative ways of exploiting existing rights-of-way).

Meanwhile, there is considerable scope for incremental gain from all access technologies and a great deal of inherent capacity in HFC (because of coaxial cable's very large theoretical bandwidth). Also, a gap currently exists between the capacity of FTTH links and the capacity of typical links to the Internet core, which means that with FTTH deployment, the capacity bottleneck is simply pushed upstream (except for applications that rely only on local bandwidth). Pervasive deployment of fiber to the premises thus awaits investor belief that the necessary demand exists, a leap of faith that the demand will emerge once very bandwidth-intensive applications take hold, or a long-term investment horizon. FTTH will be more attractive where there is either no existing infrastructure or where a provider opts to compete with the incumbents by providing a very-high-capacity alternative. FTTH is being used in green-fields developments, in some community-based initiatives, and by a few overbuilders in small-scale deployments. As a general rule, FTTH will be deployed when a combination of economics, demand, and capabilities (compared to alternatives, including the infrastructure already in place) justifies the investment.

Wireless. Wireless technology offers mobility and the most flexible deployment scenarios. In the shorter term, satellite and fixed wireless are being used to support market entry by providers that lack wireline assets. Fixed wireless may also offer a longer-term residential broadband option, especially in less densely populated areas or areas able to support a larger number of facilities-based competitors, and satellite has an obvious niche in reaching remote areas. To reach the most remote few percent of U.S. households, the high fixed cost of building and launching satellites is offset by low per-passing costs. While so-called third-generation (3G) wireless will provide more capabilities than present systems do, the throughput per user falls short of a reasonable definition of broadband. Wireless local area networking technology using the IEEE 802.11b standard is beginning to emerge as an alternative model for untethered broadband access in public places (using both commercial and noncommercial models). Looking forward, advances such as robust multicarrier modulation and space-time processing with antenna arrays will benefit wireless across the board—not only higher-performance fixed wireless, but also enhanced mobile cellular systems, which offer ubiquity and mobility, and wireless local area networks (LANs), which provide complementary "last meters" access. Wireless is expected to continue to lag wireline in bandwidth, but its greater flexibility, anticipated performance improvements that would make it "good enough" for many applications, and the equipment cost reductions that come from reaching mass-market volumes can make it a long-term competitor.

Finding 6.4. There will be substantial geographical variation in the nature of competition.

Diversity in technology will be accompanied by diversity in the competitive landscape, with different degrees of "natural" competition—competition that is facilities-based or that occurs through voluntary business arrangements with facilities owners. With broadband, local conditions are very important, and the distribution of broadband availability will be quite uneven, especially in the earlier stages. No matter what regulatory approaches are applied (short of policy embracing a single monopoly provider), all of the following outcomes are likely to occur in one or another region of the United States:

• *Type 0—no terrestrial providers of broadband.* This situation is not uncommon today despite significant deployment, but it can be expected to become less common as the near-ubiquitous public telephone and cable networks are upgraded to support broadband. There is no region of the lower 48 states that entirely lacks service today, because some form of satellite-based broadband is possible wherever the user is able to install an antenna dish with line-of-sight view of the satellite (albeit with cost and performance inferior to what would be possible with access through alternative technologies if they were to be available).

• *Type 1—one terrestrial facilities-based provider in the area (e.g., cable but not DSL, or vice versa).* This common circumstance will diminish to the extent that the incumbent telephone companies and cable operators both expand their broadband coverage. It will persist where the market is perceived to be large enough to support the first entrant but not large enough to attract a second incumbent provider.

• *Type 2—two terrestrial facilities-based providers.* This will be a common long-term outcome. The incumbent telephone and cable provider will both upgrade to support broadband, but no other provider will enter the market. One or both may choose to support multiple higher-level service providers such as Internet service providers. Alternatively, one of the incumbents and an overbuilder (using wireline or wireless technology) could provide broadband service.

• *Type 3—one or more facilities-based providers that install new infrastructure to compete with the incumbents.* This has occurred in limited fashion so far, with companies such as RCN overbuilding with HFC, and Sprint and WorldCom overbuilding with terrestrial wireless in selected markets. The financial viability of type 3 competition—and prospects for competition beyond that offered by the incumbent telephone and cable companies—will be tested over the next few years.

Finding 6.5. The vitality of the CLEC industry is in doubt, but the source of apparent troubles is uncertain.

In 2001, the vitality of the data CLEC industry, which has provided broadband retail competition in a number of markets, came into doubt. Charges and countercharges were made as to whether the CLECs or incumbents were responsible for reported difficulties and delays in establishing service, a number of Federal Communications Commission (FCC) proceedings were held on the matter, and fines were assessed against ILECs. The possibility that incumbent-deployed technology (such as fiber-fed remote terminals) might complicate or preclude copper loop unbundling added an element of uncertainty. A wave of CLEC bankruptcies and outright shutdowns disrupted service and left some consumers without any broadband alternative. It is unclear whether the CLECs' apparent woes were due to the better engineering and operational practices of the incumbents, to unrealistic undercapitalization, intrinsically flawed business models, poor management, anticompetitive practices, failures of their business partners, or insufficient added value relative to the incumbent, or to some combination of these factors. Where this alternative no longer exists, there is less price pressure on ILECs offering broadband and one less option for access to alternative ISPs.

Finding 6.6. Unlike the underlying communications technologies, the capabilities of deployed broadband are not on a Moore's law-like curve.

Unfavorable comparisons are sometimes made between sustained improvements in the performance-to-price ratio of computing and lagging improvements in the capacity of broadband local access links. From this perspective, and consistent with broadband definition 1 above, local access links are a bottleneck. The communications technologies themselves —most notably, ongoing improvements in fiber optic transmission speeds —have in fact kept pace with or surpassed improvements in computing. The gap that exists is between *deployed* access technology and computing technology, reflecting economic considerations rather than an inherent mismatch.

Finding 7. The Relationship Between Broadband and Content and Applications Businesses Is Critical and Is in Flux.

Today's debate over ISP access to cable broadband systems puts a spotlight on a more general possibility that is motivated by a range of factors—that increased ties between communications technologies and the content and applications that run over them could result in an Internet that is balkanized (even as the industry consolidates), is less open in character, or is less supportive of application and service innovation. Past experience with content-conduit relationships suggests a range of possible long-term outcomes for broadband. Telephony has long followed a common carrier model in which content and conduit have been cleanly separated. Cable operators today have considerable control over the content carried by their systems. Such content-conduit ties are cited as a source of financial strength; cable-unique services helped fuel the industry's growth beyond its community antenna television roots. These ties are also associated with business and regulatory complications.

With dial-up Internet access, the ISP and phone carrier are separate entities; customers are free to select from among a wide array of ISPs. Internet connectivity is usually understood to mean access to the full range of content and applications available via the Internet, though there are ISPs offering services ranging from full connectivity to delivery of comprehensive, proprietary content and services. The availability of services offering full connectivity, together with ISP diversity, has been an enabler of experimentation with new applications and services. Going forward, broadband Internet service providers have a choice of offering full, unrestricted connections to the Internet or evolving toward a more defined package of services (using Internet technology). In the early days, when the business side was still developing and the user base was smaller and generally more sophisticated, users expected to be able to do anything with their Internet connection, services were geared more toward these users, and with a few exceptions, the ISPs were not strongly differentiated in terms of the content or services they provided. When cable operators started offering broadband, they opted to do so through exclusive ISPs, more recently evolving to offer a set of ISP choices.

Today, the provider industry is more mature (and more consolidated, especially in broadband), users are not all technology-savvy, and providers are becoming more sophisticated about consumer behavior and about how to make money. ISPs are seeking opportunities for additional revenue streams by bundling additional services, establishing preferred content and services (even restricting access to particular content and services), and defining tiered services. These factors all suggest the rise of alternatives to traditional Internet access that offer a more limited, defined set of content and services that could change the fundamental nature of the Internet as experienced by consumers. While consumers may differ in their preference for one type of service or another, it would represent a significant shift in the communications landscape if they were to lose the option of full, open Internet broadband connectivity. Voluntary measures—and those adopted in order to obtain permission for mergers—have given cable broadband customers some choice of ISP and thus decreased restrictions on access to Internet content. These responses to critics may address concerns about the potential market power of facilities owners, but their effectiveness remains unproven.

RECOMMENDATIONS

The present policy framework for broadband, which revolves around the Telecommunications Act of 1996, is problematic and is unsuited in several respects to the new era of broadband services. The significance of broadband data communications was appreciated in general terms by some of the key players that shaped the act (and is reflected in multiple sections of the act dealing with advanced services), but the central role of the Internet (and the rapid rise in popularity of applications running over the Internet, such as the World Wide Web) in the communications landscape was not fully anticipated. Framed before the Internet was fully commercial, the Telecommunications Act of 1996 devotes much of its attention to the voice telephony market and maintains distinct rules for the various communications networks (telephone, cable, cellular, broadcasting, and so on). To stimulate competition, the act employs both facilities-based competition, in which providers compete head-to-head using their own facilities, and unbundling, in which incumbent telephone companies are required to provide network elements—most notably, the copper lines that run from the central office to each subscriber—to competitors at regulated prices.

Recommendation 1. Prioritize Widespread Deployment and Defer New Regulation in the Early Stages.

The committee is mindful that there is a tension between permitting private sector deployment of broadband to proceed without any hindrance from government intervention and society's desire to guide the outcome. Decision makers will have to balance the inevitable calls to shape broadband toward some particular end against the "natural" trajectory defined by user preferences, private sector investment, and the market. The committee's specific, pragmatic strategic preference is to promote broad deployment relatively quickly and to foster facilities-based competition.

Recommendation 1.1. Avoid present-day policy making that is based on presumptions about the final form of broadband markets.

Some forms of intervention to expand access could deter investment from taking place at all, which suggests prioritizing widespread though not universal deployment over addressing access gaps early on. Because government intervention may affect private sector investment decisions, it should be undertaken with great care in this nascent area in order to avoid unintended consequences. Also, resolving the chicken-and-egg dilemma depends on broadband reaching some critical level of penetration if new content and applications are to take off. Once a mass market is achieved—which brings with it prospects of new applications and business opportunities—there is a likelihood that demand and willingness to pay will increase, which in turn may attract new players to provide competition, and decrease the need for regulation. Also, learning more about the nature of consumer desires and the shape that the technology and associated markets "naturally" take will help inform the policy debate. It is, for example, premature to conclude that facilities-based competition is or is not feasible in many locations. As the shape of broadband deployment starts to become clearer, a firmer basis for broadband policy will be in place.

Recommendation 1.2. Complementary to favoring policies facilitating rapid deployment over intervention, develop and implement enhanced monitoring of deployment, investment, and market outcomes and develop metrics to permit independent evaluation and rating of performance.

The committee acknowledges that the approach reflected in Recommendation 1.1 is different from that of others who advocate increased early attention to ensuring access to all or who argue that it is essential to shape the behavior of incumbents (telephone or cable) or to otherwise regulate the competitive environment early on. There is, indeed, some risk that if facilities-based competition does not materialize, the committee's recommendations could lead to a stagnant scenario in which incumbents face little competition and deploy and upgrade broadband services slowly. Thus, attention should be paid to distribution and performance variations as well as to overall rates of deployment. It is also essential for regulators to watch for undesirable outcomes that would have long-term consequences—most notably, abuse of market power. Monitoring would provide a basis for distinguishing between unrealized concerns and actual provider behavior, and would help inform public debate about the need for possible regulatory intervention.

Detailed data on market penetration are hard to gather, inconsistently described, and often proprietary. Likewise, it is difficult to acquire solid data or assess commercial claims about costs and markets. To monitor the shape of broadband deployment and refine policy responses, government at all levels needs a consistent picture of data on total market penetration, the extent of competition, and other key indicators of future trajectories. Since national averages tell very little about variation in levels of local competition, these data must be gathered at a fine grain—even community by community—and they must be updated on a regular basis.

At this point in the deployment of broadband, when the mature form of the market has not emerged, it is more important to watch for signs that the market is not serving important policy goals than to predict the final outcome now. These concerns suggest the following as key indicators to track:

- *What percent of the population is situated in what sorts of competitive context—regions of type 0 through 3?* Which of these regions are expanding and contracting over time?
- *For different applications, is the performance perceived by the consumer improving or deteriorating?* This is a measure of whether, by broadband definition 1, services available are actually broadband. Sound metrics of performance and means of monitoring their trends would have to be developed and agreed to.
- *Are new applications that depend on high bandwidth emerging?* If they do not, it would be an indication that by broadband definition 2, the services being deployed are not broadband.
- *How effective are emerging alternatives to formal regulation?* Open access policies aim to limit the market power of incumbents (both local exchange carriers and cable operators) in providing broadband services, reflecting concerns that facilities-based competition may not provide a robust alternative in all circumstances and that incumbents' ability to leverage past monopoly status should be bounded. Existing unbundling and resale rules require incumbent local exchange carriers to provide would-be competitors with access to the local loop, so public attention to open access has focused mainly on cable system operators. The year 2001 saw the development of a potential template for the industry as a whole: conditions on the AOL-Time Warner merger, which were agreed to by the Federal Trade Commission, were developed in the face of significant pressures to block the merger. Ongoing scrutiny of that industry, such as that to be carried out by the appointed monitor of the AOL-Time Warner

merger, is needed, to determine if emerging alternatives to formal regulation will prove adequate.

 • *Is subscriber access to certain Internet content or services being blocked or impaired (as compared with other content)?* The open access issue is one manifestation of a broader question of the extent to which nondiscriminatory access to Internet content and services will continue with a shift to broadband. Impairment of subscriber access in any industry segment would be an indication of undesirable consequences arising from vertical integration of content and broadband communications businesses.

Recommendation 2. Structure Regulation to Emphasize Facilities-Based Competition and to Encourage New Entrants.

Recommendation 2.1. In the long term and in the case of investment in new facilities, policies should favor facilities-based competition over mandated unbundling.

Current regulation of the ILECs contemplates three forms of competition—(1) facilities-based competition, (2) competition enabled via unbundling of ILEC network elements, and (3) competition through resale of ILEC services. In facilities-based competition, providers rely substantially on their own local access facilities rather than on local access facilities owned and operated by other providers (a facilities-based provider might make use of backhaul links from other providers). Unbundling, in which ILEC network elements are made available to would-be competitors at regulated prices, was initiated as part of the 1996 telecommunications act's attempt to stimulate competition in both the local and long-distance markets and to reflect the advantages of scale and scope enjoyed by ILECs. For cable operators, the only access requirements have arisen in the context of mergers and acquisitions. Current regulation is ambivalent and sometimes ambiguous as to which is the preferred approach.

Per the taxonomy presented in Finding 6.4, the policy goal with respect to competition, simply put, should be to increase the prevalence of type 3 conditions in place of type 2, shift type 1 conditions to type 2, and so on. Increasing the extent of competition through facilities ownership (and voluntary business arrangements to open facilities) rather than relying on regulation that mandates unbundling is important for several reasons:

 • *It reduces the need for persistent regulatory intervention.* Until there are effectively competitive facilities-based alternatives to the incumbent monopolist, full deregulation is very unlikely to come about, and there will be a continued need to regulate such things as the terms and conditions of access to incumbent unbundled elements.

- *It permits the natural (i.e., competition-shaped) character of broadband service and industry structure to be discerned.* This helps define an end-point goal for regulation in those regions where competition is less robust. Otherwise, since broadband cannot be precisely defined without learning much more about consumer preferences and the shape of the market where consumers have a real choice, regulators could strive toward the wrong outcomes.
- *It promotes diversity.* Facilities-based competition better supports diversity in both the technology base (which makes broadband more adaptable to changing user needs and circumstances) and more diversity in types of cost structures (which makes broadband more robust in the face of changing business circumstances).
- *It avoids deterring competitors from investing in their own infrastructure.* While unbundling is often offered as a stepping-stone to facilities-based competition by providing a revenue stream to a start-up firm, it can also inhibit facilities-based competition by reducing the incentives for competitors to build new facilities (or upgrade existing ones).
- *It removes a disincentive to new investment by incumbents.* To the extent that the unbundling requirements are extended to new network elements deployed by incumbents to offer advanced services, such as fiber-connected remote terminals, it is a disincentive for investment by the incumbent in such enhanced facilities, because the incumbent cannot capture all of the benefits of its investment. In making this observation, the committee is not necessarily accepting at face value ILECs' assertions that their investment decisions are driven chiefly by unbundling requirements when there are other plausible explanations (such as the benefits of not having to face the threat of CLEC competition or pressures for financial results). Nonetheless, the incentive level is critical, especially if investment is to occur in lower-density or poorer areas where the business case may be less attractive.
- *It avoids costs and organizational complications associated with coordination between incumbents and competitors.* Organizational coordination problems arise because the incumbent's and competitor's interests are not aligned, a difficulty manifested in delays and confusion in provisioning DSL service. The coordination issues give rise to extended regulatory proceedings, with the associated delays and expenditure of resources.
- *It facilitates technical optimization of total bandwidth.* Crosstalk among telephone lines constrains DSL performance. Bit rates and corresponding ranges can be improved when transmissions can be coordinated so as to minimize interference. Logical-layer unbundling (see below) is another way to facilitate this.

In its focus on investment in new facilities and the long term, the committee distinguishes between how to treat the existing telephone copper plant facilities and new facilities. The case for the present unbundling of the copper plant rests on the premise that the public should benefit from past investment made when the telephone companies enjoyed a (regulated) monopoly position. Also, changing present policy would severely disrupt the business plans of today's CLEC industry. Thus, it is reasonable to maintain unbundling rules for the present copper plant.

It is when looking to the future, to investment in new facilities, that reconsideration of unbundling is most important. Because the objective is to minimize disincentives for new investment, existing unbundling rules should be relaxed only where the incumbent makes significant investment to extend service to areas not served by existing infrastructure or in facilities constructed to enable new capabilities. Investment for routine maintenance or minor upgrades should not be sufficient to result in exemption from unbundling requirements. That assessment must also take into account the extent to which an incumbent's control over the existing plant can be leveraged to gain an anticompetitive advantage in offering broadband over new facilities.

At least in more densely populated, more affluent areas, facilities-based competition appears to be possible. That is not to say that sustaining facilities-based competition will be easy, and policy should reflect this reality. If more facilities-based entrants in an area are successful, each provider will have a lower take-rate and increased facilities competition may be accompanied by higher prices. But the policy objective of competition is not simply lower prices; the aim is also to increase quality, stimulate investment in upgrades, and provide meaningful consumer choice—and consumer education about these other factors may be necessary.

Facilities-based competition can be stimulated by reducing barriers to entry. Certain forms of access—such as access to rights-of-way and (possibly incumbent-controlled) poles and conduits—stem from privileges granted or property controlled by governments and are not a direct product of the innovative activities of a competitive firm. Governments should devote increasing attention to this type of access so as to reduce obstacles to new facilities-based entrants.

Recommendation 2.2. Favor alternatives to physical unbundling.

In cases where facilities-based competition is found to be insufficient, the most common regulatory alternative is some form of mandated unbundling. An example is the currently debated opening up of cable systems to unaffiliated ISPs. When policy objectives call for the opening up of incumbents' facilities, this goal can be achieved in several ways, either at a low level, by unbundling the physical links of the provider, or by unbundling some higher-level service. In physical-layer unbundling, a competitor to the incumbent gains direct access to the electronic signals on the wire (or light on a fiber) running from the subscriber to a central office or remote terminal; can adopt whatever transmission scheme it chooses to; and is free to compete on speed, quality, and other transmission characteristics. However, the ultimate performance and reach of the physical links may be impaired by such low-level sharing. Options for enhancing DSL, such as coordinated assignment of copper pairs and coordination of transmitted signals among pairs, cannot be implemented if competitors are free to implement their own technology. Similarly, low-level unbundling of cable, for example, allocation of different frequency bands to different providers, raises the risk of interference among signals and overall loss of quality and operational stability. No individual purchaser of unbundled access has an incentive to internalize the interference problems its traffic causes for others.

Logical-layer unbundling exploits the layered way in which broadband services are implemented. It is the basis of today's cable open access initiatives. Higher-layer services concerned with transmitting bits are implemented on top of protocols concerned with transmitting electrical signals across the wire, which means that they can be implemented independent of the particulars of the physical layer connection. That is, a competitor need not control the actual signals running over the wires if it can implement its service using bit transport capabilities provided by the incumbent. In addition to facilitating measures to address the crosstalk problem, logical-layer unbundling may be a more practical way of providing unbundling as fiber is pushed deeper into the telephone network and the termination point shifts from the central office to remote terminals.

A principal disadvantage of logical-layer unbundling for the competitor is that the performance characteristics of the link implemented by the incumbent may restrict the types of services the competitor may offer and limit the competitor's ability to differentiate itself from the incumbent. Nonetheless, in the long term, particularly with respect to new facilities, logical-layer unbundling would provide a better foundation for technology-neutral broadband regulation, provided that facilities owners are not permitted to exercise market power with respect to transport.

The current situations of the ILECs and the cable providers differ somewhat. The physical links of the ILECs, specifically the local loops and subloops, are currently subject to physical-layer unbundling requirements, which has allowed a number of data CLECs to enter markets. The cable debate about open access has, in contrast, been centered at a higher service level. In the long run, a convergence toward a uniform open access policy based on logical-layer unbundling may be the best outcome. The cable industry claims that it will implement logical-layer unbundling voluntarily. If this outcome does not occur, mandated open access may well be the regulatory response (unless a much more competitive landscape appears). In the case of ILECs, regulators should consider whether the goal of robust competition among different services offered by different providers could be better achieved in the long run through logical-layer unbundling rather than physical-layer unbundling, especially as the telephone plant evolves to make increased use of remote terminals.

Recommendation 2.3. Anticipate that facilities-based competition will not occur in all places, and fashion appropriate policies to address these gaps.

While their boundaries are difficult to forecast and will likely change over time, it is reasonable to anticipate areas where there is a single terrestrial provider. These type 1 areas will generally exist where population density is lowest and the per-passing cost burden is highest, making the business case for entry by a second facility owner unattractive. In these areas, policy makers will face the challenge of how to address a noncompetitive broadband market. Questions that must be addressed in fashioning such policy include whether and how to intervene, how long to wait before assuming that a rough equilibrium situation of only a single facilities-based carrier has been reached, what impact either mandated unbundling or voluntary facilities-sharing has on the competitive landscape, and to what extent satellite-delivered broadband (with less attractive price or performance) provides sufficient competition to the terrestrial facility owner.

Local conditions may also change over time—especially early on—and thus the extent of and approach to intervention will have to change. This flexibility will challenge traditional regulatory approaches, which move more slowly. Consider the most complex case: a competitor withdraws (transforming a type 3 region into a type 2 region, for example). A result may be a need to increase regulation of the survivor. This outcome would certainly be characterized by the provider as unfair after-the-fact rule changing, but this sort of eventuality must be anticipated. Thus providers might face a changing and nonuniform set of business conditions—a situation that, while potentially confusing for providers, reflects the realities of their operating environment.

Recommendation 2.4. Ensure appropriate radio spectrum for broadband and associated capabilities.

Wireless is well suited for certain less densely populated regions, offers an additional path for entry by new facilities-based competitors, and, if suitably configured, is unique in its support for mobile use. Both licensed and unlicensed spectrum plays a role in enabling various wireless broadband alternatives as well as local area and mobile capabilities that complement and supplement wireline broadband access. The committee did not examine in detail whether current spectrum allocations are sufficient or appropriate, but notes that spectrum availability is a precondition to any wireless deployment. Nor did the committee evaluate the merits of various allocation schemes or the trade-offs between allocations for fixed versus mobile, licensed versus unlicensed, or unshared versus shared uses. Efforts to examine spectrum policy to support broadband and related services (both current and contemplated), such as those being undertaken by the Federal Communications Commission, should be continued.

Recommendation 3. Reflect the Convergent Nature of Broadband and Target Policy at the Appropriate Layer.

The Telecommunications Act of 1996, which for the most part assumes the continued existence of a number of distinct services that run over distinct communications technologies and separate infrastructure, does not fully reflect the convergent nature of broadband (different communications infrastructures are able to deliver a similar set of services using a common platform, the Internet) nor the evolution toward a common technology end point (deep penetration of fiber, complemented by short runs to the premises).

Recommendation 3.1. Move toward a more coherent, consistent policy framework for broadband.

Failure to move toward a more coherent, consistent policy framework could lead to policy-induced distortions in technology deployment. For example, even as several major cable operators have entered into open access agreements, the industry has considerably greater control over access and content than do the telephone companies, which fall under industrywide common carrier rules. A more coherent policy would also better accommodate technological innovation beyond today's HFC and DSL systems. Progress in rationalizing the overall regulatory framework (which would require revision of the Telecommunications Act of 1996)—

to address the mismatch between convergent services and stovepiped regulation—would also help reduce uncertainty and thus could stimulate investment. In the process of reconciling policy across technologies (and associated industries), policy should emphasize broad deployment and facilities-based competition (Recommendations 1 and 2) and not simply apply existing regulations that were designed to deal with circumstances particular to individual technologies (or associated business). Also, technology convergence notwithstanding, policy should be able to accommodate a diversity of business models as incumbents and entrants alike experiment with different business strategies. These realities are generally appreciated by the Federal Communications Commission as well as by the regulated industries themselves; the issue today is how and when the regulatory framework should be reformulated.

Recommendation 3.2. If regulation of a broadband-delivered service is contemplated, it should be done in a service- rather than a technology-centric fashion.

Reflecting political or social interests, various communications services—such as today's broadcasting and telephony—are subject to regulation. It is reasonable to anticipate that services delivered over broadband will be subject to similar scrutiny, and thus it is prudent to identify the most appropriate means of regulating them. Formulation of any future regulation should focus on the service rather than on the particular transmission technology.

Flexible service-centric approaches that tolerate technology diversity are essential, because broadband-delivered services are subject to faster change and greater variation—because of the general-purpose nature of the broadband infrastructure over which they run—than are conventional services. For example, if broadband is to be used to provide telephone service intended to substitute for conventional telephone service, regulators should focus on the marketing of the service to ensure that the promised reliability and 911 service are in fact delivered, rather than on the technical means by which the service is provided (whether over the Internet or otherwise). Defining regulated services this way not only encourages convergence by relying on a technology-independent way of describing the service, but it also tolerates service diversity by permitting different types of services to be defined. One might, for the purposes of regulation, define two classes of telephone service: (1) a service intended to substitute for conventional phone service (providing high reliability and 911 service) and (2) a less costly service for more discretionary uses. Another reason to move toward a service-centric approach is that the assumptions underlying regulation of services are frequently tied to the characteristics of particular technologies. For example, regulation of broadcasting has been fashioned in an environment of over-the-air channel scarcity, a condition that need not apply to broadband-delivered services.

Recommendation 4. Take Active Steps to Promote Increased or Accelerated Deployment, Including at the Local Level.

As described above, the economics associated with investment in broadband suggest that, absent some additional impetus, achieving nationwide broadband deployment may be a protracted process. In at least some parts of the country—type 0 and 1 regions—there may be little or no broadband deployment or facilities-based competition, and intervention may be required. Type 2 areas, in which the telephone and cable incumbents constitute a duopoly, are also places for government at all levels to explore intervention that would encourage new entrants where the market appears to be capable of supporting more participants. Many of these incentives should be locally based, because there is considerable local diversity in the conditions for broadband deployment.

Recommendation 4.1. Establish a federal and state policy framework supportive of local initiatives that ease market entry and foster competition.

Current broadband policy is largely federal in scope, and it assumes, at least implicitly, a uniform national approach. But the degree of natural competition and prevalence of technology will vary by region, state, and municipality, and policy at all levels will have to accommodate this diversity. Federal rules should continue to bound the range of outcomes—for example, by preventing local governments from raising unreasonable barriers to entry or from discriminating in providing access to public facilities, and by preventing a proliferation of inconsistent local rules that can complicate and deter investment. But because it is communities themselves that have the most at stake in regard to broadband service, there are appropriate forms of local decision making, based on local conditions and needs. Particularly at the municipal level, various sorts of incentives and local arrangements can encourage and even shape the form of broadband deployment that occurs (e.g., localities may target their communications purchases as a way to encourage an entrant).

Recommendation 4.2. Explore public sector initiatives that foster market entry.

Initiatives involving public sector actors may provide an alternative to imposing unbundling requirements on incumbents in order to provide increased competition in type 0, 1, and 2 circumstances. These initiatives should be articulated, researched, and evaluated with a focus specifically on reducing barriers to entering competitors by building or facilitating enabling infrastructure.

A decision to provide a publicly funded broadband service—which might be done in an attempt to introduce service where there currently is none—can affect the number of broadband providers in a given area. In cases where a market is capable of supporting only one private provider, the introduction of a public network to compete with it could have the effect of driving the private sector network out of operation. Similarly, the creation of a public network could deter future entry into a market capable of supporting only a very limited total number of players. Also, where government bodies enter into exclusive arrangements with a single company, there is the risk of regulatory capture. These factors all argue that local governments should concentrate on taking steps to encourage and facilitate competition among private sector players, rather than creating new quasi-monopolistic entities. Options include these:

• *Fiber condominium arrangements with public participation.* A locality declares its intention to build out fiber along its streets and invites any interested parties to purchase some share of the fibers installed (and possibly installs additional dark fiber for future use).

• *Customer-owned condominium arrangements.* Customers own links to a suitable aggregation point. This option would most likely take the form of a condominium arrangement in which a group of households would coinvest in new wireline infrastructure—probably fiber—that serves a neighborhood or community; this arrangement might be facilitated by local governments.

• *Partnerships with the private sector to install (and possibly maintain) fiber.* The town itself, the schools and municipal departments, businesses and other private sector players in the town, the citizens themselves, and any interested broadband providers can sign up.

• *Municipal investment in wholesale second-mile fiber facilities, or fiber conduit.* Second-mile fiber facilities provide connectivity to neighborhoods that can be shared by competing broadband providers who in turn provide broadband to individual homes and shared conduit that decreases each provider's installation costs. Municipal investment in either would be analogous to the investment in streets as an enabler for local commerce—here enabling the value-added flow of bits instead of the flow of cars and trucks.

In each case, the locality provides motivation, coordination, and resources for joint action. It may share in the cost of the common construction and may also prohibit the digging up of the streets again for some period after the construction. Typically, some provision would also be made to lease colocation space to service providers at the fiber termination points to facilitate Internet interconnection. By avoiding the extra cost of uncoordinated overbuilding—keeping down the per-passing costs —this approach attempts to provide competition at per-passing costs comparable to those of a single provider. Local and regional government or quasi-governmental agencies can also act in effect as anchor tenants that underwrite some of the cost of installing infrastructure, reducing the costs for other government agencies, private sector firms, or even individual customers.

Recommendation 4.3. Relax federal, state, and local rules to ease market entry or to stimulate investment.

Local governments can also relax rules that deter or preclude overbuilders from entering a market, such as by providing access to rights-of-way, forms of relief for opening of facilities to competitive higher-level service providers, and so on. Local policies that tend to protect the incumbents from facilities-based entrants should be strongly discouraged or even preempted at the state or federal level.

Various forms of regulatory relief—such as a relaxation of franchise fees or obligations—could be granted in return for infrastructure build-out or upgrade commitments. One option would be to provide relief from certain forms of regulation, such as mandated access in exchange for specified deployments of new or upgraded facilities. Another option would be to reduce the business risk associated with facilities construction by providing assurances that compensation would be provided for future regulatory imposition of unbundling requirements. Regulators might also provide a "safe harbor" (exceptions from heavy regulation) for providers in a type 1 situation if they behave comparably (in terms of prices and service quality) to providers in a type 3 situation. Finally, in cases where broadband providers fail, governments at all levels can take steps to expedite a transfer of assets to ensure continuity of service for affected customers.

Recommendation 4.4. Provide financial incentives for investment in underserved and high-cost areas.

Examples of financial incentives would include tax credits given for building out infrastructure in underserved areas, or incentives—including tax credits and changes in permitting and zoning rules—given to providers that invest in infrastructure upgrades exceeding specified build-out or performance targets or that make investments in training and support of developers and users. Another option would be to provide government-guaranteed loans for infrastructure upgrades and build-out in high-cost areas.

Recommendation 5. Increase Local Capacity to Promote Broadband Deployment.

The recommendations above point to a number of specific measures that local or regional governments might pursue to promote broadband deployment in their communities. These opportunities also represent a considerable challenge for many communities that lack experience and knowledge in managing the complex legal, regulatory, and economic issues these options encompass. A few communities have already taken significant initiative with respect to broadband, but the majority are just now exploring the options before them. Therefore, mechanisms to enhance local capacity can play a critical role. Because one of the motivators for broadband is demand for work- and business-related applications and associated applications such as continuing education, in some circumstances it will be appropriate to link broadband initiatives with broader economic development efforts.

Recommendation 5.1. Support planning grants for localities to explore options.

Because an exploration of the complex set of issues confronting each community requires expertise, the engagement of various sectors within the community, and input from the public at large, federal and state governments should support planning grants to communities that demonstrate serious interest in taking steps to advance broadband deployment.

Recommendation 5.2. Provide cost sharing for field trials, including local-government-sponsored initiatives.

Cost-sharing grants or subsidies for communities that have limited-performance or no broadband would support experimentation with pre-market technologies and alternative organizational models. Such trials would permit governments and private sector firms to obtain more realistic experience with the performance of technology alternatives, help industry move up the learning curve of emerging technologies, test alternative organizational approaches and access models (such as municipally owned fiber or conduit available to multiple providers), and test demand stimulation strategies (e.g., locally developed content and applications). While there may be municipalities that have existing public utilities capable of embarking on such a program, a more likely mode is through partnership with private firms.

Recommendation 5.3. Establish a national clearinghouse to raise awareness, provide technical assistance, and disseminate best practices for local and regional efforts to accelerate broadband deployment.

A mechanism for sharing best practices for local and regional policies, regulation, and planning would help communities that are facing complex decisions. For instance, model regulatory frameworks would illustrate the range of possible outcomes, provide regional and local governments a starting point in negotiating with providers, and help overcome the knowledge and experience imbalance that local and regional governments may experience. Efforts by the National Association of Telecommunications Officers and Advisors and the Association for Community Networking are promising first steps. In-depth, authoritative information will be needed if best practices are to be useful to communities across the capability spectrum. A national clearinghouse would permit maximal sharing of best practices but would not necessarily supplant state or regional efforts, which may be better positioned to focus on local circumstances and needs.

Recommendation 6. Defer Development of a Universal Service Policy for Broadband Until the Nature of Broadband Services, Pace of Deployment, Distribution of Access, and Social Significance Become Clearer.

The Telecommunications Act of 1996 devotes considerable attention to measures that continue support for near-universal telephone service. Existing universal access programs such as the high-cost fund support (which, by helping to expand or upgrade rural public telephone networks, can also provide a foundation for DSL deployment, as well as extend or improve dial-up service) and the e-rate program (which funds Internet access in many schools, libraries, and health care institutions) have helped to increase broadband access. The 1996 act has instigated efforts to develop policy for expanding broadband access (such as the Federal-State Joint Board on Universal Service).

A number of the committee's recommendations aim to increase the breadth of deployment. While the committee anticipates demands that universal service programs be extended to residential broadband, its view is that it would be premature to embark on a comprehensive new universal service program until the overall shape of residential deployment and the nature of broadband services are better understood. The committee does not believe that, at least at present, a social contract analogous to that developed for telephony would be appropriate for broadband.

It is already apparent that broadband is a desirable and useful service, and it is reasonable to presume that it will take on increasing social importance in the future. But there is a difference between a service's being useful and showing great promise, which has motivated the recommendations in this report aimed at widening deployment, and a service's being critical to meaningful participation in society (as telephone service has come to be understood). In the early stages of deployment and acceptance, policies aimed at fostering rapid, widespread deployment, complemented by broadband access through schools, libraries, and other public centers, are appropriate.

Further, defining an appropriate universal service policy will be complicated. For voice, the shared understanding of what society should expect from the telephone industry, which became the goal of federal and state regulators, has been that a more or less uniform telephone service should be available to residential customers at a roughly uniform price. However, broadband is not a uniform service. Different users have different needs, and different technologies deliver different variants with different features as well as cost and performance characteristics. Also, as the two definitions for broadband advanced by this committee indicate, as technology and use evolve, what is broadband today will not be considered so in the future. One cannot employ a simple universal definition for broadband such as "faster than 200 kilobits per second." The cost could be made uniform only through substantial transfer payments within the system—an approach that was possible in the simple, more static world of telephony but that is very hard to carry out in the less well defined, changing, competitive world of broadband. This suggests that natural cost and service variations must be accepted (which must be distinguished from exercise of market power). For instance, satellite-based service is capable of reaching essentially all parts of the country. As a result, there will be relatively few people who will literally be unable to obtain some form of broadband (assuming these services are marketed to them). Thus, the geographical access divide is much smaller if the requirements are relaxed for what must be the same across regions, and if such trade-offs as lower reliability (e.g., satellites are susceptible to rain fade), higher latency, lower data rates, or higher up-front and monthly costs are permitted.

Recommendation 7. Support Research and Experimentation.

Recommendation 7.1. Support research and development on access technologies, especially targeting the needs of nonincumbent players and other areas that are not targets of stable, private sector funding.

Much of current research has reflected the interests of incumbents. Research that looks at the needs of nonincumbent overbuilders should be specifically encouraged. Such systems will in all likelihood make use of less mature technology alternatives. And as overbuilds, they have lower levels of subscription (lower take-rates) and need to be cost-engineered to anticipate this outcome. Particular research targets include these:

- *Architectural options and other means of cost reduction in fiber access networks,* including new techniques for using coarse wavelength-division multiplexing and low-cost in-home receivers and/or transmitters.
- *Enhanced wireless capabilities,* including capacity and other enhancements for wireless that provide robust, spectrally efficient, and scalable broadband wireless access to homes; architectures for synergistic co-existence of various wireless access technologies (fixed, mobile, in-home, ultrashort-range, and so on); technologies for true mobile broadband wireless services beyond 3G; convergence of fixed and mobile Internet architectures and protocols; and new information-delivery paradigms for broadband mobile Internet services.
- *Technologies that foster the accommodation of multiple competitive service providers over facilities.* Such open access-ready systems might not be a natural research and development target of large incumbent providers but will be the preferred form for a variety of public sector or public-private deployments.
- *Quality of service for homogeneous and heterogeneous access scenarios in the local access link and home,* including for applications that make intensive use of the upstream channel.
- *System robustness and reliability,* reflecting the increasing importance of broadband services to individuals and organizations.

Because the primary objective is to develop technologies that can be practically implemented by a broadband provider, research and development programs should encompass systems and economic perspectives, not just individual technologies or components. Doing this sort of research requires overcoming several institutional problems. Much of the computer science community traditionally has viewed cost reduction as an engineering topic for industry to pursue rather than as a legitimate research topic. Further, few academic research centers devote attention to systems engineering issues, which have generally been addressed by incumbents and their equipment suppliers.

Recommendation 7.2. Support research on economic, social, and regulatory factors.

With broadband a nascent service, now is an especially opportune time to study potential social and economic implications and to develop an understanding of these factors so as to inform government policy making and industry strategies. Areas for further research include these:

- *Social and economic impacts of broadband connectivity and availability.* Such understanding will help localities assess the case for local broadband initiatives and help fashion any future broadband universal access programs.
- *Alternative business models and better understanding of consumer behavior* and its relationship to currently available and prospective applications and services.
- *Economic and regulatory barriers that may hinder the nonincumbent facilities provider.* For example, the cost of the first mile is not the only barrier to deployment. Small neighborhoods (new construction, pockets of dense development, and so on) may be able to justify the construction of new facilities. But this construction cannot occur unless there is some larger network to connect to that serves to aggregate traffic from these neighborhoods. This is what might be called the "second-mile" problem—aggregation of traffic to the point where it is economically viable to connect to the rest of the broadband world.
- *Improving our understanding of why local access performance has lagged that in other computing and communications sectors* and what strategies might help to close that gap.
- *Comparing U.S. progress with that in other countries,* and evaluating how progress abroad relates to national broadband policies and strategies.

Historically, a substantial fraction of funding for telecommunications economics research has come from industry itself. The increasing politicization of broadband (and telecommunications more broadly) argues for increased support from less directly interested parties, such as the federal government and foundations.

mission and Congress at the national level[1]—as well as in trade associations, consumer advocacy and other public interest groups, and by civic organizations, telecommunications and Internet policy scholarship forums, and groups concerned with international economic development. That such a diversity of organizations share a common interest in broadband underscores how much the Internet has become accepted as important to the U.S. economy and society, a marked contrast to the early and mid-1990s when the federal Information Infrastructure Task Force worked hard to proselytize the Internet and related services.[2] Various factions point to broadband as a compelling reason for shifts in telecommunications policy; these include proponents of both more and less government intervention. Understanding the nature of broadband and what is involved in getting it to more consumers is one of the major goals of this report.

Broadband, in the sense of high-capacity communications channels, is already present throughout much of the communications infrastructure. Fiber optic links with very large capacity are already commonplace within the networks of telecommunications carriers and are available for local access in many locations, albeit at high costs affordable by only larger businesses or organizations. The broadband challenge on most people's minds today is how to make higher-capacity connections available on a more pervasive, affordable basis. In particular, how can one best extend high-speed connectivity to users in homes, small businesses and smaller offices of larger organizations, local governments, and so forth? Widespread use—marked by new patterns of information flow—not only would benefit the individuals connected, but also could lead to qualitative changes in how people interact with family, community, and the workplace, with potentially profound social and economic implications. Broadband is viewed by some as a double-edged sword: networking could promote economic development, yet electronic commerce also has the potential to displace local businesses. (Present and potential applications and impacts are considered in Chapter 3 in this report.)

Extending the reach of broadband generally implies building on the existing communications infrastructure base, either incrementally or through significant investment in new infrastructure. It is an expensive

---

[1]Broadband-related bills introduced in the 107th Congress include S. 1056 (Community Telecommunications Planning Act of 2001), H.R. 2139 (Rural America Broadband Deployment Act), H.R. 1542 (Internet Freedom and Broadband Deployment Act of 2001), H.R. 267 (Broadband Internet Access Act of 2001), S. 150 (Broadband Deployment Act of 2001), and S. 88 (Broadband Internet Access Act of 2001).

[2]For the flavor of that period, see CSTB's 1996 report *The Unpredictable Certainty* and its 1994 report *Realizing the Information Future*, National Academy Press, Washington, D.C.

undertaking to deploy broadband to households and to small businesses and other small organizations. Each of these is a small economic unit, and most premises are located a significant distance from a so-called point of presence—which is a location where a communications service provider can get economies of scale by aggregating traffic from many customers onto its core, high-capacity links that connect to other parts of the network, including access to the Internet. (In the telephone network, these points generally are located at central offices, while in hybrid fiber coax cable systems, these points are known as head ends.)

The link between the point of presence and the customer—using either existing communications infrastructure or new facilities—is frequently referred to as the "last mile," because it represents a bottleneck that constrains the benefits the consumer gets from the rest of a network, which is literally at some distance. Greater difficulty and cost are associated with dispersed populations, whether they have low density, with homes being far apart and farther from the local point of presence, or are remote, with an entire community, whatever its density, being many miles from the nearest existing aggregation point.

PERSPECTIVES ON BROADBAND

A major goal of this report is to examine whether broadband deployment is working and what, if anything, needs fixing. There are very different perspectives on what is happening and how well the process is working. In the course of its work, the Committee on Broadband Last Mile Technology learned about several different views described below, all of which shaped its thinking:

- *Incumbents (incumbent local exchange carriers [ILECs] and cable system operators).* Deployment of consumer broadband is very costly, and dreams of "overnight" nationwide deployment are not realistic. There is good evidence of market demand, and capital is being expended at substantial rates. Sustained demand is expected to justify the continued investment. The current round of failures in certain sectors, most notably the troubles of a number of nonincumbent digital subscriber line (DSL) providers— and the associated shift in investment climate—will slow progress to some extent but do not represent a fundamental problem. Private sector investment is healthy. Fundamentally, nothing is "broken"; it is simply early in the process.

- *Consumers.* Consumers with access to broadband are experiencing much-improved Internet service compared with what dial-up provided. Some high-end, demanding users may be disappointed with the quality or predictability of their service. Many consumers are being told either

regulation developed in the contexts of older communications infrastructure continue to be applied to the new technology. That base has many faces: there are multiple communications networks, which have emerged, evolved, and coexisted in largely self-contained fashion. Thus, it is helpful to briefly review the communications past and its evolution over recent decades to a digital infrastructure capable of supporting broadband.

Traditional circuit-switched telephony is, with the exception of high-capacity lines leased by large customers, a way of providing analog narrowband last mile access. The public telephone network was originally built for voice communications but for some four decades has been used increasingly for data communications. At its core—in the channels that aggregate communications from many users—the telephone network has long had large, and growing, bandwidths. At the edges, with the exception of a few customers (chiefly larger organizations) that have been able to lease high-bandwidth private lines, customers have historically been connected through relatively low capacity twisted pair links (this is often referred to as the "local loop"). Analog telephony has evolved to digital, with high-speed digital signal transmission commonplace throughout the public telephone network except in the last mile segment. Digital transmission over the last mile has been possible for many years with the addition of dial-up modems. Integrated Services Digital Network (ISDN) never took off in the consumer market, and more recently, DSL technologies add equipment at both the customer premises and the central office to leverage the existing last mile twisted pair infrastructure in order to provide higher data rates.

Two-way wireless networks, which originated as consumer services to provide analog cellular telephony, complement these other infrastructures. Digital transmission also extends into the last mile in the current generation of cellular telephony (although analog cellular networks continue to be used). In recent years, a second generation of digital services has been deployed in more populated areas; these services support very limited data communications, including access to some Internet services. Second-generation services have grown dramatically in popularity as service prices have dropped and handsets have improved in size and battery life. So-called third-generation service, which will offer greater bandwidth (though less than the hype would suggest), inspires considerable speculation. Even with today's generation of technology, various forms of access to Internet-like services—most notably text messenging, but also including access to information and commerce—have proved popular in countries other than the United States, fueling speculation about their potential in the U.S. market.

Broadcasting in the form of radio and television has been in place for many decades. While radio and TV have very large bandwidths and may make use of digital signal transmission, none of these services fits today's common understanding of broadband. This is in part because, unlike the more general purpose, generally Internet-based broadband offerings of today, they integrate physical- and higher-layer functionality. That is, the services are aimed at particular types of communication or content (e.g., broadcast radio or television), much as the public telephone network has been designed to support a particular set of voice communications services, and they have emerged, evolved, and coexisted in self-contained fashion. Some proposed applications are data-centric, however, and may play a role complementary to the digital communications services discussed in this report. Since the 1980s, direct broadcast satellite has used satellite transmission to provide many channels of service over very wide areas, and this technology has been further developed to provide two-way broadband service delivery.

Cable television networks started out as a way of extending the reach of the broadcast networks. As this analog, one-way infrastructure grew, it began to distinguish itself from broadcasting through development of its own content. In more recent years, cable networks have joined telephony networks in the public debates about broadband because recent and ongoing upgrades have added support for two-way communication at comparatively high bandwidths.

The widespread use of computers in the home—most notably and visibly today in the form of the general-purpose personal computer, or PC—has helped to transform expectations for consumer electronics, which historically focused on entertainment and specific personal services. Computers in the home provide a broader base of support for work, education, and other nonentertainment activities within the home. The general-purpose nature of PCs implies both breadth and a multitude of options for future use. The home PC, in turn, has proliferated in part because of its potential for connectivity outside the home (today chiefly through the Internet). Capability (e.g., storage, processing speed, and support for audio and video) in home PCs and the richness of the content available through the Internet—and therefore the bandwidth needed to access it easily—have increased in tandem. These trends have been the most obvious drivers of those seeking broadband in the last mile. Forecasts of future demand involve extrapolations from the rapid growth in adoption and speed that has been experienced thus far. An important caveat is that these figures derive from the early adopters: home penetration by PCs, which grew relatively quickly in the 1990s, has been leveling off, and there is reason to believe that the explanation goes beyond simple costs.

In each of these instances, there have been well-defined roles for regulators at all levels of government. In the case of broadcasting, the air-

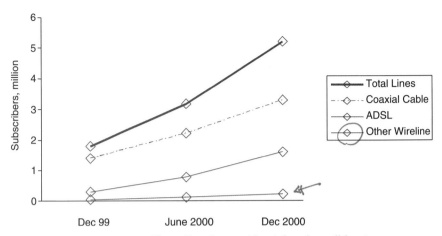

FIGURE 1.1 Penetration of broadband to residential and small business customers, December 1999 to December 2000. NOTE: (1) "Total" includes wireless, satellite, and fiber subscribers. (2) ADSL = asymmetric digital subscriber line. (3) "Other wireline" includes symmetric DSL services. SOURCE: Federal Communications Commission (FCC). 2001. *High-speed Services for Internet Access: Subscribership as of December 31, 2000.* Industry Analysis Division, Common Carrier Bureau, FCC, Washington, D.C.

infrastructure. Now, as then, there are multiple technologies and industries that can advance the infrastructure in general and broadband in particular. Optical fiber systems continue to promise the most bandwidth, but at the highest cost and risk. Private investment is still viewed as an essential ingredient, but it continues to be inhibited by uncertainty about what consumers will buy and what business models will succeed. Today, as then, it is understood that government action (or inaction) has the potential to both inhibit and promote investment.

BROADBAND DEPLOYMENT TRENDS

FCC data based on reports from carriers show rapid growth in broadband subscriptions by residential and small business customers, with the total growing from roughly 1.8 million in December 1999 to 5.2 million subscribers in December 2000 (see Figure 1.1).[5] Looking specifically at residential users, an October 2000 report from the National Telecommu-

---

[5]Interpretation is complicated because the figure includes small business as well as residential customers and because ADSL is separated from other forms of DSL, which are lumped under "other wireline."

nications and Information Administration (NTIA) indicates that 4.4 percent of all U.S. households, or 10.7 percent of households with Internet access, had broadband access as of August 2000.[6] Market research reports from 2000 provide consistent figures; for example, a November 2000 study by the Cahners In-Stat Group found that roughly 9 percent of U.S. households that access the Internet use a form of broadband Internet access.[7] Reports from mid-2001 show further growth: a total of more than 5 million cable modem subscribers and more than 3 million DSL subscribers.[8] There have, however, been hints that growth has been slowing, at least in some market segments: second-quarter 2001 reports from Verizon and AT&T Broadband show growth below the 2000 rate, and early 2001 also saw contraction in the competitive local exchange carrier (CLEC) business.[9] Penetration rates can be much higher than the average in markets where broadband has been available for several years. For example, in Portland, Maine, an early test market for TimeWarner Cable, about one-quarter of households have become cable modem subscribers.

Access rates—the fraction of households that *could* subscribe to broadband if they chose to—are substantially higher than current subscription rates. A survey of Internet users commissioned by the General Accounting Office indicated that some form of wireline broadband access was available to 52.4 percent of Internet users—25.4 percent via both cable and DSL, 16.9 percent via cable only, and 10.1 percent via DSL only—as of May 2000.[10] As of mid-2001, approximately 60 million homes reportedly had cable modem service available, and 52 million homes had DSL service available.[11] Availability and use of broadband are both correlated with town size. Nielsen/Netratings found that broadband users in the

---

[6]National Telecommunications and Information Administration (NTIA). 2000. *Falling Through the Net: Toward Digital Inclusion.* NTIA, Washington, D.C., October. Available online at <http://www.ntia.doc.gov/ntiahome/digitaldivide/index.html>.

[7]Cahners In-Stat Group. 2000. *Broadband Consumers—Profiles and Strategies,* Report No. BBWIS00-05SP. See also "Broadband Subscriptions Will Rise 77% Through 2004," *Broadband Week,* available online at <http://www.instat.com/rh/bbw/is0005sp_story.htm>.

[8]The National Cable & Telecommunications Association (NCTA) estimates 5.5 million subscribers as of August 2001. See <http://www.ncta.com>.

[9]AT&T Broadband reportedly signed up 259,000 customers during the fourth quarter of 2000, but only 131,000 during the second quarter of 2001. Verizon signed up 90,000 customers in the fourth quarter of 2000 and 120,000 during the second quarter of 2001 (Christopher Stern, 2000, "Broadband Market Growth Slows," *Washington Post,* August 28, p. E01).

[10]Determining the fraction of homes with DSL service available is more complicated than in the case of cable. DSL availability depends on central office equipment, line length, and the characteristics of the specific loop, while availability of cable modem service for the most part depends only on whether the subscriber's system has been upgraded.

[11]Remarks of Robert Sachs, NCTA, June 11, 2001; Cablevision Blue Book, Cahners Business Information, New York, June 2001.

The oft-cited penetration numbers for different communications services can mask considerable variations in the nature or quality of the service. Both basic and higher tiers of capabilities have arisen in all of the traditional or conventional communications infrastructures. For example, touchtone and multiparty capability emerged as options in telephony, FM emerged as a "higher-quality" option compared with AM in radio, and color emerged as a "higher-quality" option compared with black-and-white TV. Cable came along to provide yet another TV option, but over a different infrastructure, with service tiers determined by the nature and amount of the programming content. Even dial-up Internet access is subject to variation. The speed ceiling is limited by the audio bandwidth of the public telephone network, but the floor depends on the quality of the individual telephone line. As a practical matter, what has been universally available is a lowest-common-denominator service, although upgrades in provider networks tend to raise that floor over time (for example, touchtone service has become the norm in telephony, and party lines have gone by the wayside).

As is seen in many markets, saturation—or at least high and slowly growing levels of penetration—tends to prompt the introduction of enhanced, higher-value and higher-priced offerings in the hopes of increasing provider revenues. Sometimes this is in the form of new content or applications, and at other times it reflects upgrades to the hardware and software of the communications network itself. And, over time, new communications technologies arise that complement the existing ones, offering new or significantly enhanced capabilities. The experiences of the 20th century suggest that few new technologies completely replace earlier ones, and that whatever substitution occurs does so over a long timescale. As demonstrated by the rapid rise of direct broadcast TV, new technologies can, however, pose a significant challenge to the existing players.

Complicating an understanding of broadband in the last mile is the evolution of the community context. On the one hand, the community can compensate in part for a lack of home access by providing access to broadband capabilities in publicly owned spaces (e.g., schools and libraries) and through private organizations (e.g., businesses as employers). On the other hand, the community can stimulate home access demand by generating content and opportunities for civic interactions—as well as supporting organizational use of the Internet, telecommuting and distance learning, public awareness and education about how to benefit from broadband, and so on. The lowest-common-denominator level of communications infrastructure—basic telephone service; television via broadcast, cable, or satellite; and dial-up Internet access—may have been taken for granted in all but the areas hardest to serve. However, differences among communities raise questions about how broadband relates to local economic development for purposes of attracting broader economic opportunities (and a higher quality of life) for citizens (through access in homes as well as schools, hospitals, and libraries). There is, of course, a tension between the well-connected home as a place from which its residents can access people, information, and economic activity that may be based physically quite far away—and that same home as an entity with a specific physical location, which drives needs to access people, information, and economic activity locally. Today's islands of broadband have the potential to intensify other differentiators of home and community experience, which has led to the invocation of broadband in the evolving consideration of a "digital divide." Communities compose the social level where interhome (and intercommunity) differences in access, burden, and benefit are most apparent, and they are on the frontlines of the integration of business and nonprofit influences on local activity. Although 1990s public debates over information and communications infrastructure took a national perspective, communities may play a larger role in moving forward in the new century.

ACCESS ECONOMICS AND EVOLVING APPLICATIONS

Because many costs are per-house-passed rather than per-customer-served and because of economies of scale, individual or isolated consumers cannot induce providers to deploy expensive infrastructure at a reasonable price. Thus, investors and industries search for clusters of consumers who will pay for service before the investors and industries will commit to upgrade or deploy infrastructure. One key recurring question is what types of service the customer will pay for and at what levels. Both the reach of different services and their enhancement paths reflect differences in industry and provider business models. Consumers usually pay for the in-home hardware (and software) required to use a communications service, but it varies as to whether they purchase it directly or lease it from a service provider. Cable television reflects consumer willingness to pay for access to programming content, in contrast to broadcast content, which is for the most part paid for by advertising. Consumers who place a telephone call to an Internet service provider (ISP) pay that provider for Internet access service, in addition to what they pay for telephone service and for the equipment they use, and in addition to what they may pay to access certain kinds of content or services through the Internet. What people will pay regularly for information and communication services remains an open question as the choices proliferate. Providers of traditional services approach this question with concerns about preserving traditional revenue streams as well as cultivating new ones. Providers of new content and services have been struggling to find the

synchronous satellites has introduced a new option for broadband. It is unclear at present to what extent uncertainty in some segments of the business could contribute to an overall slowdown in investment, and caution should be exercised in projecting long-term prospects for broadband based on the present downturn.

SCOPE OF THIS REPORT

The world of broadband is significantly more complex than that of the traditional or conventional communications infrastructures. This report is designed to assess the nature of broadband, its deployment and acceptance, expectations about future deployment, and the potential longer-term technical and social implications of broadband access. The challenging and sometimes necessarily speculative nature of this analysis makes it inherently imperfect. Notwithstanding these limitations, an additional goal of this report is to make useful recommendations about how best to maximize the potential impact and rewards of broadband, generally exploring what will be required to achieve ubiquitous broadband access, in the sense of both expanding the geographical reach of broadband facilities and addressing affordability issues.

The focus of this report is on providing access to fixed (i.e., nonmobile) users, but the label "last mile" also applies to mobile applications, and the report touches on mobile issues as appropriate. For example, to the extent that one wishes to support near-seamless communications across fixed and mobile locations, the two are coupled.

Broadband poses many analytical challenges that go beyond the complex technical and economic landscape. One problem is the lack of a common information base: detailed information is often proprietary; information presented in governmental proceedings is tailored to those proceedings; and systematic detailed data on deployment are hard to come by. Perhaps an even bigger challenge relates to the generally poor track record of both those within industry and outside observers in forecasting information technology (IT) developments or its economic parameters. Finally, basic assumptions will continue to shift. For example, changes underway include the nature of installation (do-it-yourself/off-the-shelf versus professional installer) and the specification of what can be shared (e.g., a shift from built to leased wireless towers or from single-user to shared conduit or fiber bundles). The future may well see change in licensing requirements (e.g., per-site versus per-system licensing of wireless service). Finally, the roles of the key players—consumer, community, communications-industry sectors, and all levels of government from town to federal—continue to be in flux.

Notwithstanding these and other challenges, the Committee on Broadband Last Mile Technology has attempted to put forth, by consensus, views about the broadband last mile that seek to have value in the 2- to 10-year time frame. While such a time frame might seem to be daunting in the face of the rate at which some of the basic technologies are advancing (Moore's law and its kin), the processes of deployment and acceptance have always proceeded much more slowly, and there seems to be no particular reason to expect a significant change in these time constants going forward.

ample, two recent Swedish governmental commissions took a look at this same question (but without having to factor in the U.S. statutory language, as did the FCC) and adopted substantially higher-speed thresholds: symmetric 2 Mbps and 5 Mbps.[5] In the end, neither the definitions of the FCC or those of the Swedish commissions are entirely satisfactory (indeed, FCC staff speaking at the committee's 2000 workshop acknowledged difficulties associated with the FCC definition).

Defining broadband is more than an academic exercise. Numerous groups would stand to benefit from workable definitions of what constitutes broadband. They include:

- *Consumers*, who would like to be able to evaluate service offerings to see if the offerings are likely to meet their needs;
- *Service providers*, who would like to develop, invest in, and deploy services that consumers will need and want;
- *Application and content developers*, who would like to understand and track the connectivity performance options available to consumers;
- *Policy makers or regulators*, who seek to monitor broadband service deployment and measure the impact of policy or regulatory decisions on deployment, define the characteristics of services eligible for tax credits or loans, or define the characteristics of services required in build-out commitments associated with regulatory relief; and
- *Public interest groups*, which seek to evaluate capabilities available to consumers and to understand the implications of alternative policy approaches that influence those capabilities.

Framed in this way, defining the term "broadband" in some sense also involves (1) identifying the kinds of applications that consumers are likely to find useful and desirable and (2) determining the benefits that different segments of the public anticipate from access to broadband services. The definition of broadband used by each of these groups will reflect that group's expectations and, consequently, can have a significant effect on decision making. Too limited a definition, such as establishing too low a data transmission rate as the broadband threshold, could result in a mismatch between expectations and capabilities, while a definition that is unrealistic in terms of technological capabilities, costs, or consumer demand could prompt inappropriate or poorly aimed policy interventions. The absence of a consensus on definitions will confuse political

---

[5]Swedish Special Infrastructure Commission (June 1999): Broadband should be defined as at least 2 Mbps (symmetrical) to the user. Swedish IT Commission (November 1999): Minimum 5 Mbps to the user.

debate on the subject and require ongoing debates about what definitions to use.

OVERVIEW OF THE TECHNICAL CHARACTERISTICS OF BROADBAND

Communications capacity, or speed, is only one of a set of performance characteristics of a service. That it is not the whole picture is easily seen in the contrast between dial-up access, where the modem must place a telephone call and negotiate a connection with the ISP's modem, and the services available today that are generally considered broadband—which frequently offer "always-on" connectivity as well as high speed. Along with speed and always-on are additional parameters such as bandwidth symmetry and addressability that are important components of a definition of broadband. Each of these is considered in the sections that follow.

Speed

The speed or bandwidth of a service—the rate at which one can transfer data to and/or from the home—is a function of multiple factors. Because the effective bandwidth reflects the capacity of the end-to-end connection between sender and receiver, the speed seen by a user can be constrained at any one of a number of points between the user's computer and the computer providing a particular service. However, speeds within the core network have been rising, at least in the United States and other developed nations, and the capacity of the network link between the user and the broadband provider's network is one of the crucial factors that determines how the broadband service can be used.

The better-than-dial-up criterion for broadband assures that a service is at least a little better than what was available before, but it does not address the question of whether the service is good enough. And while a 2- or 5-Mbps threshold would seem ample for most applications envisioned today, it might, on the one hand, prove inadequate in the future, or, on the other, raise questions about whether its costs today would exceed what customers are willing to pay for today. Later, this chapter explores several approaches to answering the fundamental question, How fast is fast enough?

As indicated earlier, the effective speed for interacting with an Internet host is not merely a function of the performance of the broadband local access link—it depends on the entire path between the host and the user, and also on the loading on the host computer. As a result, depending on the circumstances, improvements in the performance of one link does not necessarily improve overall performance—it may only shift the bottle-

particular stream (delivery of packets for playback in near-real time), is even more asymmetric.

While Web browsing has been a dominant application of residential broadband, accompanied by more limited audio/video streaming, peer-to-peer applications have surged recently. These applications, which use many individual computers instead of a central server to distribute content, require significant upstream capacity for each computer. They have, as a result, presented ISPs with traffic loads that are at odds with the ISPs' assumptions about asymmetric traffic[7] and have raised questions about what shape user demand will take in the long term. Similar pressures result from other applications in which users host content on their local machines, creating upstream demand whenever this content is requested. These pressures, at odds with the capabilities of today's networks, have also led some broadband ISPs to prohibit customers who subscribe to consumer/residential services from running servers on their computers.

It is not clear at this point how traffic patterns will evolve as applications mature and as the population of broadband network users moves beyond early adopters. There is at least some reason to believe that the traffic patterns will in fact be asymmetric, though perhaps not as strongly as some of the broadband ISPs initially assumed in their network design and pricing models. But it is also important to recognize that some of the demand for symmetric bandwidth is a political rather than a business or engineering proposition. If the networks are designed to make it impossible, or very expensive, for individuals to originate the kind of traffic associated with the provision of services or content to significant audiences, it would foreclose the possibility that high-traffic upstream services will emerge on a highly distributed, grass-roots basis. This prospect points toward a model of the future broadband-enabled Internet as an environment dominated by commercially provided services connecting to customers—an outcome that in the view of some would fall short of broadband's full potential.

More generally, while much of the focus on broadband has been on its potential as a channel for delivering information, broadband also provides a more general communications channel (into and out of the premises). On the one hand, e-mail and instant messaging are prominent examples of communications applications that do not depend on large amounts of upstream bandwidth (or downstream, for that matter), but

---

[7]For example, according to Jim Hannan of Sprint Wireless at the committee's June 2000 workshop, "As a point of data, in our experience, we would love it if [the ratio of downstream to upstream] were 10 to 1. You know, our network model said worst case: 8 to 1. Unfortunately, our experience is 2 1/2 or 3 to 1, downstream to upstream."

that provide evidence of demand for convenient, Internet-based communication. On the other hand, as consumers start transmitting video clips (produced using increasingly inexpensive digital video cameras), bandwidth requirements could increase significantly. On the horizon are a number of communications applications—telephony being the most obvious—that place increasing demand on the upstream channel.

The detailed discussion of application classes below suggests that the jury is still out on the long-term implications of such applications for symmetry demands in broadband services. Nevertheless, a number of pressures for increased upstream capacity are evident.

Always-On

In addition to higher bandwidth, a broadband connection also generally provides an always-available connection to the Internet. One principal implication of always-on broadband service is that, for the first time, residential users have nearly instant access to Web or other Internet services on demand. Before the advent of broadband services, residential and many small business Internet users were confined to using a dial-up line to access the Internet. With dial-up, the user faces a noticeable delay—the sum of the time it takes to place a call between the user and ISP modems, the time it takes for the two modems to negotiate a connection, and the time it takes to log in (generally by authenticating the user via a password) to the ISP. The delay is increased if the user makes a habit of turning off the PC between sessions, since the time it takes the computer to boot up must also be added to the time it takes before a user can access the Internet. By eliminating the need to place a telephone call, broadband services greatly reduce the time required. While there is some delay associated with negotiating communications parameters when the customer's modem is powered up, these devices are designed to be left on all of the time, meaning that there is continuous connectivity between the modem and the network to which it is attached. Laptop computers have had power management features for some years; more recently this capability has been added to desktop computers. Power management capabilities make it possible to have computers "sleep" (quickly switched to a low-power state) and then be reawakened whenever the user wishes to access Internet resources.

The term "always-on" might conjure up visions of some sort of compelled use in which computers or applications must be left running all of the time. Always-on does not imply this; it refers merely to a characteristic of broadband networks that *enables* network communications to be initiated at any time. Users remain free to close software programs or shut down computers as they wish. Of course, some applications and com-

BOX 2.1
In-Home Networking Technologies

Wired Ethernet

This is the industry-standard networking technology commonly used in office and business settings. Ethernet today routinely runs at 100 Mbps, which provides adequate performance for many applications, even video applications. (Quality-of-service management, which is not provided by standard Ethernet, may, however, be required for very-high-end applications.) The primary difficulty with using wired Ethernet is that most homes are not wired with the requisite category 5 wiring. There are long-term efforts aimed at promoting the installation of networking-compatible wiring in new construction;[1] rewiring of existing dwellings is generally restricted to early technology adopters who are willing to deal with the cost and disruption associated with installing new wires within a house. With a wired infrastructure in place, Ethernet is a very inexpensive solution, with interface hardware available from many vendors and frequently incorporated into computers. It also offers ample headroom for future speed upgrades (1 gigabit per second [Gbps]s has been demonstrated over four category 5 twisted pairs of 150 feet). For the slowly growing set of users that have the requisite wiring, Ethernet is a likely technology of choice.

Phone Line Networking

Phone line networking operates by using a high-frequency carrier superimposed over a home's existing analog voice telephone wiring, allowing any standard phone jack within the house to become a network port. For homes that have phone jacks already installed in locations where networked devices are likely to be located, as is the case in many U.S. homes, this is an attractive solution. An industry standards group, the Home Phoneline Networking Alliance (HPNA), has defined two standards: HPNA 1, which provides a 1-Mbps data rate, and HPNA 2, which increases the data rate to 10 Mbps while maintaining backward compatibility with the first version. The HPNA specification does not interfere with the normal voice operation of the phone line, and it operates in a different band from a G.992.2 asymmetric digital subscriber line (ADSL) (G.lite) so that it can coexist with that standard as well. HPNA products are currently offered by a number of vendors for attachment to existing computers via parallel port, universal serial bus (USB), or via a peripheral component interconnect (PCI) add-in card. Additionally, a number of PC vendors are shipping home PCs with HPNA integrated into the system directly. The technology is relatively inexpensive and HPNA is being bundled with home computers today, much as most home PCs include analog modems. HPNA has the drawback of interfering with broadcast radio and some, but not all, types of DSL.

---

[1]Wiring America's Homes, sponsored by the Home Automation Association.
See <http://www.homeautomation.org/wah.html>.

Wireless Networking

Wireless solutions are very attractive in that they require no wires to be installed. They allow networked computers to be located anywhere within the home, and they support mobility within the house. In the past, wireless technologies suffered from being too expensive for broad consumer acceptance, had lackluster performance, and were too power-hungry for use in battery-powered devices. More recently, two standards using the unlicensed 2.4-gigahertz (GHz) band that overcome these shortcomings have emerged: 802.11b and HomeRF. 802.11b has been defined by the Institute of Electrical and Electronics Engineers (IEEE) and supported by the Wireless Ethernet Compatibility Alliance industry consortium. It uses direct sequence spread spectrum rather than frequency hopping, and operates at up to 11 Mbps for data. A number of vendors have announced 802.11b products. 802.11b is also being widely supported in business environments and public access points and is also being used in a number of community access initiatives. With both standards, there are issues of interference with other uses and other technologies that make use of the same radio spectrum.

Products using a new standard from IEEE (802.11a), which use the 5-GHz band and promise data rates of 54 Mbps, are under development. Another wireless LAN standard operating in the 2.4-GHz band, 802.11g, would boost speeds to as much as 54M bit/sec while proving backward compatibility with the 802.11b. Another relevant wireless standard is Bluetooth. Currently Bluetooth targets data rates of less than 1 Mbps, although work is ongoing to define higher-speed versions. However, it focuses now and probably in the future on short-range "personal area networking," at less than 10 meters (m). While Bluetooth will likely have applications in the home, the range may restrict it from being a general-purpose solution for home networking. Also, because both Bluetooth and the current generation of wireless LANs use the same spectrum, there are still unresolved issues of how to efficiently share the spectrum and avoid interference.

Powerline Networking

Because power outlets are ubiquitous in homes, there has been long-standing interest in technology that would provide high-speed networking over household AC power wiring. However, there is a great deal of interference present on power wiring, because these wires are used to supply power to motors and other very electrically noisy devices. In addition, many homes utilize both phases of the supply power in different circuits within the home; communicating across outlets connected to different phases requires installation of bridges between the phases, which may be difficult for consumers themselves to install.

In multidwelling units there are also potential interference problems, analogous to those faced in wireless networking, associated with multiple users using common lines. To date, the most common use of networking over the powerlines has been for X-10 home control devices that permit remote operation of lights and the like. In the year 2000, several companies began shipping, or announced, powerline-based data networking products, with claims of data rates up to 10 Mbps. The HomePlug Powerline Alliance available online at <www.homeplug.org> has been formed and is promoting its 10-Mbps baseline standard. Field trials and certification lab are reportedly approaching.

practice, motivation, and perceived impacts that varies with point of view. The issues are outlined here because they contribute to both perceptions and realities of commercial broadband offerings, which will be implemented based on choices made by providers that must decide among technological and strategy options. Given the newness of the marketplace, it is easy for critics to assume intent based on experience with traditional media, especially cable, and it is hard to predict what practices will succeed in the broadband marketplace, regardless of their fate with traditional media. About the only certainties at this point are that the service providers are trying to make money, that content providers seek access to users, and that provider policies and practices are evolving at the same time as the technologies and businesses.

Already, there are various models for Internet service, ranging from the ISP that provides only basic IP connectivity to the ISP that provides a modest bundle of services and content, to ISPs such as America Online (AOL) and Microsoft Network (MSN) that aim to provide a wide range of products and services. Providers can seek various degrees of control over particular applications that run over their service or restrict access to particular content, perhaps simply by making it much easier to access preferred content. This may happen for various reasons, and the effects may be either primary (to promote use of certain content) or secondary (to make use of certain content less convenient).

If some content (e.g., from sources with business relationships with providers) is cached and easily accessed, other content may appear to be harder to get to. Uncached Web content will, for example, be slower to load—especially if the source is far from the user and/or on a network with poor connectivity to the user's. In the extreme case, access to non-cached content might be poor enough to make it seem effectively filtered; consumer advocates express this concern about the fate of content from nonprofit sources, but the concern remains hypothetical.

Service providers provision bandwidth, especially upstream, based on a particular business model—which makes assumptions about who is sending how much of what to whom—or on the assumption that a certain fraction of traffic can be cached. Or, providers might use restrictions— such as restrictions on virtual private networks or on operating household-based servers—as a means of value stratification, charging more to those who value, use, and will pay for more flexibility or capacity.

Actions that restrict upstream communication raise concerns about innovation enabled by end users' being able to originate content or applications. A targeted approach by ISPs might alleviate some concerns. For example, a provider that is concerned with upstream bandwidth scarcity might more effectively deal with excessive bandwidth use (relative to provisioning assumptions) by applying measures that monitor or restrict bandwidth consumption rather than by prohibiting all users from, say, running servers. While some legacy equipment might not support bandwidth monitoring or control, most ISP equipment today would permit this. Opinions will differ as to whether restrictions reflect legitimate operational considerations; valid business decisions to differentiate customers; or unreasonable attempts to limit customer access to applications, content, and services.

Assessment of provider conduct should distinguish between the use of caching and similar techniques, which are aimed at improving access to some content by moving it (via distributed copies) to locations closer to users, and the use of filtering, which limits access to some content entirely. Steering or restricting customers to certain content runs counter to the traditional Internet model, in which Internet service is deemed synonymous with access to all Internet content. The success of these "walled-garden" models depends on whether consumers want the preferred content (or, in the view of critics, have no alternative). Actual consumer preferences and reactions to their experiences as users confronting differential ease of access to content are an important but unknown factor.

Implications of Network Design/Architecture

Another parameter that deserves consideration is whether "broadband" refers exclusively to Internet service or is a more inclusive term that refers to a set of data communications services. Is the point of broadband to bring the Internet to the home or small business at much higher speed and with characteristics such as always-on, or is broadband really about delivering to the home a bundle of digital services, which include IP service, that are demultiplexed at a gateway? Cable television systems today deliver both IP data and digital television signals. Higher-quality pictures and greater system capacity than analog cable systems could deliver were the original motivation for deploying hybrid fiber coax (HFC) in cable systems—IP data capabilities were added later. This video via MPEG (a standard for video compression from the Motion Picture Experts Group) streams is largely one-way (possibly with a low-capacity return channel to allow the selection of content or other interactive features), and the content is offered through various service bundles and pay-per-view options defined by the service provider. Looking forward, to what extent will services be delivered using plain-vanilla IP versus more specialized protocols and architectures? Running video and audio over plain IP, for example, is not without problems today, and these, together with business considerations, may well lead providers to devise other network protocols and systems to deliver audio and video alongside IP (for other applications), perhaps coming out of the set-top box into

investment in the local access link will not improve application performance. (Other strategies may be used in such circumstances, such as caching or replication within the network of the access provider.)

Broadband Definition 1, however, gives an answer that is only correct for a given set of applications at one point in time. What happens when new applications come along? In fact, the performance of broadband access will be a key factor influencing the emergence of new applications, since new applications that demand higher transfer speeds cannot take off until there is a critical mass of users with the access capacity to use them. This motivates an alternative definition of broadband:

Broadband Definition 2. Broadband services should provide sufficient performance—and wide enough penetration of services reaching that performance level—to encourage the development of new applications.

This definition implies that a broadband access system is defined both by a technical evolution path and an economic evolution path that will allow it to play its part in the chicken-and-egg application cycle. The subscriber link is viewed as a potential bottleneck that inhibits innovation and constrains the development of new services elsewhere in the network. Those providing services over the Internet who feel constrained by the premises-link bottleneck may not be able to fully incorporate the benefits of relaxing this bottleneck in their own investment decisions (i.e., their incentives to "subsidize" broader deployment fall short of the true collective benefits)—because they are unable to internalize the benefits realized by other service providers.

One example of how this view comes into play is the asymmetry of broadband services. Anticipating a number of new applications that require greater upstream capacity, one can project increasing demand for upstream bandwidth arising from new applications. Yet, if connections remain highly asymmetric over the long run, then applications that need significant upstream capacity will be slower to appear. Because it takes into account the dynamic interplay between deployed technology and applications as well as the interplay between technology and economic developments, this second definition is likely to be the more useful one in planning and policy making.

Whichever of these definitions one adopts, it is quite apparent that a single number—be it 200 kbps or 2 Mbps—is not a useful definition of broadband (even if one focuses only on the bandwidth issue). However, not all values (from zero to infinity) will be equally meaningful. Applications such as those discussed in Chapter 3 tend to cluster into classes characterized by bandwidth and other performance requirements. This suggests that there will be a series of milestones along the way, with multiple peaks that may well correspond to, or catalyze, application and infrastructure deployment milestones.

Today's residential broadband capabilities, which are typified by several hundred kilobits per second to several megabits per second downstream and several hundreds of kilobits per second upstream, support such applications as Web browsing, e-mail, messaging, games, and audio download and streaming. These are possible with dial-up, but their performance and convenience are significantly improved with broadband. At downstream speeds of several tens of megabits per second, new applications are enabled, including streaming of high-quality video, such as MPEG-2 (a standard defined by the Moving Picture Experts Group) or high-definition television (HDTV), download of full-length (70- to 90-minute) audiovisual files in tens of minutes rather than hours, and rapid download of other large data files. Reaching this plateau would enable true television-personal computing convergence. With comparable upstream speeds, computer-mediated multimedia communications become possible, including distance education, telecommuting, and so forth. With FTTH, a new performance plateau with gigabit speeds both up- and downstream would be reached. The applications that would take full advantage of this capacity remain to be seen.

TABLE 3.1 Mapping Between Broadband Service Capabilities and Application Classes

Broadband Capability	Application Class
Large downstream bandwidth	Streaming content (e.g., video)
Large upstream bandwidth	Home publishing
Always-on	Information appliances
Low latency	Interactive games

example, shared sports viewing requires substantial upstream and downstream bandwidth simultaneously. Furthermore, the composite broadband use in a home may be made up of multiple applications being used simultaneously by different family members.

Faster General Internet Access and General Internet Applications

Browsing and Related Activities

The primary motivation today for residential broadband access is simply to improve the performance of the overall Web browsing experience. While many factors actually influence the perceived speed of Web browsing—including, most notably, the performance of the server itself and the performance of the server's connection to the rest of the Internet—moving from dial-up speeds to broadband speeds on a consumer's Internet access link will almost always provide dramatic perceived speed improvements in general Internet usage.

In addition to making the general Web experience more enjoyable, this speed improvement can also mean that new types of content become usable by the consumer. There is, for example, a widely held belief among commerce site operators that it is essential to minimize page-load times.[1] Commerce sites thus depend on network performance in designing their pages, and any increase in that performance (either on average or for specific users that they can identify) means that they can increase the richness (and hence possibly the value) of their pages. For example, small images might be replaced by higher-resolution pictures that more closely approximate the quality available in print catalogs.

---

[1]One rule of thumb, the "8-second rule," states that if it takes longer than 8 seconds for a page to appear on the consumer's screen, there is a high likelihood that the consumer will abandon the site. See, for example, Zona Research, 1999, *The Economic Impacts of Unacceptable Web Site Download Speeds,* available online at <http://www.zonaresearch.com/deliverables/white_papers/wp17/>.

Other Web usage, such as simply reading long articles (for example, from online news sources), becomes more enjoyable with greater bandwidth, and hence the Web is a more attractive medium when the effective speed of information display approaches that experienced in physical page turning. Finally, certain types of real-time applications, such as streaming stock quotes, depend upon speed and timeliness to be valuable. Such applications can often run continuously in a part of the screen and attract user attention intermittently. However, to be effective, bandwidth must be sufficient for the performance of these applications and that of whatever other network interactions the user may be involved with.

Messaging

Messaging of various kinds continues to show up in surveys as an important application. For example, a Jupiter MediaMetrix assessment of AOL usage for January 2001 reported that of 22 billion minutes spent on AOL's online service, 4.7 billion were spent on AOL e-mail, 2.8 billion on internal instant messaging, and 6.2 billion minutes on AOL instant messaging with users outside of AOL's online service; this contrasts with 2.1 billion inside all AOL content channels.[2] Although many saw it as an application geared toward entertainment, messaging is also seeing increased use in a variety of business environments. While not demanding in terms of bandwidth (dial-up bandwidths are sufficient), broadband enhances messaging because it is always on.

Fast File Downloading

Many users are familiar with downloading e-mail attachments or software upgrades. But many bulk file transfers are simply not practical without broadband. For example, downloading an entire application that might otherwise be delivered on a CD would require many hours over even the best dial-up connection—a 60-megabyte (MB) file would take about 4 hours on a link with a sustained 35-kbps transfer rate. For most people, this length of time is simply impractical, particularly if the dial-up line is also used for voice communications or is subject to periodic disconnection. On the other hand, a constant connection to the network at even modest broadband speeds may make such transfers reasonable.

It is important not to underestimate the impact of fast file-downloading capability on a very wide range of applications, including audio and video. Streaming is complicated compared with file downloading, and

---

[2]See "AOL's Minutes." 2001. *The Washington Post*, March 8, p. E11.

on bandwidth or on consumer acceptance of a model in which the individual does not own the software. In many cases (for example, tax preparation software), users may want to control the data locally for privacy and security reasons. Other applications, such as games, could be obtained through rental, and there would be no such concerns.

Network Storage

Network storage applications provide users with an alternative to storing data on local hard drives or on removable storage media such as floppy disks or CD-ROM. There are two major advantages to this service. First, people use network-based storage rather than run their own local servers to do such things as sharing photos. It is hard to know whether storage will migrate into the home or out of the home when material can be stored in either place—much undoubtedly depends on pricing, confidence about access controls for out-of-the-home storage for certain kinds of materials, and so forth. Second, network-based storage provides redundant off-site storage. This is likely to be attractive to small and home businesses and to people who require disaster recovery (which might well include anyone with a PC who has had a disk crash). Privacy issues can be handled by only placing encrypted data on the remote store. For small business it seems likely, for reasons of performance, management, and support, that content will be hosted remotely by commercial Web hosting services rather than at the small business site.

The requirements depend on what sort of data is being stored. For example, photo (or video) storage may require relatively high upstream capacity to permit uploading in a reasonable time (and not tie up the connection). But file-system backups, which normally need to transfer only periodic, incremental updates, depend more on the always-on nature of the connection rather than the bandwidth (unless the volume of modified data is very large). One can imagine the emergence of a generation of operating systems with automatic continuous backup across the network as an option—greatly reducing the likelihood of data loss due to disk crashes or other computer failures.

Static Image Delivery

Several interesting video applications depend on the ability to deliver still photos or short video clips. The emergence of inexpensive—albeit more expensive than their analog counterparts—digital still and video cameras enables easy capture of photos.

Audio

Because many audio applications do not demand especially high bandwidth, in notable contrast to video applications, they often work with at least some level of functionality over a fast dial-up connection. All of the currently deployed broadband technologies are fast enough to support the key audio applications that have emerged to date. These include conventional voice similar to telephony; voice as a complement to games and other interactive applications; and a full range of sound applications, beginning with music but including other types of content (e.g., news and other spoken word). As a result, some experience has been gained with the delivery of audio applications over the Internet in general, and via residential broadband in particular. This experience supports a key theme of this chapter—for many applications, the bandwidth provided by broadband services is a necessary but not a sufficient condition by itself to make an application work effectively. Factors such as which home networking technologies are used, the availability of special-purpose appliances, and the nature of user interfaces are also critical enablers of widespread use of audio applications. While there is much interest in broadband for video delivery, this chapter devotes considerable attention to audio as well, both because it is an important application and because understanding of audio applications is better grounded than that of video applications, given early efforts to deploy various audio applications.

Audio Delivery

Fundamentally, there are two ways to approach audio delivery—a file can be downloaded to a local computer and then played, or the data can be streamed from a remote computer to the local computer, played more or less as it is received. Clearly, the file transfer model is appropriate only for distributing prerecorded material; conversations by their very nature have to be conducted in a streaming mode, and streaming is also essential for "live" content that has high time value (such as commentary on a sporting event). The use of streaming delivery does mean that the audio is necessarily listened to in real time. While some streaming applications use encryption to make it difficult to keep a copy, some streaming applications permit a copy to be saved to a file for replay or other later use.

Streaming audio requires an end-to-end network connection that is fast enough to handle the actual encoded size of the audio file on a second-by-second basis (one end may be at a content server located some-

While acceptable spoken voice quality is provided by a data rate as low as 4 kbps, music playback covers a wider range of data rates. Present storage and transmission costs generally mean that the maximum practical compressed signal data rate for many applications is 32 to 64 kbps. MP3-type encoding is commonly used today to compress audio at a variety of compression ratios. MP3 at 64 kbps provides a quality roughly analogous to (analog) FM radio quality—acceptable in some applications, particularly if it is to be played back through a low-quality system, but not as good as a CD played using high-quality equipment. Compact disk (CD) quality using today's compression algorithms requires 128 kpbs.[7]

The gap may also be growing between what generally available bandwidth supports and state-of-the-art audio. Consumer electronics companies are currently beginning to promote a series of super-high-fidelity recording schemes using higher-capacity DVD (digital versatile disk) media that provide a much higher quality than that of CD audio. Multichannel sound proposed for future HDTV-class applications would require a higher bit rate, with 320 kbps being a conservative figure for 5-channel sound.[8]

The wide range of bandwidth-quality trade-offs for sound is illustrated by radio broadcasting that is being streamed across the Internet. At the low end, services such as spinner.com stream sub-FM radio quality music at roughly 20 kbps. Much content is streamed at rates in the range of 20 to 100 kbps, with the low end serving dial-up users and the high end aimed at users in the workplace or with residential broadband. Toward the high end of that range, the quality lies somewhere between FM radio and CD quality. And at the high end lies uncompressed full-fidelity radio broadcasting at a data rate of 1.4 Mbps, as was demonstrated at the October 2000 meeting of the Internet 2 consortium. The majority of applications moving audio over the network today, however, operate toward the lower end of the quality-bandwidth curve.

The range of technology options today supports the observation that there are very different thresholds for what constitutes "minimally acceptable" music quality and what constitutes "high" quality. This is a very subjective matter—many people are willing to listen to AM radio, a large number find FM radio acceptable, and some significantly prefer CDs over FM because of the quality difference. In addition, acceptability varies from one recording to another; some lossy algorithms work reason-

---

[7]Released in 1980, the CD audio specification (the so-called red book standard) makes use of an inefficient compression scheme that requires about 1.5 Mbps. Today, considerably better compression algorithms are available.

[8]Fortunately, the bit rate grows less than linearly with the number of channels.

ably well most of the time, but occasionally, particularly for certain types of music, they produce artifacts that are very audible and annoying to some minority of listeners, who will reject the compression strategy on this basis.

Applications such as telephony also require two-way delivery to and from the home. The same coding issues that arise for other audio also arise here, and there are tighter constraints posed by the more limited upstream bandwidths in today's broadband technologies. However, data rates alone will not compensate for inexpensive or poorly positioned microphones or for ambient noise. If one is to use a broadband connection to the Internet to substitute for conventional voice telephony conversations, a good handset will still be needed. It will, for example, be problematic to hold conversations having good sound quality using the PC analog of a speakerphone that is not close to the speaker's mouth, just as it is with conventional telephony.

Specific Audio Applications

To better understand the requirements of audio-based applications over broadband, it is important to examine a set of specific applications and practicalities of each application, including what consumers are likely to expect.

Playback of Music. Today's music-playback applications are attractive to people who like the convenience of playing music on their computers, who want free music via peer-to-peer applications, who want to listen to radio stations that do not broadcast in their geographic region, or who want to listen to events that they cannot get access to in other ways. This content is often not reproduced on high-fidelity equipment. As noted above, options for music content distribution available today are also generally inferior in quality to that of a well-produced audio CD. In order for network-delivered audio to substitute for audio CDs, at least for people who are particular about sound quality, it will be necessary to move up the quality-bandwidth curve somewhat from where typical applications are today.

While a number of PC-based audio applications have enjoyed widespread use, it is unlikely that consumers will want to be forced to sit near a PC whenever they listen to music. The configuration of a home will depend on household income, personal preference, and the like, but most homes have devices in various locations. For example, the average number of radios per U.S. household in 1998 was 5.6.[9] Multiple audio CD players are also commonplace, and many homes have one or more high-performance stereo systems. Normally, each of these is controlled locally

say, half-hour of a broadcast to permit selecting a particular song or other material for local storage and later playback (there are, of course, interesting intellectual property rights issues to be worked out in this sort of scenario).

Network-Based Voice Telephony. In recent years, there has been growing interest in running telephony over general-purpose data networks, including the public Internet, instead of over the public telephone network. As an application of dial-up Internet service, Internet telephony arose as a less expensive alternative to conventional telephony. The decreased costs to users are a result of several factors: (1) by utilizing the Internet, which is typically made available to residential users on a flat-rate basis, Internet Protocol (IP) telephony avoids the per-minute charges generally assessed by long-distance carriers; (2) because a long-distance call can be placed with these services through a local call to an ISP, these services allow bypassing the per-minute access charges that long distance companies are required to pay local exchange carriers to terminate long-distance calls. From an overall industry perspective, there are also players moving toward replacing specialized telephone gear with IP-based equipment, seeking both to reduce costs and to introduce new functionality. There may also be efficiencies that result from running data and voice over a common network. IP telephony is being used today by some households and within some enterprise networks; it is increasingly also being used internal to the networks of a number of telecommunications carriers. Both deployments raise a series of complex policy issues.[10]

With residential broadband, which offers much greater bandwidth and always-on connectivity, IP telephony has the potential to move from a relatively marginal, hard-to-use application to a mass-market application. Depending on the architecture of a particular service, it might be a service that consumers run over their Internet connections simply by installing additional software and possibly making arrangements with a third party. Or, it may be a value-added service offered by the broadband service provider. In either case, IP telephony provides a way to bypass the local exchange carrier for telephone service. Price may not be the only selling point: Because IP telephony permits much more rapid innovation in services, the ease with which new features can be added may prove an additional customer draw.

Voice telephony applications do not require especially high bandwidth, with 64 kbps—or less with compression—in each direction being

---

[10]See Chapter 4 of Computer Science and Telecommunications Board, National Research Council, 2001, *The Internet's Coming of Age*, National Academy Press, Washington, D.C.

sufficient to provide the quality that people are used to from the conventional phone system. But these applications are much more sensitive than the pure "listening" applications in terms of network delay, jitter, and packet loss. Multiway conference calling raises additional architectural and performance issues. There are several ways that this can be done: as a series of point-to-point connections between individual participants and a control unit, or on a distributed basis using multicasting. For multiway conference calling control of delay and jitter is even more critical because of the number of sites involved. Whether meeting these requirements is best done by increasing network capacity or by incorporating quality-of-service mechanisms into network—and if the latter, which sort of mechanisms at what places in the network—is an open question.

Unlike conventional telephony, IP telephony comes in many varieties. In one major class, conversations are transmitted across the Internet end-to-end. Another possibility is to use IP-based voice service part of the way, perhaps only on the local access link, and connect calls to the traditional voice telephone system through a gateway. Here again the key barriers to acceptance are not bandwidth but the integration of network-based voice telephony with convenient handsets and "dialing" (call setup) devices. Given the popularity of cordless phones, it is unlikely that placing and receiving calls from PCs will find mass-market acceptance (although one might speculate about a PC role as a kind of base station). Other features that are important enablers of widespread adoption include the integration of ancillary services such as answering machines, voice mail, caller ID, and call waiting.

A number of companies have deployed IP telephony solutions, and it is a service that some broadband providers have chosen to add to their service bundles. But it is also possible that residential IP telephony may turn out to be a red herring. Voice telephony is important enough to most people that they are not willing to replace it with an unreliable service unless there is a compelling economic justification. Also, the voice telephone system works well—it is reliable, easy to use, and inexpensive (and getting more inexpensive every week it seems, at least within the United States). Except for people who are tremendously sensitive to the modest costs of long distance today (with rates of $0.05 to $0.07 per minute available as part of various calling plans) or who often place costly international calls (where IP telephony can effectively skirt the very steep tariffs still imposed by some countries), IP telephony may not be attractive unless it comes as an absolutely simple and seamless by-product of a broadband connection.

Audio Filtering and Searching. Audio, radio, and telephony are, for the most part, translations of existing applications to the network environ-

---

BOX 3.1
Internet, Television, and the Multiple Meanings of "Internet TV"

Trends in both television and Internet technologies make clear that the Internet and television will become increasingly intertwined in the future. The label "Internet TV" has multiple meanings, all of which deal with some form of convergence between conventional television and Internet service. Following are the definitions of four principal options:

1. *Delivery of conventional television or Internet-specific content over the Internet.* Rather than watching television programs broadcast over the air or over cable, television programs would be accessed over the Internet and then watched using either streaming for real-time viewing or file transfers for delayed viewing. Today, this sort of content would have to be viewed on a computer, but the technology could be incorporated into future television sets (or provided through an external adapter) to facilitate television access over the Internet.

2. *Adoption of an Internet-like (e.g., browser) interface for identifying and selecting television content.* In this case, the Internet would be used to enable a more interactive approach to controlling the television experience and would supplement the television content with additional information.

3. *Internet content that complements television content.* Subscription services—including WebTV and AOL TV—complement the traditional television viewing experience by allowing viewers either to interact with TV programs or to access complementary information via the Internet. Television stations and networks increasingly also have Web sites with information that extends, complements, and promotes their programs and schedules.

4. *Use of a home TV set to view Internet sites, as offered by WebTV, perhaps in conjunction with conventional television viewing.* These kinds of applications of Internet TV create an interactive television experience. This technology could be an intermediate stage toward realizing option 1.

SOURCE: Adapted in part from A. Michael Noll. 2000. "Infrastructure Implications of Internet TV." *TV over the Internet: Implications for Infrastructure, Content, Policy, and Strategy.* Columbia Institute for Tele-information, New York, November 10.

---

into some personal computers and by the advent of digital video recorders—complement the capabilities described above.

Video applications face many of the same issues as audio applications in terms of getting video content to the correct appliances through in-home distribution networks—the computer, the television, or perhaps some type of "videophone" appliance—as well as similar issues of integrating control with actual content distribution. But video permits a number of possible variants with interesting implications for both users and the broadband providers that carry these applications. These include:

- *Interactivity.* Another trend is toward interactivity—transforming video from a passive experience into an active one. Interactive television is providing exposure to consumer options for, say, selecting a camera at a sporting event. Such early experience with interactivity raises questions about the locus of control (at the transmitter or the receiver), the relative costs of bandwidth and the other technology needed to implement the interaction, and the potential for approximations to interactivity, such as broadcast of navigable objects.

- *Video for social communication.* Another possibility is the combination of traditional entertainment with social communication. The scenario is that people are watching a sporting event, with the traditional live broadcast coming into the home—but also sharing live video with friends who are watching the same game at the same time in different cities or simply different homes. This implies fairly high bandwidth peer-to-peer video communication in conjunction with passive video delivery. It is a very different concept—implying very different behavior—from today's scheduled videoconferences.

- *Home and community video.* Developments in video capture and editing technology enable new options for user-generated video.[12] One obvious application is home movies. Another is further decreasing the technical barriers to community access-type video production and delivery.

- *Large numbers of simultaneous video streams.* People can interact with video content quite differently from how they interact with audio. One audio signal per room (or perhaps one per person if headphones are used) at a time is a basic limit—playing 10 radio channels at once simply creates cacophony. But with enough display screens, a room or an individual can make use of many video signals at once. People can divide their attention by simply looking from one screen to another. One can imagine people receiving a number of different video signals continuously (for example, multiple TV-type feeds) with the sound usually suppressed. Another source of multiple video streams could be a new class of video display devices—video picture frame appliances that periodically download images for display from the Internet. With the always-on capabilities of broadband and an in-home network, one can easily see these evolving into video portals that look out on favorite scenes, into the homes of family and friends, and the like—perhaps at fairly high resolution, but with a relatively low frame rate.

---

[12]Hal Varian. 2000. "Cool Media: A New Generation Is Turning the Tables on Television." *The Industry Standard.* November 20, p. 293.

Whereas teleconferencing brings to mind a fairly formal notion of communication, similar to a telephone call, telepresence can enable much more informal interaction. For example, in a business setting it may enable casual interactions between lab spaces that could permit easier collaborations. Though early telepresence trials were constrained by technical shortcomings, this work also pointed to the significant role that social practices play in their acceptance and usefulness and suggested that it is difficult to predict when telepresence applications will be successfully implemented.[13]

In a personal setting, telepresence may enable a parent to have a continuous window on a child at a day care facility, thus enabling a closer ongoing relationship, even with working parents. Telepresence could possibly enable new forms of extended-family relationships over distances. An interesting attribute of telepresence is that it potentially poses higher bandwidth demands than one might expect from videoconferencing applications. This is because the premise of telepresence is that the window is always open, to enable spontaneous observations and interactions. One example that is a simple evolution of telephone use today is school children holding shared homework sessions, connecting their respective homes for many hours of working, chatting, and collaborating on assignments.

Telepresence can encompass not only audio and video, but also haptic interaction, force feedback, and control of remote devices (teleoperation). One especially demanding application of telepresence has been seen in experiments with distributed music performances, which require minimal latency and jitter. Telepresence for music is under consideration for concerts, studio production, and master classes.[14]

Thus, the bandwidth requirements for telepresence are not limited by the number of people actively engaged in watching the video stream at any given moment. One can easily hypothesize the need for more video streams to be maintained to or from a location than the number of users at that location. Ultimately, such casual real-time applications may drive much higher bandwidth requirements.

---

[13]See Steve Harrison and Paul Dourish. 1996. "Re-Place-ing Space: The Roles of Place and Space in Collaborative Systems." *Proceedings of the ACM Conference on Computer-Supported Cooperative Work CSCW'96* (Boston, Mass.). ACM, New York. Draft version available online at <http://www.parc.xerox.com/csl/members/dourish/papers/place-paper.html>.

[14]Chris Chafe, Stanford University, personal communication, briefing on digital music-making to CSTB Information Technology and Creativity Committee, January 12, 2001.

Telemetry

Telemetry applications involve primarily numerical data streams. They are expected to grow with the proliferation, and networking, of embedded computing and communications systems—smart appliances and so on—as well as networking capabilities within and from the home. Sensors and controls are being developed for a variety of functions in a household, such as temperature and energy management, utility monitoring, appliance operation, and security. More sophisticated health-monitoring systems are also being developed. For example, it may become possible to undertake skin cancer screening from home, which requires an ability to capture and send high-resolution images.

There is growing interest in telemedicine services that require broadband access. Possible connections include patient-to-doctor (e.g., in rural health care, where travel to the doctor's office is difficult), patient-to-physical therapist (e.g., supporting rehabilitation after a patient returns home following hip surgery), and patient-to-family (e.g., to allow a family to watch a newborn in neonatal intensive care).

Telemetry applications rely critically on the always-on characteristics of broadband and the ability of broadband to multiplex many data streams (for example, to allow a medical device or an appliance to emit and transmit a data stream regardless of what else is going on over the broadband connection), in contrast to dial-up connections. In many cases the data streams involved are low bandwidth. However, some applications, such as webcams or health-monitoring devices that transmit images, could result in demand for capacity that is higher upstream than downstream. Although primarily deployed for planning communication with a medical service, the same broadband connections might also support emergency response capabilities similar to or enhancing today's telephone-based systems. Such services presume, of course, reliable always-available connections.

New Kinds of Publishing

Peer-to-Peer Applications

Peer-to-peer communication was the original design premise of the Internet. Particularly with the rise of the Web, the focus of communications on the Internet shifted to the client server as central Web servers became the primary residence of Internet content. Recently, however, peer-to-peer communications among end systems on the Internet has undergone a renaissance, owing at least in part to the grass-roots movement toward sharing content.

Napster, developed as a way of exchanging MP3-encoded music files, became a widely used peer-to-peer content distribution application. By offloading the file transfer to exchanges between individual computers, it relies much less on third-party servers than would be the traditional practice of many users downloading content from a single server. Napster still relies on a central directory server to provide people with pointers to content, but other peer-to-peer applications have emerged that largely remove this constraint. Gnutella, for example, is a Napster offshoot that allows users to conduct a search among linked, decentralized computers offering content; however, it still depends on some means for users to obtain the Internet address of at least one such linked computer (whether through a Web page, e-mail, or instant messaging). Although these recreational services have received a lot of attention,[15] and their fate rests in part on the outcome of litigation and negotiations with the publishing industry, similar technologies have taken off for research activities.[16]

The motivations for deployment of these applications are several. Technical arguments include immunity from single-point failure and distribution of traffic load throughout the network. Much of the interest in Napster has, however, stemmed from another factor—the relative protection that peer-to-peer models offer from attempts to control the content distribution. A central Web server is a relatively easy target if one seeks to suppress undesired or illegal activity—in the case of Napster, the distribution of music in violation of copyright—while a distributed network of computers exchanging files is harder to detect and, because it potentially involves thousands or millions of participants, to take action against.[17]

There are additional compelling arguments for peer-to-peer applications. By their nature, they do not require the installation of servers or arrangements with businesses that offer hosting services (or other capabilities). Thus they offer a speed and ease of deployment applications much in the spirit of the Internet's pure end-to-end model—a new application depends only on software running on the individual computers and adequate network performance, and not on the installation of software on a hosting server. The appeal is twofold: nimbleness that comes from not having to coordinate with any other party when rolling out

---

[15]Similar services have also been introduced, such as AIMster, which leverages AOL's Instant Messenger for file transfer.

[16]Intel has been encouraging such applications through the Intel Philanthropic Peer to Peer Program (see <http://www.intel.com/cure/program.htm>).

[17]For an examination of technical and other factors surrounding intellectual property rights in a networked world, see Computer Science and Telecommunications Board, National Research Council. 2000. *The Digital Dilemma*. National Academy Press, Washington, D.C.

content or applications, and the freedom and control over one's own content that come from not having to involve a third party. Given such attributes, pilot efforts are underway to use the technology in business, the scientific community, and so forth.[18]

"Local Interest" Content, Including Video

Although the mass appeal of community-access television is debatable, cable has provided a vehicle for communities, organizations, and individuals to gain some experience and to experiment with video content production. Broadband promises to generalize and build on that experience by enabling a more varied menu of content not constrained by finite studio and broadcast time slots. In the short term, constraints on long-haul bandwidth may preclude wide-area transmission, but most of the interest would be local in any event. Local-interest video programming requires high bandwidth within a community, suggesting that it is most likely to take off with fiber and most likely to be linked early to community-wide fiber networks. The traveling parent who wants to watch the local Little League game will have to settle for very low quality video, or pay very dearly (if that is even possible, since the limiting factors will be community connectivity to the core net, not just the traveling parent's connectivity). However, the ability for remote family and friends to see (literally) local activities is socially valuable; the sharing of family photos, Web sites for children (beginning prenatally in some instances), and other grass-roots activity begun with narrowband suggest the potential for growth.

Home Content Hosting

There are many applications—distinguished by their not requiring delivery of information that changes in real time—that lend themselves to either a model of local hosting or a model in which users upload content

---

[18]The surge of popularity in peer-to-peer applications also raises speculative questions of whether the Internet really is evolving toward being the basis of a distributed computer. If the answer is yes, then one might think of computer bus speeds as giving some sort of an upper limit to broadband speeds. Today, the 32-bit bus of a 1.5-GHz Pentium 4 runs at 48 Gbps in both directions (peak, or at least half of that speed in both directions). This view would support the eventual migration toward a fiber to each home (which, as is discussed elsewhere in this report, is something that may take some time to happen). There may also be an accompanying trend that, as speeds increase beyond the human limits of audio and video, the bandwidth demands become more symmetric.

to content servers. These include, for example, Web page hosting, making photos available for others to download, sharing music. (In contrast, there is no substitute for upstream capacity for applications that depend on transmission of delay-sensitive real-time content out of the home, as is required for telephony, videoconferencing, or webcams. Also, home control and other applications that access sensor information and then take control actions must access the actual home.) The content-hosting alternative still requires upstream capacity, but it involves the transfer of content only once each time it is modified; those accessing the content download or stream it from one or more third-party servers located somewhere in the Internet.[19] Use of hosting services is a common practice for both business and personal content, and a number of businesses provide services in this area. Third-party hosting offers several advantages. The provider, who specializes in that sort of service, takes on responsibility for appropriate interconnection and colocation arrangements to ensure good performance for users throughout the Internet. A third-party hosting provider also generally provides other desirable functionality, such as redundant facilities, backup power, and data backup.

The choice between these two alternatives—local hosting or use of a hosting provider—depends on many factors. First, there are trade-offs, depending on how often things change versus how often they are used. For example, a home webcam might change once per minute and have to push a new image to a server at that point, but if the image is only accessed rarely, then most of those server updates will have been pointless and the network would be less loaded if users directly accessed the camera. Consumer preference, including such considerations as wishing to maintain personal control over content, also plays a role. The emergence of a "Napster culture" suggests demand for the local hosting approach, but the future of this model is unclear, as is the future of peer-to-peer itself, in part because many of today's broadband services provide limited upstream capacity and because ISPs may discourage or prohibit users from running their own servers or consuming large amounts of upstream bandwidth. The balance might tip as significantly more upstream bandwidth is made available in the local access segment.

---

[19]Note that this model can also be applied to near-real-time content, such as audio or video broadcasts of live events; one copy of a stream can be pushed out to buffers on local content servers for multiple users to access, as demonstrated by Akamai's technology for streaming video. However, unlike uploaded content, streamed uploading implies a steady-state demand for upstream content.

Push Content

Various business models assume an ability for different kinds of parties to push content into homes—that is, rather than await a specific request, always-on connectivity would enable these parties to transmit content into homes on a variety of schedules. Some of these arrangements would be highly functional—updates to device software, regular and automatic updates to databases maintained in the home, diagnostic probes (which would trigger responses), and so on. Other arrangements may be part of the "price" of a device or service, such as advertising.

Multiplexing Applications Demand in Homes

Understanding how demand for networked capabilities and services will evolve is extraordinarily difficult. It is apparent that there are multiple broadband applications of interest and that some sort of composite of this is likely to typify future broadband use. To complement rampant speculation, a number of scholarly and corporate entities have begun to develop model homes of the future, which are laboratories, showcases, or both, for potential windows into new options for home life. These possibilities leverage many developments, as explained in a variety of speculative media pieces:

> The fusion of technology and materials is making new forms possible. Add the potential of artificial intelligence, biometric sensing, robotics and mass customization, and it's little wonder that designers are imagining a new generation of houses in which people rule their environments, rather than submit to them. Web-linked companies already are rolling out model homes with all the click-and-drag amenities available today. They trumpet a lifestyle in which work, play and shopping are only a palm-held device away. It's the profusion of gadgets, and the dependence on them and the linkages among them, that will define the future of this house.[20]

These visions imply bandwidth demand associated with both individual household members and devices; people will use networks to communicate with each other, and devices will communicate with each other (and with people) directly, too. The descriptions suggest movement toward more symmetric communication capability—in the limit, equal upstream and downstream capacity—for homes; but how much remains an open question. In the meantime, the descriptions clearly argue for in-home

---

[20]Linda Hales. 2001. "Blobs, Pods and People." *The Washington Post Magazine*, March 25, p. 37.

Distributed Work and Education

Distributed work and education—which depend on e-mail, file transfer, and sometimes on audio- and videoconference capabilities—have long been touted as applications for information networks; both have already benefited from narrowband Internet access. Following significant growth in the 1990s, a sizable minority of companies are believed to offer a telecommuting option to some employees, presumably as a result of the proliferation of personal computing and communications options as well as the impetus provided by a variety of situations (e.g., California earthquakes) that have increased transportation problems.[22] At the same time, there have also been reports of dissatisfaction on the part of both employees and employers.

Forecasts have included expectations of growing use of multiple media (e.g., enabling simultaneous transmission of data and voice or of at least two streams of data) and of conferencing involving multiple media, including video as well as audio links. One enabler would be availability of connectivity comparable to the 10 Mbps typical of low-end office local area networks, with more symmetric bandwidth enabling more symmetrical use.

One small study examined reactions of people working at home to a transition to DSL service and found overall satisfaction based on the increase in their productivity attributed to higher-speed connectivity; people also noted that the productivity benefit depended on whether other home-based workers with whom they collaborated also had such connectivity.[23] That kind of comment underscores the potential for qualitative change in an activity from widespread availability of a capability—change not visible when availability is unevenly distributed among a population, such as a group of teleworkers.

Distributed education, like distributed work, involves remote access to information and communications. Discussions of distributed education are more likely to involve use of still and moving images with broadband; they also involve conferencing for interaction among multiple students. Note that distributed education is expected to benefit both adults and children.

---

[22]Patricia Riley, Anu Mandavilli, and Rebecca Heino. 2000. "Observing the Impact of Communication and Information Technology on 'Net-Work'." *Telework and the New Workplace of the 21st Century.* U.S. Department of Labor, Washington, D.C. Available online at <http://www.dol.gov/dol/asp/public/telework/p2_3.htm>.

[23]Riley, "Observing the Impact of Communication Technology," 2000.

"Tele-webbing"

A new sort of composite application that some have begun to call "tele-webbing," which combines Internet access with conventional television viewing, is beginning to appear. Simplistically, accessing the Web while also watching television would qualify for this description, and indeed it is common for people to engage in other activities while also watching entertainment television that has low attention demands. Thus, the consumer who scans e-mail while watching a sitcom could be said to be tele-webbing. More interesting, however, are cases now emerging where the television watching and Web access are interrelated. For example, many sports Web sites now provide real-time Web applications that feed game statistics to a browser. Having such a site open while watching a televised sports event provides a deeper experience of the event. For an even more real-time experience, experiments have been done with making race-car telemetry information available concurrently with a race broadcast. This allows a measure of user selectivity in how the race is experienced, since the user can focus attention on a particular driver. Finally, various levels of viewer interactivity have been evaluated for making television game shows (which have long elicited vicarious play-along-at-home experiences) truly interactive. All of these ideas involve taking advantage of a second screen that the user can selectively use for added experiences. Importantly, all these applications involve constraints on tolerable latency for the data streams relative to the primary video streams. This class of applications may be another example of where the total bandwidth demand to a home may exceed what the user can consume at any instant because the value of these applications lies at least in part in the user's ability to instantly shift attention from one video feed to another screen full of information.

Communities and Community Networks

Community networking efforts to date provide a window into the interactions and synergistic possibilities presented by greater networking capabilities among people in a given area, who presumably have at least some shared interest in a common set of information or in communicating with each other. With disappearance of a number of the pioneering bulletin-board-type community networks, network communications have tended to become less geographically focused. And as dial-up Internet access via commercial ISPs has become widespread, community networking initiatives have, for the most part, focused less on building local infrastructure and more on content and services. Contemporary approaches to community networks are likely to emphasize a variety of service activities that accompany deployment and facilitate use, such as information resources and training, economic incubation, pilot and demonstration projects, and development of public-private partnerships. But regardless of how it is labeled, the attention to local interests has persisted; it is expressed in the various Web sites established by local governments, schools, libraries, athletic consortia, religious institutions, and so on—a diverse group of sources that defies the categorization of the more controlled local access cable television or local radio station and that offers the potential of upgraded offerings where capabilities are available.

Note that on a small scale, multiunit dwellings (e.g., apartment buildings) can serve as microcommunities: the availability of broadband to individuals in the component units is constrained by decision making of the owner; where the owner is supportive, all units can have this capability, but the reverse tends to be true as well. Also, in some communities, special centers have been established that offer broadband capabilities together with the hardware and software to take advantage of them—a physical portal.[24] These communications centers complement the concentrations of demand in such public-interest (and often publicly supported) facilities as medical and education centers of different kinds. Thus, it is important to recognize that community networks have both infrastructural and content dimensions.

SOCIAL FACTORS AND IMPACTS OF BROADBAND

There is much potential for future applications that enrich or complement traditional content and communications channels, but excitement about them should be tempered by an appraisal of the time frame in which these applications could be realized and the nontechnical obstacles that retard their deployment. Much of the expectation surrounding broadband involves more than new technology—it also requires a transformation of societal structures, media, and other institutions. This section briefly discusses some of these factors.

Availability of Content

One obstacle is the availability of content. A recent television commercial from Qwest exemplified the expectations—being able to access every book ever published in any language and every movie ever made

---

[24]Richard Civille, Michael Gurstein, and Kenneth Pigg. 2001. "Access to What? First Mile Issues for Rural Broadband," white paper; see Appendix C.

available, on demand over the Internet. In reality, we are some time away from widespread video-on-demand; thousands of channels of "radio" over the Internet; abundant, high-quality educational video content; and so forth.[25]

In addition to technical obstacles, the familiar chicken-and-egg phenomenon comes into play. Without a mass market of consumers with broadband access, it is hard to develop a business model that justifies investment in new content (or translating old content). One new media businessperson, Andrew Sharpless, addressed the committee from his vantage at that time of developing new online services for Discovery Communications. He suggested that at least 10 million households would need to use broadband before meaningful content would emerge, and he noted that cable experience shows that serving 50 million customers is key to lining up advertisers (with online services, a top rating by Jupiter Media Metrix had become key to advertiser interest by 2000).[26]

Intellectual property rights issues are another large factor—the interests and holdings of broadband providers, users, and rights holders are not necessarily aligned. The 2000-2001 rise of Internet radio raised a set of issues related to content use fees, and the popularity of Napster and other content-sharing technologies heightened rights holders' concerns about control over their intellectual property, making intellectual property more prominent in the development of business plans.[27]

Finally, although content availability affects demand for broadband, one should not underestimate the volume and value of customer-provided content. Broadband is not only a mass media technology; it is also an interpersonal technology. As noted above, messaging and e-mail are both very popular applications, illustrating the value of broadband for

---

[25]Unrealistic expectations have been rampant when it comes to home technology, if not the Internet generally. For example, the *Washington Post* published an article in 1994 that suggested that going online will not support new relationships, online banking, real-time game-playing, "basking" in multimedia, hobnobbing with celebrities, and online shopping, most of which has, in fact, happened, at least to some degree even with low bandwidth. See Jim Kennelly. 1994. "9 Ways Going On-Line Can Change Your Life and 6 Ways It Can't," *The Washington Post: Fast Forward*, September, pp. 9-13.

[26]Andrew Sharpless, personal communication, briefing to the committee, November 1999. He discussed how Discovery Online scaled back its content expectations because of these considerations.

[27]For an in-depth exploration of the issues surrounding intellectual property rights in a digital, networked environment, see Computer Science and Telecommunications Board, National Research Council, 2000, *The Digital Dilemma*, National Academy Press, Washington, D.C.

communication as well as content delivery.[28] Multiplayer games, one of the few profitable Internet applications today, rely on user-provided content. Telemedicine will rely, in large measure, on user-provided content, plus some professionally prepared patient education materials. Families will generate and want to distribute pictures and home movies.

Broadband Impacts

One category of impact on quality of life derives from broadband's interaction with consumption of media: broadband is associated with the allocation of more time to media consumption overall, in part because it puts Internet use on a par with TV and radio use.[29] Whether the increase in media consumption is transient or long term, and what it may imply for (or as a result of) other activities that may receive less time than media consumption, remain to be seen. It is not known whether the home is truly an infinite sink for bits over time or whether there is some limit that one can compute, based on something like human perception or expectations about other things going on in the home. In terms of general information access, one could argue that broadband provides limited content beyond that available through dial-up. There is little unique content available only to broadband users that is not duplicated on cable television today (e.g., CSPAN). In terms of applications, the prominent examples deal with entertainment—access to interactive games, or even a broader assortment of music than one can find on the local radio channels is unlikely to compel public policy support, but these applications, along with day-trading tools and e-commerce, exercise the technology (and, sometimes, the law) and build an experience base for the underlying capabilities.[30] Attention to individual categories of information or applications can obscure the larger development, which is a shift to an expectation of ubiquitous access to a variety of information and applications. But ubiquity does not imply endless variety: experience with television shows

---

[28]Some argue that the value of communications applications such as messaging is underappreciated compared to content delivery. See Andrew Odlyzko. 2001. "Content Is Not King." *First Monday* 6(2)(February). Available online at <http://www.firstmonday.org/issues/issue6_2/odlyzko/>.

[29]Pierre Bouvard and Warren Kurtzman. 2000. *The Broadband Revolution: How Superfast Internet Access Changes Media Habits in American Households*. Arbitron Company, New York. Available online at <www.arbitron.com> and <www.colemanresearch.com>.

[30]One might draw a limited analogy to the supply of simple games with the Windows operating system and Palm devices to help people get used to manipulating a mouse in the former case and the Graffiti writing system in the latter.

that consumers limit themselves to seven to nine channels, implying high cost in searching for acceptable content—and that aids in effecting such search may be an important complement to content innovations per se. The oft-made contrast between children who are exposed to computer-based technology early on and adults who are introduced to it at older ages underscores the potential for cumulative experience to change people's expectations and behavior.

Several emerging applications described above may be more compelling from a policy perspective. Telecommuting can have positive impacts on the environment, local economies, and people's ability to earn a good living. Telemetry and monitoring applications can enhance health care delivery. Basic communications and telepresence applications can help keep children and elderly parents connected. And broadband can be used to deliver more sophisticated (multimedia and interactive) educational content. But many of these applications remain more promise than reality.

There is time to consider and act on possible negative impacts (from the obvious questions about privacy and security to the more idiosyncratic ones relating to cases of excessive use). For example, public- and private-sector attempts to deal with spam originating in the narrowband context are likely to take on new urgency in the broadband context. If any kind of communications of the past is any guide, people will send information whether there is demand or not, and the prospect of video spam may arouse people even more than fax and e-mail spam have. Security concerns have arisen, associated with the always-on nature of broadband. But with anticipated assimilation of broadband into a technology-intensive household, other concerns will arise. For example, just as people change physical locks after, say, a divorced spouse leaves, a kind of virtual door is developing with broadband, and there may be a kind of virtual set of keys to change, too. This is also a time to address the implications of technology options for the disabled: Some of the envisioned capabilities will make it easier for people with disabilities to remain in their homes; some may require appropriate design for effective use by people with disabilities. Consideration of differences in abilities leads naturally to consideration of human-computer interaction and user interfaces; progress in these areas may facilitate use by all.

While the lag in compelling applications may contain growth in demand for broadband, its silver lining may be to limit the impact of disparities in access and use. Measurements of the disparity are in flux, given progress in deployment and adoption, but significant differences have been noted by region, locality, racial and ethnic groups, income, educational attainment, and age.[31] Income and educational attainment

---

[31]See NTIA's *Falling Through the Net* series.

4

Technology Options and Economic Factors

Although great technical and business strides have been made in improving the data transmission speeds of communications networks, the local access technologies that make up the last (or first) mile connections in the network have mostly lagged far behind. Enhancing the local access infrastructure to bring high-speed services to residences and small businesses requires upgrading or building infrastructure to each premises served. There are a variety of technology options with different characteristics and cost structures and variation in willingness to pay among potential customers. This chapter explores the characteristics of the various local access technologies and the interplay among relevant economic considerations.

LOCAL ACCESS TECHNOLOGIES IN CONTEXT

While this chapter focuses on local access, the other network elements through which content, applications, and services are provided also contribute to the total cost and performance characteristics of broadband service. Local access links carry communications to and from points at which communications from multiple premises are aggregated and funneled onto higher-capacity links that ultimately connect to the Internet or other broadband services. The first point of aggregation, also known as the point of presence, is most commonly located at a telephone company central office, cable system head end, or radio tower (which may be at a considerable distance from the premises) but may also be in a piece of equipment in a vault, pedestal, wireless antenna site, or pole-top device located nearby to the premises. Circuits installed or leased by the provider in turn run from the point of presence to one or more public or private access points for interconnection with the Internet. The so-called second mile connects local access facilities with upstream points of aggregation. In connecting to the Internet, broadband providers either pay for transit service or establish peering agreements with other ISPs to exchange traffic on a settlement-free (barter) basis. Caches, e-mail and content servers, and servers supporting specialized services such as video-on-demand or voice telephony are located at points of presence and/or data centers. Routers located in points of presence and data centers take care of directing data packets on to the next point in the cross-network trip to their eventual destination.

ESSENTIAL FEATURES OF THE LOCAL ACCESS TECHNOLOGY OPTIONS

The future of broadband is sometimes described as a shootout among competing technologies that will result in a single technology dominating nationwide. This view, however, is simplistic and unrealistic; there is no single superior technology option. Broadband is going to be characterized by diverse technologies for the foreseeable future. There are a number of reasons for this:

• *Incremental investment in existing infrastructure.* While some firms may have access to large amounts of venture capital, the expectations of investors in existing firms is for short-term payoffs. As a result, the technological approach chosen by an incumbent is likely to make use of existing equipment and plant, and the deployment strategy must be amenable to incremental upgrades. The infrastructures of the various incumbents in the broadband marketplace—telephone local exchange carriers with copper loops, cable television companies with coaxial cable, cellular companies with towers for point-to-point wireless telephony—will continue to make incremental improvements unique to their respective technologies to provide and enhance broadband services.

• *Continued exploitation of skills.* Technologies require distinctive skills and knowledge—those needed, for example, to design, launch, and operate a satellite. Similarly, cable and telephone companies understand the technological challenges associated with their respective systems. Companies that know how to do one or another thing well will attempt to find market opportunities where these skills give them an advantage.

• *Different demographics and density.* The United States (and world) population is very diverse in topography, density, wealth, and demand for communications services. The particular economic and technical characteristics of each broadband technology will provide specific advantages in serving certain geographical areas or demographic groups. Some may have an economic advantage in particular locales owing to the nature of the infrastructure already in place or to inherent physical attributes of the environment. Planning should reflect the existence of a diverse set of solutions that depend on particular circumstances rather than a technology monoculture.

This section discusses the salient characteristics of each technology option and provides a brief road map of how existing technology and anticipated research and development will play out in coming years.

Wireline Options

In rough terms, access technologies are either wireline or wireless. Wireline includes telephone network copper pairs and the coaxial cable used for cable television service. Incumbent telephone companies and cable operators are both in the process of upgrading their infrastructures to provide broadband services. Wireline infrastructure is also being built in some areas by so-called overbuilders, who are building new wireline infrastructure in competition with the incumbent wireline providers. In the United States, this has largely been through deployment of hybrid fiber coax to provide some mix of television, data, and voice services. There are also a few overbuilders that are using or plan to use fiber.

The wireline technologies all share the feature that labor and access to a right-of-way are significant components of the cost. These costs are more significant where infrastructure must be buried than where it can be installed on existing poles.[1] The other major component is the electronics at each end of the line, where costs are subject to rapid decreases over time as a result of Moore's law improvements in the performance-to-cost ratio and increasing production volumes. Labor, on the other hand, is not subject to Moore's law, so there is no obvious way within the wireline context for dramatic declines in cost for new installation (though one cannot rule out very clever solutions that significantly reduce the labor required for some elements of the installation).

---

[1]One estimate provided to the committee is that aerial installation is almost twice as inexpensive as when the infrastructure must be buried.

Hybrid Fiber Coax

Cable systems pass 97 percent of the homes in the United States.[2] The older generation of cable technology uses a branching structure of coaxial cables fanning out from a central point or head end to the buildings in a community (see Figure 4.1a). The older systems rely on long chains of coaxial cables and amplifiers, with each segment feeding into a smaller coaxial segment.

Hybrid fiber coax (HFC) is the current generation of cable system technology. HFC systems carry analog signals that feed conventional television sets as well as digital signals encoded onto analog signals that carry digital video programming and up- and downstream data. In the new architecture, the system is divided into a number of small coaxial segments with a fiber optic cable used to feed each segment or cluster. By using fiber instead of coax to feed into neighborhoods, the system's performance and reliability is significantly improved.

Another benefit of an HFC upgrade is that the resulting system can carry two-way data communications, such as Internet access. Additional equipment is installed to permit information to flow both to and from the home (see Figure 4.1b). Internet service is provided using a device called a cable modem in the home and a device known as a cable modem termination system in the head end. The ability to offer competitive video, voice, and high-speed data services using the present generation of technology has attracted several nonincumbent companies to enter a few markets as overbuilders using the HFC technology.

Over 70 percent of the homes in the United States are now passed by this upgraded form of cable infrastructure. The fraction of homes served by HFC is continuing to increase as cable companies upgrade connections to all homes in their franchise areas and can, with continued investment in upgrades, increase until it approaches the 97 percent of households that currently have cable service available at their property lines.

A technology standard for cable modems known as DOCSIS has been adopted industrywide. Developed by an industry consortium seeking a quicker alternative to the more traditional standards development process then underway under the auspices of the IEEE, the DOCSIS standard is stable, and more than 70 modems have been certified as compliant. Standardization has helped modems become a mass-market product. The standard provides consumers the assurance that if they purchase certified modems at retail, or have them built into PCs or other appliances, cable operators will support them across the country. Further helping push down costs, several competing suppliers have developed highly inte-

---

[2]Paul Kagan Associates. 2001. *The Kagan Media Index*, Jan. 31, 2001.

(a) Tree and Branch Architecture

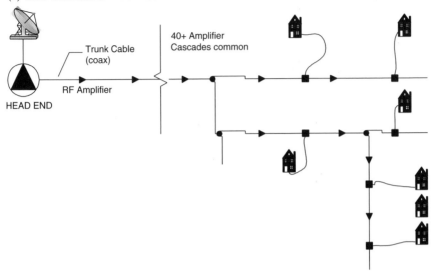

(b) HFC Architecture

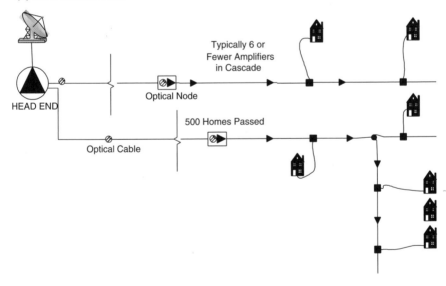

FIGURE 4.1 Evolution of cable systems to support two-way data. SOURCE: James Chiddix. 1999. "The Evolution of the U.S. Telecommunications Infrastructure Over the Next Decade. TTG2: Hybrid-Fiber-Coax Technology" (IEEE workshop paper).

grated silicon, and single-chip DOCSIS solutions are available to modem manufacturers. With increasing volumes, a single standard, and single-chip solutions, the cost of a cable modem at wholesale has already dropped to $150 or less and can be expected to continue to drop as volumes increase.

Digital Subscriber Line

Digital subscriber line (DSL) is the current method by which twisted copper pairs (also known as loops), the decades-old technology used by the telephone companies to reach the residence, can be upgraded to support high-speed data access. In some newer builds, analog transmission over copper wire is only used between the premises and a remote terminal (which may be at curbside or, more commonly in a pedestal or underground vault within a neighborhood), while a digital loop carrier (DLC) generally using fiber optic cable connects the remote terminal with the central office. In a traditional, all-copper plant, the first segment of the loop plant is referred to as the "feeder plant," in which hundreds of phone lines are bundled in a cable that runs from the central office to a smaller distribution point. From the distribution point, smaller cables containing fewer phone lines run to pedestals or cabinets within a neighborhood, where they in turn connect to the twisted pairs that run to the customer premises (see Figure 4.2).

All transmission of data over wire involves coding these data in some way consistent with the carrying capacity and noise conditions of the wire. The familiar dial-up modems code (and decode) data in such a way that the data can pass through the traditional switches and transmission links that were designed to carry voice, which more or less limits speeds to today's 56 kbps. DSL uses an advanced coding scheme that is not compatible with existing switches. Consequently, new electronics known as a DSL access multiplexer (DSLAM) has to be installed in any central office where DSL is to be offered. The DSLAM must in turn be connected to a switched data network that ultimately connects the central office to the Internet (see Figure 4.3). DSL service enables the transmission of packet-switched traffic over the twisted copper pairs at much higher speeds than a dial-up Internet access service can offer. DSL can operate at megabits per second, depending on the quality and length of the particular cable. It is thus the upgrade of choice to bring copper pairs into the broadband market.

DSL standards have existed since 1998, and new versions of these standards, which add enhancements to asynchronous transfer mode (ATM), IP, and voice services over DSL, are expected in 2001 or 2002 from the International Telecommunication Union (ITU). Large interoperability

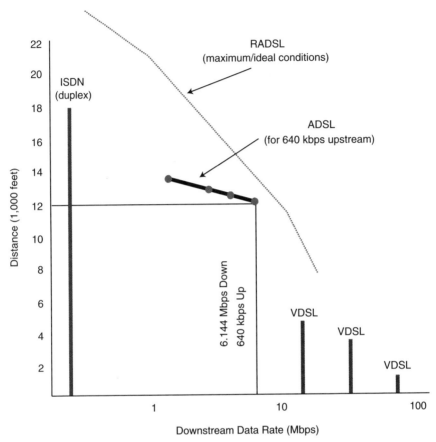

FIGURE 4.4   Rate and maximum distances for various flavors of DSL. SOURCE: Adapted from a figure provided to the committee by Ted Darcie, AT&T Research.

support DSL. More significantly, DSL does not work over wires longer than a certain distance (18,000 feet for the primary flavor used for residential service today, ADSL). It should be noted that wire lengths are substantially shortened by the deployment of remote terminals.

Crosstalk—the coupling of electrical signals between nearby wires—gives rise to interference that degrades the carrying capacity of each copper pair. The level of crosstalk depends on the number of pairs within the bundle carrying DSL, their proximity, and the power and bandwidths they use. It is even possible for DSL signals from adjacent lines to create signals larger than the intended DSL signal on the line. The interference has the effect of reducing the maximum data rate at a particular loop length (or the maximum loop length for a given data rate). In essence, an issue of spectrum sharing within the cable bundles arises. The term "spectrum" is appropriate because the crosstalk and interference effects depend on how the signals on the different pairs make use of the different frequencies used for transmission over the lines. Today, incumbents and competitive providers using unbundled loops are free to choose among a number of flavors of DSL, without regard to how the spectrum used by one service affects services running over other copper pairs.

At the request of the FCC, a working group of carriers and vendors worked to develop a spectrum management standard for DSL. The present standard, released in 2001, places forward-looking limits on signal power, bandwidth, and loop length.[3] By establishing thresholds with which the current DSL technology is generally compliant, the standard seeks to prevent future escalation (where each DSL product or service would try to "out-shout" the others) and thus place a bound on the level of crosstalk that will be faced in the future. While the standard is currently voluntary, it is generally expected that it will provide the technical basis for future FCC rulemaking. Issues that the standard does not address—which are being explored by a Network Reliability and Interoperability Council subgroup under American National Standards Institute (ANSI) T1 auspices that is developing guidance to the FCC on crosstalk—include how many DSL lines are permitted per binder group, what standards apply to lines fed from digital loop carriers, how products should be certified or self-certified, and how rule compliance should be enforced.

Advanced Wireline Offerings—Fiber Optics in the Loop

Optical fiber has a theoretical capacity of about 25,000 GHz, compared to the roughly 155 megahertz (MHz) possible over short copper pairs, the roughly 10 GHz[4] capacity of coaxial cable. (The relationship

---

[3]Working Group on Digital Subscriber Line Access (T1E1.4). 2001. *American National Standard for Telecommunications—Spectrum Management for Loop Transmission Systems (T1.417-2001)*. Standards Committee T1. Alliance for Telecommunications Industry Solutions, Washington, D.C.

[4]The practical upper limit for data transmission over coaxial cable has not been well explored. The upper cutoff frequency for a coaxial cable is determined by the diameter of the outer copper conductor. Smaller cables (1/4-inch- to 1/2-inch-diameter) probably have a cutoff frequency well in excess of 10 GHz. It is unclear what the upper limit is on modulation efficiency. The 256 quadrature amplitude modulation (QAM) currently in wide use allows 7 bits per hertz, but in short, passive runs in neighborhoods, much more efficient modulation schemes are possible, suggesting that HFC could evolve to speeds exceeding 100 Gbps to small clusters of customers.

between hertz and bits per second depends on the modulation scheme; the number of bits per hertz typically ranges from 1 to more than 7.) This very high capacity and consequent low cost per unit of bandwidth are the primary reasons why fiber is preferred wherever individual demand is very high or demand from multiple users can be aggregated. Other considerations in favor of fiber include high reliability, long service lifetime,[5] protocol transparency, and consequent future-proof upgradability.[6] Thus, fiber predominates in all of the telecommunications links (voice and data) except the link to the premises, where cost considerations come into play most, or for untethered devices. Because of their large demand for bandwidth, an increasing fraction of large businesses is being served directly by fiber links. There is also increasing attention to fiber technologies for local area and local access networks, as evidenced by recent development of new technologies such as gigabit Ethernet over fiber.

One important use of fiber for broadband is that of increasing the performance of other wireline technologies through incremental upgrades. Both HFC systems and DSL systems benefit from pushing fiber further into the system. To increase the performance of DSL, the copper links must get shorter. As penetration and the demand for higher speed increase, the upgrade strategy is to push fiber deeper, with each fiber feeding smaller service areas in which shorter copper connections run to the individual premises. So a natural upgrade path for copper infrastructure is to install electronics ever closer to the residence, to a remote terminal located in a pedestal or underground vault or on a telephone pole; to run fibers from the central office to this point; and only to use copper

---

[5]In the 1970s, researchers worried about the possibility of fiber degradation over time. A number of experiments were conducted and no degradation effects were found. Thus— barring an accidental cut—the only reason fiber is replaced is when some new transmission scheme reveals the old fiber to have too much eccentricity of the core or too much material dispersion. These factors have only come into play in very particular situations. For example, when OC192 (10 Gbps) transmission was introduced, there were concerns that old fiber with an out-of-round cross-section would cause problems. But in the end, only a limited amount of fiber required replacement to support the new, higher-speed transmissions.

[6]"Protocol transparency" refers to the ability to run any communications protocol over the fiber by changing the end equipment and/or software. Other communications media display some degree of protocol transparency, but with fiber, the large RF spectrum on an individual fiber is entirely independent of other fibers (in contrast to DSL, which has crosstalk issues; wireless, which has obvious spectrum-sharing; and HFC, which also has shared spectrum). This transparency property only holds true over the fiber segments that are unshared—where passive splitting is done, all must agree on at least the time division multiplexing (TDM) or wavelength division multiplexing (WDM) scheme, and where active switching is used, all must agree on the packet protocol. True protocol transparency— and true future-proofing—is thus greatest in a home-run architecture.

between the remote terminal and the home. Similarly, to deliver higher performance over HFC, the number of subscribers in each cluster must shrink, so that the total capacity of a single coaxial segment is shared by a smaller number of subscribers and the per-subscriber performance goes up. This also requires that fiber be installed farther out into the distribution tree.[7]

A basic upgraded architecture is apparent: fiber optic cables radiate out from a central office or head end to local distribution points that serve small clusters of buildings. At each cluster, a relatively compact set of electronics couples the fiber to a local distribution plant. For HFC, a short segment of coax runs from this distribution point to feed a cluster of homes, while for DSL this is a short copper twisted pair. As the cluster size continues to decrease, from the hundreds of homes commonplace in much of the industry today down to tens of homes, HFC and copper pair systems will come to resemble each other. The networks will not, to be sure, be the same in all details. For example, different networks will have different "active elements" in different parts; some networks will have active switching deep into the network, while cable networks will likely place less emphasis on remote switching in favor of carrying traffic back to the head end before aggregation or routing. Where active components are located has implications for where power must be delivered, and thus implications for cost, ease of installation, and so forth. But the essential feature is a continuing trend toward pushing fiber deeper into networks.

Fiber-to-the-curb (FTTC) is a general term for this class of system. FTTC is also a label for a specific class of technology that makes extensive use of fiber for local distribution and that local exchange carriers are using to build or rebuild their telecommunications. A technology being used in new construction today, it will in turn be a basis for incremental upgrades of the telephone infrastructure in the future.

Whether as the final upgrade step in the incremental path described above or for installation by another player, another alternative is to run fiber to the premises themselves, dubbed fiber-to-the-home. The term FTTH encompasses multiple architectures. The factors that control what speeds are actually provided are the technology components that are

---

[7]Deployment of fiber deeper into incumbent telephone networks also raises interesting questions about how one would implement unbundling, which was originally premised on unbundling a copper loop running from the central office to the subscriber. Issues such as colocation become more complicated when the loop terminates at a curbside pedestal or controlled environment vault. Colocation is even more complicated if fiber is pushed deep enough that it reaches to the poletop or even into the home. Aesthetic and practical concerns limit the size and number of these remote terminal units, which in term complicates the provision of colocation space.

installed at the end points of the fiber—the residence and the service provider's point of presence, which may be located at a head end, central office, or remote terminal. The three principal forms of FTTH are these:

- *"Home run" systems*, where there is a separate fiber or fiber pair that runs all the way from each residence to the central office or other point of presence. Because there is no sharing of fibers, this scheme has a higher cost of installation, but offers the highest ultimate performance with the appropriate system design and terminal equipment and the most flexibility. Providers can deploy the technology of their choice independent of other providers (there are no spectrum-sharing issues, as is the case, for example, with wireless, and no crosstalk problems, as is the case with DSL). Also, the end-point equipment attached to each fiber (at the central office and home) can be upgraded independently.

- *The Passive Optical Network (PON) architecture*, in which a single fiber runs from a central office to a simple optical divider, called a passive splitter (hence the "passive" in PON), which may be quite compact, from which individual fibers in turn run to each of a group of homes. The absence of active electronics in the field and the overall simplicity yield lower life-cycle costs.[8] The PON architecture also avoids the complications and expense associated with providing robust power at the remote switching point. Unlike switched fiber or home runs, the format of the information on the different paths in a PON system is not totally independent. This implies that there may be some upgrade strategies that are not backward-compatible and would require simultaneous upgrades of head-end and terminal equipment. Just how must flexibility for upgrade and change is available in a PON system depends on the details of the design. As part of an effort to reduce costs, an ATM-specific realization of the PON architecture has been standardized in the ITU (the Full Service Access Network or ATM PON standard).

- *FTTH systems with fully active (electronic) elements in the path from the central office to the residence*, in which fiber runs from the central office to one or more stages of remote terminals at which the signals are switched among fibers that go on to feed individual premises. Two examples of this approach are switched Ethernet and HFC using active switching. Switched Ethernet systems are beginning to be used by companies providing fiber to the home and businesses, extending what is normally a local area network technology over a metropolitan area. HFC systems of the future, instead of using a passive splitter, might have a fiber connect-

---

[8]Paul Shumate provided estimates to the committee of 20 percent lower capital expenses and a $500 life-cycle cost savings.

ing to some electronics that serves a small cluster of homes, using fiber instead of coaxial cable to connect to individual homes. Unlike the other two architectures, this approach requires special attention to how to power the remote switching points, especially where reliability requirements (and associated regulatory requirements) demand robustness in the face of power grid failures.

These various forms of FTTH have different cost structures and present different opportunities for incremental upgrade.

FTTH is seen by some as the "holy grail" of residential access. From a technology perspective, it is a high-performance end point, with enormous headroom for future upgrades. As a result, the sentiment is often expressed that the nation should strive to deploy that solution directly, without spending time and diverting investment dollars in intermediate technology of an incremental nature that might, eventually, be obsolete.

From a business perspective, a direct move to FTTH raises several issues. There is a significant investment in telephone and cable infrastructure that can meet many of today's broadband Internet access needs with modest incremental expense.

Business choices among the alternatives thus hinge on such factors as the investment horizon and forecasts for bandwidth demand. While both DSL and HFC can evolve toward higher performance, it is still unclear whether the pace of improvement in these technologies will continue to meet customer needs. A second issue is whether the performance benefits of FTTH over those of other alternatives would be of sufficient value to consumers to support the prices needed to cover the at least somewhat higher costs. The familiar case of the recent slowdown in new PC sales may offer a useful illustration of this point. New PCs are faster and have a variety of capabilities that older models do not, but it seems, at least at present, that many buyers find the older models more than adequate for what they want to do. If this is the case, then some new, compelling set of applications that requires those capabilities will have to emerge to really boost PC sales.

The total cost of deploying FTTH is, of course, substantial, involving both the basic costs associated with wireline infrastructure deployment and the premium associated with fiber. Areas being newly developed (so-called green-field areas) offer an especially attractive market for fiber, to the extent that the additional costs are modest compared with the basic installation costs of any local access technology. Indeed, the total life-cycle costs for fiber are believed to be lower than the costs of alternatives for new installations. When new wireline infrastructure is installed (e.g., in a new housing development), FTTH at present costs more to install, by at least several hundred dollars a home, than alternatives. The total cost includes the costs of installing the wireline itself (digging trenches, hanging on poles, and so on), which are similar in magnitude for any wireline overbuilder whatever the specific technology.

Unlike copper wires or coaxial cable, however, non-home-run fiber architectures require that fiber be spliced together. Splices are more time-consuming than electrical connections and require specialized expertise and/or complicated equipment to produce. Not surprisingly, this has been an area of considerable attention, and increasingly sophisticated techniques and equipment have been entering the market, but costs remain higher. The significant improvements made in splicing technology and techniques over the past few years mean that this is likely to become less of an issue; moreover, home-run FTTH systems do not require splicing in the access network. In addition, there are increased costs associated with the terminal equipment (the lasers and other electronics that transmit and receive light signals over the fiber). Costs here exceed those of terminal equipment for DSL or HFC, in part because of the higher costs associated with the optoelectronic components and in part simply because of lower product volumes typical of any new product. There have been significant improvements in the cost and performance of fiber distribution technology over the last few years as a result of technical advances and increased deployments in gigabit Ethernet, wavelength division multiplexing (WDM), passive optical networks, and optical switching, but there is still a good bit of room for cost improvements in terminal equipment, splicing, and trenching.

A small number of new private sector entrants are planning or starting to deploy FTTH as an overbuild. For them, becoming a facilities-based provider would require installing infrastructure in any event. In addition, the higher performance potential of fiber and, in light of its longevity and future-proof quality, a total life-cycle cost not dissimilar to that of alternatives, are viewed as giving these entrants a competitive advantage in the market.

Other deployments are taking place in a different economic context; these include, for example, municipal deployment; deployment as a part of new residential construction; or deployment as an offshoot of fiber installations for government or business customers. These scenarios alter the economic calculus and hence the set of technology choices that can be justified. Once the high up-front costs of laying fiber are paid, the incremental costs for upgrades are predominantly *per-subscriber* and not *per-passing*. In return for the high initial investment comes a measure of future-proofing, as the same fiber can provide decades of useful service. This sort of economic model will make sense for an investor with a long investment horizon. For instance, it may be attractive to a municipality that has to float a bond issue for a one-time investment, and then live with the resulting investment for the life of the bond. The technology also allows the municipality to place responsibility on the individual consumer to make any future incremental investments. It might also make sense for an individual to finance the fiber installation, much as houses are financed through decades-long mortgages. This economic model makes much less sense to a corporation seeking to make continuous incremental investments with a goal of showing short-term returns each quarter.

In the long run, all the wireline alternatives have the option of converging on FTTH, if the market demands it. For those with existing infrastructure, the issues are the incremental costs of getting there and the question of whether the intermediate steps are sustainable. For those contemplating installing new infrastructure, the issue is the cost-effectiveness of fiber compared with other technology alternatives available to them, and whether fiber offers them sufficient advantage in the marketplace.

Powerline

The pervasiveness of powerlines has led to consideration of using them to provide broadband connectivity to the home and within the home, with speeds of 20 Mbps and 1 Mbps, respectively, typically envisioned. Several experiments have been conducted[9] and proposals have also been made to develop both national and international standards for powerline communications technology. There has been less of a push to use powerline connectivity in the United States, in part because the U.S. power distribution system, in which each secondary transformer serves only a few households (on the order of 5), makes the per-subscriber capital costs much higher. In contrast, this ratio is on the order of 50 in Europe, reflecting the higher voltages and lower currents in the European distribution systems; this difference has tempered continual interest in this technology on the part of U.S. companies such as Nortel and Intel. From an economic viewpoint, powerline communications for the last mile competes against well-established multimegabit per second wired and wireless options described in this chapter. In addition to questions about the

---

[9]One example of recent explorations is a 1999 pilot test by the German company VEBA (now part of e.on), which demonstrated a 2-Mbps per customer result in a trial involving eight households. Results were found to be good enough to suggest more extensive testing and plans for commercialization (involving AVACON A.G., a regional utility). This service uses a device attached at the meter that in turn provides connectivity at each power outlet in the household, providing Internet data and telephone and other value-added services.

cost-effectiveness of powerline data transmissions, there is an overarching and long-standing concern about the interference from powerline communications to wireless applications, including amateur radio, home stereo, and emergency broadcast services. The United Kingdom, for example, has discouraged powerline communications for this specific reason. Powerline communications will not experience widespread deployment until questions about acceptable operating frequencies and interference thresholds are resolved. For in-home networking, powerline technology has to compete with more mature wireless—802.11b (11 Mbps today, with aggregate speeds up to 100 Mbps possible); Ethernet (commonly 10 or 100 Mbps, but capable of speeds up to 1 Gbps); and phone line networking (10 Mbps). These are difficult technical figures to overcome for the powerline medium, even before considering the cost of deploying it. Intel backed out of the HomePlug system for home distribution, partly because of an underwhelming nominal aggregate speed of 14 Mbps but mainly because of the potential interference issues mentioned earlier. In short, powerline communications may yet play some role (last mile or in-home), but it is too immature compared with alternatives to characterize its importance or impact, absolute or relative, as a broadband technology.[10]

Wireline Roadmap

How can wireline providers offer greater bandwidth in the future? Both DSL and cable modem technologies have demonstrated that they can work in mass deployment and as a business proposition for providers. The existence of standards and interoperation among equipment from different vendors is a signal of technology that is mature in the marketplace. The cable industry has a roadmap for performance innovation that does not depend on substantial technical innovation, but only on the business decisions to deploy upgrades that have already been tested in the field. Similarly, the DSL industry has a roadmap for performance improvements that depends on redesign of the access network to install remote electronics in order to shorten the length of the copper pairs. In both cases, the technologies are relatively mature, so the rate of actual—as opposed to potential—performance improvement will depend mainly on

---

[10]For more on powerline communications technology, see David Essex, 2000, "Are Powerline Nets Finally Ready?" *MIT Technology Review*, June 21, available online at <http://www.technologyreview.com/web/essex/essex062101.asp> and John Borland, 2001, "Power Lines Stumble to Market," CNET News.com, March 28, available online at <http://news.cnet.com/news/0-1004-200-5337770.html?tag=tp_pr>.

the costs of upgrade, the depreciation cycle of investment, and competition from other providers.

Improvements to DSL performance will run up against the crosstalk interference problem. The current ANSI standard for DSL spectrum management falls short of addressing the long-term challenge. The problems will become much more significant as the penetration of DSL grows and as the higher data rates contemplated in the DSL upgrade path—which are more sensitive to interference—begin to be widely implemented. The concern, looking forward, is that spectrum management problems will complicate and curtail installment and progress of DSL if the current line-level unbundling regime is maintained. On the horizon are methods for controlling power levels and bandwidth in ways that mitigate the effects of crosstalk. These include coordination of spectrum use within a carrier's DSLAM (this does not, of course, address intercarrier crosstalk) and advanced signal processing technology that partially compensates for crosstalk.

While there are many unresolved questions about how one would actually implement such a process—especially given the contentious relationships among incumbent and competitive carriers—further aggregate performance improvements could be gained through some sort of systemwide coordination of spectrum use. Indications are that with appropriate coordination, symmetric data rates at least 3 times faster than the fastest asymmetric DSL data rates available today would be possible as fiber moves closer to the home. There are other possible advantages. With coordination, the DSLAM and modem equipment could be less complex (and thus less costly), and coordination would permit dynamic partitioning of bandwidth to users on demand that exceeds the factor of 3 indicated above. All of this presumes, of course, some change in the rules of the game. Making improvements in this area will require new regulatory approaches (e.g., how and whether to unbundle), new management strategies, and new technology.

While both HFC and DSL share the same general feature—an intrinsic limit to the data rate of the nonfiber portion of their networks—the limit is much higher for coax, which offers the cable industry more options for incremental investment to obtain incremental performance improvements. Companies providing data over cable have upgrade roadmaps that illustrate the cost and performance benefits of various options. In rough terms, the HFC infrastructure is capable of offering the consumer a factor-of-10 improvement over the next 5 years—by decreasing the number of homes in each cluster and/or increasing the capacity allocated to data services—at relatively low incremental cost. The total capacity of a coaxial cable segment, including both the entertainment TV and data segments, is several gigabits per second. Beyond this point, the potential of HFC to scale is not clear. The incremental deployment of fiber in the HFC infrastructure would imply that the long-term trend would be to replace the coaxial link to the home with fiber if performance gains in the range of 100 times current broadband were required. From today's vantage point, it would be accompanied by the costs and complications associated with deploying fiber to the home.

While one can confidently predict that fiber will increasingly be found deeper and deeper within access networks, and can foresee that fiber will reach an increasing number of households, it is difficult to predict how fast this will happen. Fiber-to-the-home has labor costs that are not likely to yield fully to technical innovation, but the option of technical relief of these costs is very appealing and should justify research in support of creative proposals.[11] The other major cost component is in optical components—for example, lasers and modulators. Right now, there are trends toward both higher performance (seen in wide area fiber optic networks) and lower cost. The industry speculation is that the costs of lasers for consumer premises devices can come down markedly when the volume demand is demonstrated for the specific elements. The presence of very cheap lasers in CD players and the falling cost of lasers in local area networks (e.g., gigabit Ethernet) illustrate at least the potential for inexpensive components.

A significant shift in the costs of fiber would probably require significant architectural innovation, not just improving the individual technology components of present systems. This sort of systems research works to find new ways of combining components into more cost-effective and flexible access systems. PON is an example of an architectural idea introduced in the past that had the effect of significantly reducing costs while offering other deployment advantages (it requires no active electronics and no power supply between the central office or head end and the customer premises). Further innovation is possible, and there are several fiber metropolitan area network companies claiming that they have a better architecture overall based on shared media access, optical switching, IP over SONET, or other innovations. The possibility remains that a sufficiently low cost solution will emerge from this sort of work to make fiber viable to the residence in the short-to-medium term.

It seems quite likely that within the next 5 to 10 years there will be significant FTTH deployment beyond initial field trials. Fiber is also likely to become an important technology for new installation and major upgrade deployments. Whether the amount of fiber deployed will represent a significant fraction of the installed base during this period is unclear, as

---

[11]Efforts in this direction include systems that install fiber in existing sewer pipes.

it will depend on many factors, both technical and economic. Fiber will come to each part of the network when a combination of economics, demand, and capabilities versus alternatives justifies it. The market will continue to test whether or not that time has come, and will continue to push the capabilities of other technologies as far as economically practical as well. Finally, it is worth noting that some caution is in order when making predictions on this subject. Some 15 years ago, there were claims by both infrastructure operators and fiber vendors that FTTH was coming soon, but high costs, uncertain demand, and other factors meant that these forecasts did not pan out (though green-fields situations are especially attractive on a total life-cycle cost basis).

Wireless Options

There are actually many different systems that make use of wireless communication; they are divided here into fixed terrestrial wireless, mobile wireless, fixed satellite service, and wireless local area networking. Fixed wireless service is being readied for direct competition with DSL and cable in major markets, while third-generation mobile and wireless local area networking alternatives aim to deliver services to mobile professionals. Over time, these seemingly disparate market segments are likely to overlap and converge, as portable computing devices and hybrid personal digital assistant (PDA) cell-phone-type devices proliferate further. In the long run, broadband wireless access may be expected to migrate toward the more unique task of supporting connectivity to the growing proportion of portable end-user devices. The relative roles of these wireless options will differ depending on market-demand factors, availability of capital, competitive strategies, and regulatory issues. The focus in this discussion, however, is on shorter-term prospects for broadband residential access, which is generally construed to be a fixed service.

Fixed Terrestrial Wireless

In contrast to mobile services, fixed wireless services provide connectivity from a base station to a stationary point, such as a home.[12] Per-passing costs are more favorable, especially because the cell size can be made large initially, and then decreased as subscription rates increase. As a result, fixed wireless will be an attractive option for providers that do

---

[12]Connectivity may be either to a single gateway within the home (which in turn is connected through a home network to computers within the home) or directly to individual computers within the home. (As home networks become more commonplace, some of which themselves use short-range, low-cost wireless links, the former will likely dominate.)

not own last mile infrastructure in a desired service area to become facilities-based competitors. First-generation, proprietary systems providing data rates of about 1 to 10 Mbps are commercially available. These make use of spectrum set aside for and thus referred to as local multipoint distribution service (LMDS) and multipoint multichannel distribution service (MMDS). The LMDS spectrum, located above 20 GHz, is allocated for point-to-point voice, data, or video transmission. MMDS, which uses spectrum in 2.1- and 2.5- to 2.7- GHz bands, was traditionally used to provide so-called wireless cable video services, especially educational/instructional programming; but a rule change by the FCC in 1998 opened the door to two-way data service delivery over MMDS frequencies, and the channels have been made available to wireless providers for broadband services.[13] LMDS, which offers very high data rates but has more limited range and requires more expensive equipment, is used primarily for high-speed business services. The longer range and lower frequencies of MMDS reduce both infrastructure and customer terminal costs, making it suitable for competing with DSL and cable in the residential market.

Several operators (including Sprint and WorldCom) have been deploying first-generation broadband fixed wireless networks (using MMDS spectrum) with the objective of providing Internet access with speeds of roughly 1 Mbps to homes and small businesses. In these systems, each antenna serves a large service area, and line of sight between the antenna and receiver is required. Coverage in these systems is roughly 50 to 60 percent of potential subscribers, with the exact figure depending on the topography and foliage density. Customer premises equipment costs are in the neighborhood of $500 to $1,000. The total cost of a base transceiver station is roughly $500,000. Assuming typical coverage over about an 8- to 10-mile radius, the per-passing cost is roughly $2,000 per square mile. The actual range that can be achieved will differ significantly depending on the topography, presence of buildings and trees, and so forth. The area and number of customers served by a base station (and thus the cost per subscriber) depends on signal range, desired bandwidth per customer, and channel capacity.

As of early 2001, service providers are testing second-generation products that use smaller cells to increase system capacity and enhanced signal processing to enable non-line-of-sight service. These products are ex-

---

[13]In response to a proposal submitted by participants in the old wireless cable industry, the FCC amended the rules to permit licensees to provide high-speed, two-way services, such as high-speed Internet access, to a variety of users. With wireless cable distribution of video entertainment programming proving a nonstarter, the commission concluded that two-way wireless could produce a continuing stream of leased channel revenues for the educational licensees (viable competition for hardwire cable was also a consideration).

pected to bring the coverage rate up to about 80 to 90 percent. The cost per-passing will be considerably higher because the cell sizes are smaller (3 to 5 miles), but the systems will have considerably higher overall capacity and coverage. Standards for second-generation LMDS and MMDS have been initiated in standards bodies such as IEEE 802.16. The technology of choice for mass-market MMDS is being explored in standards bodies and the marketplace, but it is likely that a variation of orthogonal frequency division multiplexing (OFDM) will be adopted at the physical level. At this point, deployment appears to be gated more by the availability of investment capital and the initial cost and performance of the technology than by the lack of standards, but agreement on a standard would permit component vendors to drive prices down farther and, in turn, could prompt more investment.

Other technologies (e.g., wideband code-division multiple access [CDMA]-derivative radios operating at several megabits per second, ultrawideband radio, and free space laser beams) are also under consideration for fixed or semimobile high-speed Internet access. As of 2001, there are several venture-funded companies (e.g., Iospan Wireless, BeamReach, and IPWireless using radio frequency transmissions, and Terabeam using free space laser transmissions) developing broadband wireless Internet access technologies, and some of these activities may lead to significantly improved cost and performance for fixed wireless.

Another alternative for broadband wireless is to extend technologies developed for wireless local area networks, which make use of low-power transmitters in unlicensed frequency bands. These have improved substantially in the past few years, with the mass-market IEEE 802.11b standard supporting speeds up to 11 Mbps in the 2.4-GHz band. Although the coverage area for wireless LANs is limited to small areas (microcells with a typical radius of less than several hundred feet, though favorable topography and directional antennas can extend this range), rapidly improving cost-performance makes it a viable option for public services in locations such as airports, shopping centers, rural communities, and dense urban areas. Future 802.11 and European Telecommunications Standards Institute (ETSI) Hiperlan II standards, which are still under development, are intended for use in the unlicensed 5-GHz band to provide speeds of roughly 50 Mbps.

There has been a dramatic surge of interest in 802.11b wireless local area network (WLAN) deployment (by individuals, community networking activists, and corporations) during the period of this committee's work. Much of this investment is driven by the fact that WLANs can be readily deployed at a grass-roots level with modest investment: a few hundred dollars for a home, increasing to a few thousand dollarsfor a small office building or campus. This investment provides mutimegabit (nominally 11 Mbps for recent 802.11b equipment) access capability to both fixed and mobile computing devices within the coverage area, as long as there is an appropriate broadband backhaul service such as Ethernet, HFC, or DSL to connect the access point. Depending on the number of users sharing the WLAN infrastructure, the costs per user can be relatively low (hundreds of dollars, as compared with thousands of dollars for other forms of broadband access), so long as average traffic contributed by each user is not too high. This favorable deployment cost model, along with the strategic advantage of being able to handle both fixed and portable devices with the same access network, seems to be driving a great deal of commercial interest. Most of the activity is of a grass-roots nature—building, store, and mall operators, individual homeowners, and community networking activists are installing their own WLANs that over time could provide fairly ubiquitous, though not uniform, coverage in populated areas, in a fashion reminiscent of the early deployment of networking within communities and educational institutions. Note that the use of WLAN for "last 100 meters" access does not eliminate the need for broadband wired access such as HFC, cable, or fiber, which is still needed for backhaul of traffic. WLAN may help the overall economics of each of these wired solutions by increasing the end-user's utility and facilitating sharing of the wired link among multiple devices and/or subscribers. This also applies to rural areas where a single T1 connection along with WLAN access might be more affordable than DSL or cable service to each home, depending, of course, on the density of the population cluster.

Scalable deployment of public unlicensed band services poses additional challenges, such as improvements in spectrum etiquette to prevent destructive interference among multiple operators. The year 2001 also saw reports of breaches in the default 802.11b security technology that will require attention. Looking to the long term, one can anticipate that access could be provided by a heterogeneous mix that combines short-range wireless access points (using technologies such as 802.11, Bluetooth, and new higher-speed solutions) with the more traditional DSL/cable/fiber/fixed wireless solutions.[14] This scenario becomes of particular interest if a large base of users comes to value mobile devices.

Mobile Wireless

While fixed wireless is an important near-term broadband access alternative, it is generally agreed that over time, wireless technologies and

---

[14]See, for example, David Leeper, "A Long-term View of Short-Range Wireless," 2001, *IEEE Computer*, June, pp. 39-44.

the spectrum associated with them will be aimed increasingly at communications for next-generation portable and mobile communication and computing devices rather than at fixed broadband. Users are likely not only to seek mobile service but also to look for broadband services that work in a more seamless fashion between home and mobile environments. As market demand and performance expectations grow, fixed wireless will be at a performance (or cost-to-performance ratio) disadvantage compared with wireline alternatives in most areas. At the same time, providers will likely find it more profitable to use spectrum for the mobile market, which wireline cannot serve. (This presumes regulatory changes in the licensing rules for that spectrum.) As a result, fixed wireless will have a long-term niche only in areas of low to medium population density, where wireline options will remain costly and the bandwidth feasible with fixed wireless is sufficient to meet demand.

In the mobile arena, solutions for third-generation (3G) digital cellular systems based on wideband CDMA have been standardized at the ITU, and early deployments are expected in 2001-2002, particularly in Japan and Europe. Deployment is expensive, requiring that the provider install new infrastructure and that the consumer purchase new phones or other receiver equipment. The 3G standard, which provides a theoretical 2-Mbps user bit-rate, is in practice limited to medium bit-rate services up to hundreds of kilobits per second due to both system capacity constraints and realistic wireless channel properties. Thus, 3G mobile, while a major step forward from current digital cellular systems, is unlikely to meet the needs of the full range of broadband access requirements that might be expected in the mobile services arena over the next 5 to 10 years. However, given that 3G chipsets will be available in the mass market within 1 to 2 years, there are efforts underway to leverage its wideband CDMA core technology to provide several-megabit fixed wireless access as well. There are also interim "2.5G" solutions, going by the names EDGE, GPRS, and HDR, which provide packet data services at moderate bit-rates (~10 to 100 kbps per user) using available "2G" digital cellular infrastructure.

Although the speeds of 3G represent a significant improvement over second-generation digital cellular in terms of peak bit-rate, the 3G service appears likely to fall short of consumer expectations for broadband services when they reach the marketplace. Despite the hype—and their usefulness for certain applications notwithstanding—3G services may turn out not to meet either the capacity or performance needs of truly scalable mass-market services that deliver several megabits to each mobile device. This indicates that there will be continued attention to developing broadband mobile technology. One interesting possibility is that derivatives of WLAN technologies—802.11, Hiperlan, or new standards—will be able to supply high bandwidth more effectively, so long as additional features to support mobility, user registration, and the like are gradually added in. In contrast to the 3G model, in which large carriers are using government-allocated spectrum, the WLAN scenario is a bottom-up, small-operator approach that leverages unlicensed spectrum. There is the potential for rapid growth owing to the lower capital investment requirements; the ability to target service to urban areas, airports, and the like and to expand as needed; and the absence of spectrum licensing costs.

Satellite

Broadband local access via satellite provides another wireless alternative. Satellite services have been available for many years, based on geosynchronous Earth orbit (GEO) satellites. These satellites have been used for telephone communications, television distribution, and various military applications. Satellite access clearly has significant advantages in terms of rapid deployment (once a satellite is launched) and national coverage, but has cost and performance limitations and system capacity limitations, particularly for uplink traffic. The utility of satellite's broadcast capabilities (one-way broadband) has already been seen in digital video via satellite (e.g., direct broadcast satellite [DBS]), which became pervasive in the 1990s. This has also been leveraged to deliver a mixed-technology Internet access service (e.g., DirectPC) with satellite downlink and dial modem uplink. A bidirectional service, in which both the uplink and the downlink use the satellite, requires the solution of significant technical problems at the same time that costs are kept low enough to be attractive to consumers. An example of such a service is the recently introduced Starband service, which promises a peak rate of 500 kbps downstream and 150 kbps upstream, using a 2- by 3-foot antenna, at a current price of $70 per month plus $400 initial investment (figures that may change as the market grows).

While their coverage is very broad, GEO satellite systems possess a number of limitations. Power constraints and dish size (which is limited to a roughly 2-ft diameter for mass-market installation) limit the downlink transmission from a GEO satellite to about 100 to 200 Mbps today (systems under development for launch in the 2003 time frame are being designed to offer at least 400 Mbps downstream). Statistical multiplexing effects permit this capacity to be shared over more users than is suggested by simply dividing this number by the peak load per user, but the total number of customers that can be served per satellite is nonetheless limited. While other performance characteristics of satellites have increased significantly (along Moore's law-like curves), the efficiency of power panels on satellites has not increased substantially over recent decades. New frequency bands can also be used to increase system capacity given a finite number of orbital spots. Spot beams and on-board switching would provide roughly a factor-of-10 improvement in capacity at the expense of reduced geographic coverage and a heavier and costlier payload. There have been several attempts to develop commercial satellites of this sort earlier, but there seem to be various technical and cost problems in each case.

Even though GEO satellites may have a limited total capacity for broadband on a national scale, they may occupy a long-term market niche if the demand is restricted to a small, bounded set of (mostly rural) subscribers. In this respect, the GEO systems clearly provide an illustration that the broadband market will be served by a range of technology options, not a single technology winner.

GEO satellite systems also have a high round-trip transmission delay. The propagation time (speed of light) up to the satellite and back is about 250 milliseconds (ms), so the round-trip delay is 500 ms. This compares with a terrestrial cross-country round-trip delay over a fiber link of between 75 and 100 ms. This has caused some to conclude that GEO satellites are useless for data purposes. In fact, whether this delay matters depends on the application being used. For Web access the delay may be noticeable, but it does not seriously degrade the experience so long as the end-node software is properly set up. For other applications, the satellite delay is a more serious issue. For Internet telephony, the long delays cause a real degradation in usability, since there are well-known human-factors issues that arise when the round-trip delay in a conversation approaches 200 ms.

An alternative that has received a great deal of attention over the last several years is to use low Earth orbit (LEO) satellites, which in contrast to GEO satellites do not occupy a constant position in an assigned orbital slot, and to rely on multiple satellites to provide coverage. LEO satellite proponents claim that power limitations are less serious than those with GEO satellites, though both types of system are constrained by power considerations. LEO satellite technology, while challenging, can be fielded, as the pioneering Iridium and Globalstar deployments have demonstrated. LEO satellite deployment for broadband data services requires the solution of additional difficult technical problems, such as antennas that can track a moving satellite at a price point suited for a consumer.

However, the feasibility of LEO satellites for mass-market broadband access is constrained more by economic considerations than the technology challenges. A LEO satellite system requires the launching of many satellites, because in their low Earth orbit, the satellites are in rapid motion overhead, and there must be enough of them that one is always in range. This means that the system has a very high initial cost to build and launch, which in turn implies that there must be a significant user pool to

m" are mostly wireless. The cost and performance of broadband wireless access networks will thus be crucial to the user's overall experience.

In that context, it is worth noting that there are significant challenges associated with delivering true broadband services, as defined in this report, to mobile devices. For example, a 5-MHz chunk of 3G spectrum can support only about 10 simultaneous broadband users per cell, a number that has to increase by orders of magnitude to make the service viable beyond narrowband uses. Research and development (R&D) challenges faced by developers of "4G" wireless standards include higher speeds (on the order of 1 to 10 Mbps), maintenance of service quality under mobile fading conditions, integration of mobile and fixed network architectures, and greater spectral efficiency, capacity, and scalability. There has been recent interest in mobile Web access, media streaming applications aimed at portable devices, and the like, but consumer demand and the shape of the market are still evolving. Significant R&D investment will be needed to reach the scalability and cost and performance levels appropriate for ubiquitous mobile/portable broadband wireless deployment. Supportive FCC spectrum regulation policies that encourage efficient spectrum usage and easier access to new spectrum, rapid technology evolution, and market competition will also be needed to drive this important scenario forward.

The Diverse Technology Landscape

The different technology options—including HFC, DSL, fiber, wireless, and satellite—are different in detail. Some have higher delay, some have lower overall bandwidth, some may have higher prices, and so on. Different technology can be deployed to advantage in different circumstances. In dense urban and suburban areas, the present generation of wireline broadband—HFC and DSL—is being utilized successfully today. Fiber will be used in access networks wherever a combination of economics, demand, and capabilities (compared with alternatives, including the infrastructure already in place) justifies it. Fixed wireless is being used to support market entry by providers that do not own or have access to existing wireline assets. In less densely populated areas, fixed wireless may offer a longer-term solution for broadband access. Finally, in the most remote areas, a small percentage of the U.S. population may best be served by satellite where the very high fixed cost of construction and launching satellites is offset by the very low per-passing costs, given the enormous area that a satellite system can serve. One of the consequences one may have to accept for living in rural areas is that the available broadband service has some particular characteristics, such as higher delay and greater cost per unit of bandwidth. This may be an issue for certain applications, but one should look at this as just one consequence of technology diversity, not as a fatal flaw of one or another technology.

The market will continue to test whether or not the time has come to deploy fiber, and it will also continue to push the capabilities of other technologies as far as economically practical. In different parts of the nation (and the world), with different demographics and population distribution, these different technology options will play out in a different mix, but each will play a role in the diverse world of today.

LAYERING AND UNBUNDLING

This chapter devotes considerable attention above to the characteristics of different technology options for broadband access. But consumers do not normally care about the communications technology for its own sake; they care about the services that can be delivered over it—Internet applications (Web, audio, video), entertainment television, and so on. Hiding these details and separating the underlying communications technologies and the applications and services accessible to end users are accomplished through the engineering practice of layering. Communication systems are often designed (and described) in a layered fashion: that is, with a physical layer at the bottom that differs, depending on the particular communications technology chosen; a top layer that represents the specific applications that users run over the network; and some intermediate layers that help organize the engineering of the overall system.

As a simple example, consider the problem of sharing the total capacity of a cable system among a number of users and applications. At the physical layer is a coaxial cable capable of carrying radio frequency signals. The capacity of the cable system is divided into a number of channels of 6-MHz bandwidth, each capable of carrying a TV channel or other information. At the layer above that, one or another form of content is assigned to each frequency. Most channels are used today to carry a single TV signal, but channels can also be used for the Internet or for telephone service. Also, using new digital representations, multiple TV channels can now be carried in a single 6-MHz channel.

The Internet's design is layered so that it works over a wide range of communications technologies, including all of the wireline and wireless broadband technologies discussed above. Consider Internet transmission over a cable system. First, one or more physical channels are assigned to Internet transmission. Then, at the lowest layer of the Internet's design, the data to be transmitted over an individual cable system channel are divided into a sequence of small messages called *packets*. Multiple users share a single channel by sending their own packets one after another. Finally, the packets used by each user are assigned to one or another "application," such as Web access, e-mail, or streaming audio. So the layers of sharing for the Internet over cable are as follows: a physical cable, which is divided into channels, then divided into packets, which are each in turn assigned to a particular user and application.

To the user of the Internet, the details of layering are largely irrelevant. But the detail does matter in the debate about unbundling. The term "unbundling" is used to describe the situation in which the owner of physical facilities is required to make some portion of that resource available to a competitor. Unbundling of the incumbent local telephone company facilities is required by the Telecommunications Act of 1996. There are two distinct ways of unbundling the local loop: physically and logically.

In the case of the copper infrastructure of the telephone company, one form of unbundling is physical, where an actual copper pair is assigned to a competitor. In this way, the competitor has direct access to the electronic signals being carried over the wire (or to the light carried over a fiber) and can adopt whatever transmission scheme it chooses. For use of the loop, the competitor pays the rate negotiated with the incumbent or, in the absence of a negotiated agreement, the rate established by regulators through arbitration, and in turn directly implements the service and bills the customer. Physical-layer unbundling requires that the competitor have the ability to colocate equipment and upstream connectivity at the network termination point of the loop (typically but not exclusively at the central office).

Physical-layer unbundling offers several potential advantages for the competitor. First, it provides the competitor the freedom to select the type of transmission technology it chooses to implement over the copper loop, independent of whatever decisions the incumbent may make, permitting the competitor to compete with the incumbent on the basis of a variety of attributes, including speed, quality, and maximum loop length. Second, in the case of a loop running from the central office to the subscriber, it is in some sense a well-defined, easily separable network element.

Physical-layer unbundling may also impair the ultimate performance of the copper plant. While it holds true for voice signals, the assumption that copper loops are fully separable is not correct for high-speed data transmission using DSL because of crosstalk among wires within the telephone plant. This means that ultimate performance and reach are hampered because corrective measures—such as coordinated assignment of copper pairs and coordination of transmitted signals among pairs—cannot be implemented if competitors are left free to implement the technology of their choosing.

Unbundling also raises new issues when applied to new facilities. As an initial matter, an unbundling obligation may deter an incumbent local exchange carrier (ILEC) from pushing fiber farther into the neighborhood. In addition, plant access on the network end of the loop today is generally at the central office. To improve the performance and reach of DSL service, it is natural to deploy fiber deeper into the telephone network. Then the copper pair terminates at a remote terminal, which may be a curbside pedestal or even a small box on a telephone pole. Issues raised in this context include these:

• Unbundling at remote terminals is problematical because of space limitations and because the relatively small number of subscriber lines terminated at each remote terminal make colocation and interconnection (linking the copper loop to the competitor's network) more difficult to achieve here than was the case at the central office.
• As fiber is pushed deeper into the network, the copper loops become shorter, each remote terminal serves fewer customers, and (if only the copper is unbundled) each provider would need to separately provision fiber to interconnect at the remote terminal. The fiber running to the terminals might also be unbundled, which would require some sort of time-division multiplexing (i.e., each provider has its own time slots) or wavelength division multiplexing (each provider has its own wavelengths) of the incumbent-owned fiber.
• Continuation of physical-layer unbundling requirements complicates establishment of technology-neutral rules because unbundling rules must take into account the particular details of each new communications technology used by incumbents.

The other unbundling option is logical—above the physical layer. Higher-layer services concerned with transmitting bits are implemented in some fashion on top of protocols concerned with transmitting electrical signals across the wire, which means that they can be implemented independent of the particulars of the physical-layer connection used to provide the higher-level service. That is, a competitor need not control the actual signals running over the wires if it can implement its service using bit transport capabilities provided by the incumbent. With logical-layer unbundling, the incumbent specifies the customer-premises equipment and operates the termination equipment.

Logical-layer unbundling offers several advantages. Colocation requirements are confined to those necessary for the competitor to interconnect with the incumbent's network. Another advantage to logical-layer unbundling is that it may be easier to verify service-level agreements between the incumbent and competing service provider, because data on logical-layer service (throughput, quality of service, and so on) can be compiled more readily. Finally, with logical-layer unbundling, one avoids much of the argument over such hard-to-measure issues as whether incumbent personnel "made life difficult" for CLEC employees while installing equipment or agreeing on a frequency plan.

A principal disadvantage of logical-layer unbundling for the competitor is that the performance characteristics of the link implemented by the incumbent may restrict the types of services the competitor may offer, and limits the competitor's ability to differentiate itself from the incumbent. While the motivation of incumbents is certainly a matter of speculation and debate, it is often suggested that one reason incumbents have favored the lower-speed, asymmetric DSL technology is that symmetrical high-speed DSL service for business customers could undercut profits on more expensive T1 data service. Incumbents might also select a transmission technology that accommodates the typical copper loop but which may not be optimal for subscribers with longer loops. A competitor restricted to logical-layer unbundling cannot provide a symmetrical service or otherwise compete with the incumbent by offering higher performance than the incumbent's system permits.

The nature of the local access technology affects what unbundling options are viable. In the case of the cable infrastructure, one could propose that different frequencies could be allocated to different providers, or that different providers could be assigned a share of the packets being sent in a single frequency, and so on. In practice, allocation schemes have not proved workable, and cable open access is being implemented at the packet level. So the fact that there are different ways of sharing at different layers, and that different technologies have different layering structure, makes the debate about unbundling complex.

ECONOMICS OF INFRASTRUCTURE INVESTMENT

Like any other business, revenue, at least in the long term, must be sufficient for a broadband service provider to be profitable (or at least to break even, in the case of a public sector enterprise). As the previous discussion suggests, different technologies have different cost structures that shape their attractiveness in different market segments. At the same time, uncertainty about demand for broadband, consumer willingness to pay, and the interaction of these factors with different business models shapes investment in broadband deployment.

Understanding Costs

Broadband deployment costs fall into two broad categories: fixed (or per-passing costs), which are roughly independent of the number of subscribers, and variable (or per-subscriber) costs. Fixed costs include those of upgrading or installing wireline infrastructure within the neighbor-hood and installing or upgrading central office or head-end equipment. For wireless, the costs of acquiring wireless spectrum licenses are another per-passing cost. The most significant variable costs are the per-subscriber capital costs, including line cards, customer-premises equipment, and the costs of upgrading or installing connections to individual premises. Other variable costs include installation at the customer premises (which drives shifts to customer-installed solutions) and customer support and mainte-nance. Providing upstream connectivity involves both fixed costs, such as installation of regional or national transport links, and variable costs asso-ciated with provisioning regional and national connectivity to support the traffic load imposed by customers.

These costs are greatly shaped by density and dispersion. Where new wireline infrastructure is installed, more remote or sparsely populated areas will have significantly higher per-passing costs, reflecting per-mile constructions costs, that make investment riskier, and the lower per-pass-ing costs of satellite or other wireless systems will be more attractive. Each particular circumstance will involve its own set of cost trade-offs, however. For instance, because installing remote terminal equipment im-poses substantial costs, home-run fiber to the premises could turn out to be cheaper than a fiber-to-the-cabinet strategy in some rural cases.

Take-Rate Tyranny

Perhaps the most important implication of per-passing costs is the "take-rate tyranny" that dominates investment decisions. Because costs are dominated by the dollars-per-mile cost of installation, investment in wireline infrastructure has a cost structure in which most of the cost is determined by the number of houses passed, and a minority of the costs is determined by the number of subscribers. (Because they lend themselves to a strategy in which the cell size can be scaled to the take-rate, wireless systems can have an advantage, though the cost of spectrum must also be factored in.)

A very simplified cost model indicates the general shape of the finan-cial dilemma facing those who invest in broadband infrastructure. If there are two providers instead of one—assuming no differentiation between the products, no first-mover advantage, and that costs are per-passing—the costs for each are unchanged but the revenues are halved. As a very rough example, if a provider makes an incremental investment in the distribution infrastructure that has a cost of $200 per passing and must recover this investment in 3 years, this is approximately $5 per month per passing. If the provider has the whole market and 50 percent of the homes

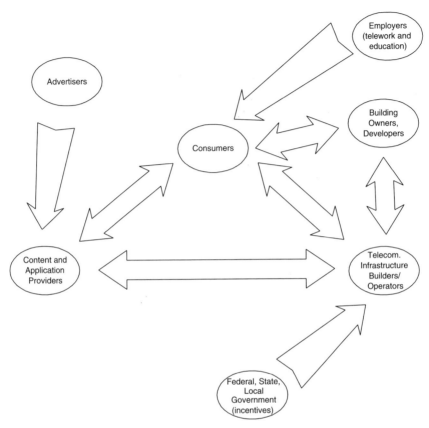

FIGURE 4.5   Paying for broadband.

Focus on the Consumer

The factors discussed in the previous section notwithstanding, the consumer is the pivot around which all of the economic issues swing. Without consumer demand and a (somewhat) predictable willingness to pay (or evidence that advertising will be a large source of revenue), there is no market. Evidence from early deployment demonstrates demand. The national average penetration (somewhat more than 8 percent as of summer 2001) reflects and masks an uneven pace of deployment. In localities where the service has been available for a reasonable time, cable industry reports on markets that have had cable modem service available for several years suggest considerable demand.[17]

Although the committee is not aware of definitive studies of consumer willingness to pay for broadband (and the notion proposed in the past, that consumer willingness to pay for entertainment and/or communications is a fixed percentage of income, is generally discounted by economists today), the general shape of the market for communications, entertainment content, and information technology is beginning to emerge. Over 50 percent of homes in America have some sort of PC, with prices that averaged near $2,000 in recent years, and which are now dropping below $1,000 for lower-end machines, illustrating that many consumers are willing to make a significant investment in computing hardware and software. In rough terms, a typical $1,200 home computer replaced after 4 years costs around $25 per month.

A majority of the homes that have PCs are going online and connecting to the Internet, and it is a reasonable projection that only a very small fraction of machines will remain offline in the coming years. Using the primary residence phone line, and purchasing a somewhat more limited dial-up Internet service, the price approaches the $10 per month (providers have also experimented with service and PCs that are provided free, so long as the consumer will allow advertisements to be displayed during network sessions, although recent reports from this market segment put in question the long-term viability of this approach). The entry price today for broadband is not dramatically different from that for high-end dial-up service. A separate phone line costs as much as $20 per month, and unlimited-usage dial-up Internet service generally runs $20 or more per month. Of course, the market offers a range of price and performance points from which the consumer can pick. At the high-end, high-speed DSL can cost up to several hundred dollars per month, and business-oriented cable services are offered at a premium over the basic service.

The total consumer expenditure for such a computer plus basic broadband service is potentially as much as $90 per month, of which the Internet provider can expect to extract less than half. From this revenue base a business must be constructed. If 100 million homes were to purchase broadband service at $50 per month, this would result in total annual revenues to broadband Internet providers of more than $50 billion, which is similar in magnitude to current consumer expenditures on long-distance services.

---

[17]For example, information supplied to the committee by Time Warner Cable is that take-rates have reached 17.5 percent of subscribers in Boston, Massachusetts, and 25 percent of subscribers in Portland, Maine.

One question that the market has not yet explored is whether the consumer would make a significant capital investment, similar to the $1,000 to $2,000 that a computer costs today, as part of obtaining Internet service. For example, if there were a home-run system with fiber running to the residence (making it a relatively future-proof investment), but the consumer had to activate that fiber by purchasing the end-point equipment, would this be an attractive option if the equipment costs were comparable? Would residents be willing to finance the capital costs of installing that fiber in the first place? While there is no hard evidence, wealthier consumers, who have demonstrated a willingness to make purchases such as multiple upscale multimedia PCs and expensive consumer electronics, might well be willing to make such investments, and some residential developers have opted to include fiber.

The Pace of Investment

The rapid evolution of some aspects of the Internet can lead observers into thinking that if something does not happen within 18 months, it will not happen. But the phenomena associated with deployment cycles measured in months have generally been in the non-capital-intensive software arena. The cost of entirely new broadband infrastructure—rewiring to provide fiber-to-the-home to all of the roughly 100 million U.S. households—would be some $100 billion, reflecting in considerable part construction costs that are not amenable to dramatic cost reductions. Even for cable and DSL, for which delivering broadband is a matter of upgrading existing infrastructure, simple economics gates the pace of deployment. For both new builds and incremental improvements, an accelerated pace of deployment and installation would bring with it an increased per-household cost. Some broadband deployment will be accomplished as part of the conventional replacement and upgrade cycles associated with telephone and cable systems. In some cases, this process will have dramatic effects—two examples are HFC replacement of all-coaxial cable plants and aerial replacement of copper with fiber as part of a complete rehabilitation of old telephone plant—but in many others cases, the improvements will be incremental. To accelerate beyond this pace means increasing and training an ever-larger workforce devoted to this task. As more new people are employed for this purpose, people with increasingly higher wages in their current jobs will have to be attracted away from those jobs. Similar considerations apply to the materials and manufacturing resources needed to make the equipment that is needed.

The investment rate also depends critically on the perspective and time horizon of the would-be investor. For an owner of existing facilities—the incumbent local exchange carriers and cable multiple system operators—realistic investment is incremental, builds on the installed base, and must provide return on a relatively short timescale. The tendency to make incremental upgrades to existing telephone and cable plants reflects the view that a replacement of the infrastructure (such as with fiber) would necessitate installation costs that can be avoided by opting to upgrade. The perception is that users would not be willing to pay enough for the added functionality that might be achieved with an all-fiber replacement to offset the extra costs of all-new installation. Changes in either costs or perceived willingness to pay could, of course, shift the investment strategy.

Once the provider has a broadband-capable system, it will only have incentives to spend enough on upgrades to continue to attract subscribers and retain existing customers by providing a sufficiently valuable service. Where facilities-based competition exists, these efforts to attract and retain customers will help drive service-performance upgrades. From this perspective, the level of investment associated with building entirely new infrastructure is very difficult for the incumbents to justify. Viewing the incumbent's incentives to invest in upgrades from the perspective of the two broadband definitions provided above, investment to meet definition 1 will be easier than that to meet definition 2. That is, it is easier to justify spending so that the local access link supports today's applications, while it is harder to justify spending enough to be in front of the demand so as to stimulate new applications.

Two types of nonincumbent investor have also entered the broadband market, tapping into venture capital that seeks significant returns— and generally seeks a faster investment pace. One is the competitive local exchange carrier, which obtains access to incumbent local exchange carrier facilities—primarily colocation space in central offices and the copper loops that run from the central office to the subscriber—to provide broadband using DSL. The other is the overbuilder, which seeks to gain entry into a new market by building new facilities, most commonly hybrid fiber coax for residential subscribers, but also fiber-to-the-premises and terrestrial wireless. Satellite broadband providers in essence overbuild the entire country, though with the capacity to serve only a fraction of the total number of households. The 2000-2001 drying up of Internet-related venture capital has presented an obstacle to continued deployment, and the CLECs have also reported obstacles in coordinating activities with the ILECs that control the facilities they depend on.

Because public sector infrastructure investment generally is based on a long-term perspective, public sector efforts could both complement and stimulate private sector efforts. The key segment of the public sector for such investment is likely to be subfederal (state, local, regional), though the federal sector can provide incentives for these as well as private sector investment. But decision making for such investments is not a simple matter, and, if present trends are any indication, such investments will be confined to those locales that project the greatest returns from accelerated access to broadband or possess a greater inclination for a public sector role in entrepreneurship.

Investment, Risk Taking, and Timelines

The myth of the "Internet year," by analogy to a "dog year," is well known. Where the Internet is concerned, people have been conditioned to expect 1-year product cycles, startups that go public in 18 months, and similar miracles of instant change. The 2000-2001 downturn in Internet and other computing and communications stocks dampened but did not eliminate such expectations. In fact, some things do happen very rapidly in the Internet—the rise of Napster is a frequently noted example. These events are characterized by the relatively small investments required to launch them. Software can diffuse rapidly once conceived and coded. But this should not fool the observer into thinking that all Internet innovation happens on this timescale.

As noted earlier, broadband infrastructure buildout will be a capital-intensive activity. In rough figures, a modest upgrade that costs $200 per passing would cost $20 billion to reach all of the approximately 100 million homes in the United States. Broadband deployment to households is an extremely expensive transformation of the telecommunications industry, second only to the total investment in long-haul fiber in recent years. In light of these costs, the availability of investment capital, be it private sector or otherwise, imposes a crucial constraint on broadband deployment—it is very unlikely that there will be a dramatic one-time, nationwide replacement of today's facilities with a new generation of technology. Instead, new technology will appear piecemeal, in new developments and overbuild situations. Old technology will be upgraded and enhanced; a mix of old, evolving, and new should be anticipated. Whether national deployment takes the form of upgrades or new infrastructure, the relevant timescale will be "old fashioned"—years, not days or months.

As a consequence, observers who are conditioned to the rapid pace of software innovation may well lose patience and assume that deployment efforts are doomed to fail—or that policies are not working—simply because deployment did not occur instantly. One should not conclude that there is something wrong—that something needs fixing—when the only issue is incorrectly anticipating faster deployment.

Much private sector investment, especially by existing firms, is incremental, with additional capital made available as investments in prior quarters show acceptable payoff. As a result, the technological approach chosen by an incumbent is likely to make use of existing equipment and plant, and the deployment strategy must be amenable to incremental upgrades. The evolution of cable systems is a good example. The previous generation of one-way cable systems is in the process of being upgraded to hybrid fiber coax systems, and these in turn are being upgraded to provide two-way capability, greater downstream capacity, and packet transport capabilities. The various incumbents now in the broadband marketplace have very different technology and business pasts—the telecommunications providers selling voice service over copper, the cable television companies using coaxial cable to deliver video, the cellular companies constructing towers for point-to-point wireless telephony, and so forth, and each will evolve to support broadband by making incremental improvements to its respective technologies and infrastructure. Incumbents seeking to limit regulators' ability to demand unbundling have an incentive to avoid technologies that facilitate such unbundling.

Because they exist to take greater risks but possibly provide much greater returns by identifying new promising areas, venture capitalists seek to invest in opportunities that offer high payoff, not incremental improvements. So it is no surprise that the more mature technologies, such as cable and DSL, have attracted relatively little venture capital in recent years. Another investment consideration for the venture capitalist is the total available market, with niche markets being much less attractive than markets that have the potential to grow very large. Finally, because the eventual goal is usually to sell a company (or make an initial public offering) once it has been successfully developed, venture capitalists must pay attention to trends in the public equity markets.[18]

Uncertain Investment Prospects in the Private Sector

Over the past few years, broadband infrastructure has to some extent followed the overall trend of technology-centered enthusiasm for venture capital investment and high-growth planning. Broadband may similarly be affected by the current slowdown in investment and by the more careful assessment of business models to which companies are now being subjected. At this time, broadband providers, as well as Internet service providers more generally, are facing problems of lack of capital and cash flow. This could lead to consolidation, and perhaps to a slowdown in the overall rate of progress.

---

[18]In a white paper written for this project in mid-2000, George Abe of Palomar Ventures characterized venture capital investing as "faddish" and observed that "there is a bit of a herd mentality." There are hints that with the 2001 market drop, venture capitalists have adopted a longer-term view and are seeking well thought-out opportunities rather than chasing fads.

telephone system, inability to book flights at the holidays, and slowdowns within the Internet. As these examples illustrate, congestion may be a universal phenomenon, but the way it is dealt with differs in different systems. In the telephone system, certain calls are just refused, but this would seem inhumane if applied to an emergency room (although this is sometimes being done—emergency rooms are closing their doors to new emergencies and sending the patients elsewhere). In the Internet, the "best effort" response to congestion is that every user is still served, but all transfers take longer, which has led to the complaints and jokes about the "World Wide Wait."

Congestion is not a matter of technology but of business planning and level of investment. In other words, it is a choice made by a service provider whether to add new capacity (which presumably has a cost that has to be recovered from the users) or to subject the users to congestion (which may require the provider to offer a low-cost service in order to keep them).

Shared links can be viewed as either a benefit or a drawback, depending on one's viewpoint. If a link is shared, it represents a potential point of congestion: if many users attempt to transmit at once, each of them may see slow transfer rates and long delays. Looked at in another way, sharing of a link among users is a central reason for the Internet's success. Since most Internet traffic is very bursty—transmissions are not continuous but come in bursts, as for example when a Web page is fetched—a shared communications path means that one can use the total unused capacity of the shared link to transfer the burst, which may make it happen faster.

In this respect, the Internet is quite different from the telephone system. In the telephone system, the capacity to carry each telephone call is dedicated to that one connection for its duration—performance is established a priori. There is still a form of sharing—at the time the call is placed, if there is not enough capacity on the links of the telephone system, the call will not go through. Callers do not often experience this form of "busy signal," but it is traditionally associated with high-usage events such as Mother's Day. In contrast, the Internet dynamically adjusts the rate of each sender on the basis of how many people are transferring data, which can change in a fraction of a second.

The links that form the center of the Internet carry data from many thousands of users at any one time, and the traffic patterns observed there are very different from those observed at the edge. While the traffic from any one user can be very bursty (for a broadband user on the Web, a ratio of peak to average receiving rate of 100 to 1 is realistic), in the center of the network, where many such flows are aggregated, the result is much smoother. This smoothness results from the natural consequences of aggregating many bursty sources, not because the traffic is "managed."

With enough users, the peaks of some users align with the valleys of other users with high odds. One of the reasons that the Internet is a cost-effective way to send data is that it does not set up a separate "call" with reserved bandwidth for each communicating source, but instead combines the traffic into one aggregate that it manages as a whole.

For dial-up Internet users, the primary bottleneck to high throughput is the modem that connects the user to the rest of the Internet. If broadband fulfills its promise to remove that bottleneck, the obvious question is, Where will that bottleneck go? There has a been a great deal of speculation about how traffic patterns on the Internet will change as more and more users upgrade to broadband. Some of these speculations have led to misapprehensions and myths about how the Internet will behave in the future.

Cable systems have the feature that the coaxial segment that serves a particular neighborhood is shared. This has led to the misconception that broadband cable systems must slow down and become congested as the number of users increases. This may happen, but it need not. Indeed, shared media in various forms are quite common in parts of the Internet. For example, the dominant local area network standard, Ethernet, which is a shared technology with some of the same features as HFC cable modems, has proved very popular in the market, even though it, too, can become congested if too many people are connected and using it at once. Cable systems have the technical means to control congestion. They can allocate more channels to broadband Internet, and they can divide their networks into smaller and smaller regions, each fed by a separate fiber link, so that fewer households share bandwidth in each segment. Whether they are, in fact, so upgraded is a business decision, relating to costs, demand, and the potential for greater revenue. Of course, less sharing would tend to reduce the cost advantage of HFC relative to other higher-capacity solutions such as FTTH.

DSL is generally thought to suffer from fewer access network congestion problems because the user has a dedicated link from the residence to the central office. It is true that the user will never see contention from other users over the dedicated DSL link; however, it also means that the user can never go faster than the fixed dedicated capacity of this link, in contrast to being able to use the total unused capacity of a shared system.

Both the cable and DSL systems bring the traffic from all their users to a point of presence (central office or head end), where this traffic is combined and then sent out over a link toward the rest of the Internet. This link from the termination point to the rest of the Internet is, in effect, shared by all of the subscribers connected to that point of presence, whether the broadband system behind it is a shared cable system or a dedicated DSL system, making the link a common source of congestion for all of the subscribers. The cost of the link depends on both the capacity of the physical link and the compensation that must be paid to other Internet providers to carry this traffic to the rest of the Internet. The cost of these links can be a major issue in small communities where it is difficult to provision additional capacity for broadband. So there is an incentive not to oversize that link. The economics and business planning of this capacity are similar for a cable or a DSL system.

The fact that the links from the point of presence to the rest of the Internet are often a source of congestion illustrates an important point. The number of users whose traffic must be aggregated to make the total traffic load smooth is measured in the thousands, not hundreds. So there may be a natural size below which broadband access systems become less efficient. For example, if it takes 10,000 active users to achieve good smoothing on the path from the rest of the Internet, then a provider who gets 10 percent of the market,[19] and who can expect half of his users to be active in a busy hour, needs a total population of 200,000 households as a market base in a particular region.

Even if the broadband local access links themselves are adequately provisioned, bottlenecks may still exist, owing to such factors as peering problems between the broadband service provider and the rest of the Internet, host loading, or other factors. Performance will also be dependent on the performance of elements other than the communications links themselves, such as caches and content servers located at various points within the network (or even performance limitations of the user's computer itself). These problems, which will inevitably occur on occasion, have the potential to confuse consumers, who will be apt to place blame on the local broadband provider, whether rightly or wrongly.

---

[19]For an examination of the smoothing phenomenon, see David D. Clark, William Lehr, and Ian Liu, "Provisioning for Bursty Internet Traffic: Implications for Industry Structure," to appear in L. McKnight and J. Wroclawski, eds., 2002, *Internet Service Quality Economics*, MIT Press, Cambridge, Mass.

5

Broadband Policy and Regulation

This chapter provides an introduction to the policy context surrounding broadband deployment and discusses specific issues that have shaped the reasoning of the Committee on Broadband Last Mile Technology and that underlie its recommendations. A more detailed history of U.S. regulation related to broadband appears in Appendix B, which is recommended for any reader not familiar with the complex regulatory context within which broadband is being deployed. Note that this chapter *does not* contain the committee's policy recommendations, although it lays part of the foundation for them. The committee's findings and recommendations are presented in "Summary and Recommendations" at the beginning of this volume.

THE CONTEXT FOR BROADBAND POLICY

Broadband—as an extension or phase of the Internet—has been imbued, in media coverage and popular debate, with revolutionary promise that cuts across traditional policy segmentation. Residential broadband has ushered in an era of considerable technological innovation and flux. At the same time that a diverse set of technologies, which are characterized by different performance characteristics (bandwidth, symmetry, transparency, and so on), are available for reaching customers, a powerful convergent platform—the Internet and its core technologies—is increasingly favored for delivery of content, applications, and services. Enabled by this flexible, general-purpose delivery platform, a multiplicity of applications and content supported through a variety of business models has emerged. The combination of technological and associated business changes generates considerable uncertainty and questions about what regulatory or other approaches are suited to meeting desired goals in light of this uncertainty.

Broadband has been targeted by traditional political players in the various policy arenas, and it has catalyzed the formation of new political alliances. It is subject to past policy developed in part for other telecommunications technologies and is the focus of a number of efforts to shape new telecommunications policy. The previous chapter explained how the characteristics of the different technology options are just a piece of the broadband puzzle. Because the profitability and growth prospects of different kinds of entities are affected by government decisions about what kind of entity can provide what kind of service, and when and where and how it can do so, the policy context has a significant impact—there are no pure investment decisions, and political activity aimed at shaping the context is rampant. While many speak of a desire to deregulate, the nature and terms of regulation have become part of the competitive process. Moreover, there is something fundamentally highly political in the nature of communications technologies and services, beginning with the importance of communications media in the political process itself.[1] The recent introduction of a number of pieces of legislation aimed at promoting broadband is another indicator of heightened interest and sometimes intense politicization. Proposed measures include tax credits, grants, subsidized loans, and other financial incentives for deployment in underserved or rural areas; support for research on broadband technologies for rural areas; grants for community planning efforts; changes in the regulation of incumbent local exchange carriers; and changes in universal service fund rules.[2]

Viewed through the lens of telecommunications policy, broadband involves a system with players and rules at federal, state, and local levels and a long history of political activity that features industry associations old and new, consumer- and issue-advocacy organizations (and consider-

---

[1]For example, the original schemes for allocating radio and television licenses had a political connection, with licenses allocated geographically.

[2]Bills that would provide financial incentives include H.R. 267, Broadband Internet Access Act of 2001; H.R. 1415, Technology Bond Initiative; H.R. 1416, Broadband Expansion Grant Initiative; H.R. 1697, Broadband Competition and Incentives Act; H.R. 2139, Rural America Broadband Deployment Act; H.R. 2401, Rural America Digital Accessibility Act; H.R. 2597, Broadband Deployment and Telework Incentive Act; H.R. 2669, Rural Telecommunications Enhancement Act; S. 88, Broadband Internet Access Act; S. 150 Broadband Deployment Act; S. 426, Technology Bond Initiative; S. 428, Broadband Expansion Grant

able activity by lawyers and lobbyists for all parties) seeking to influence legislation, administrative rule making, and court decisions. Organizations addressing broadband as part of their lobbying activity have proliferated; they range from mainstream telecommunications trade associations (such as the United States Telecom Association, the National Cable and Telecommunications Association, and the Organization for the Promotion and Advancement of Small Telephone Companies) to associations of new telecommunications competitors (e.g., the Association for Local Telecommunications Services and the Competitive Telecommunications Association) to technology-specific associations (e.g., DSL Forum and the Home Phoneline Networking Alliance), broadband issues-focused associations (such as the Competitive Broadband Coalition and the OpenNET Coalition), and consumer advocacy organizations (such as Consumers Union, the Center for Digital Democracy, and the Consumer Federation of America). At issue are considerations such as pricing, service definitions, interconnection terms, and rules for the use of public resources (e.g., radio spectrum and rights-of-way) as well as a variety of special needs that are usually met outside of normal market action (e.g., universal service and public safety). Broadband is also associated with issues of privacy, security, and access by law enforcement; the complexity of these particular issues necessitates separate examination, and they are not discussed in this report.

Viewed through the lens of competition policy, the economic regulation associated with telecommunications policy is complemented by antitrust and other matters associated with the structure and conduct of provider industries. The action centers on administrative authorizations (with or without conditions) and legal decisions related to mergers and acquisitions. At issue are basic questions of market power and related conduct, such as interconnection and access to directories.

Initiative; S. 966, Rural Broadband Enhancement Act. Bills that would support research include H.R. 2401, Rural America Digital Accessibility Act, and S. 430, Broadband Rural Research Investment Act.

Bills that would change ILEC regulation include H.R. 1542, Internet Freedom and Broadband Deployment Act; H.R. 1697, Broadband Competition and Incentives Act; H.R. 1698, American Broadband Competition Act; H.R. 2120, Broadband Antitrust Restoration and Reform Act; S. 1126, Broadband Deployment and Competition Enhancement Act; and S. 1127, Rural Broadband Deployment Act. S. 500, the Universal Service Support Act, would extend universal service fund coverage for broadband. S. 1056, the Community Telecommunications Planning Act, would provide support for community planning grants. (National Journal's Technology Daily. 2001. *Broadband Bill Status.* National Journal, Washington, D.C. Available online at <http://nationaljournal.com/pubs/techdaily/briefroom/billstatus/broadband.htm>.)

structure that are given priority through public policy decisions (e.g., 911 emergency services, law enforcement access capabilities,[5] and disability access). Early on, the government posture with respect to the market dominance of AT&T evolved to reflect evidence that AT&T devoted, without a government mandate but with protected revenue, considerable resources to improving the efficiency and capabilities of its network through technological advances. Later, government efforts to open previously closed markets motivated equipment manufacturers and service providers to develop and deploy equipment and facilities that could take advantage of those commercial opportunities.[6] Today, for example, literally scores of firms are deploying fiber-optic cables and advanced switches and routers in local and long distance networks to provide voice and data services, a phenomenon that (along with mobile wireless) has been fueled recently by tens of billions of dollars in venture capital. Rather than mandate particular technological solutions, the FCC has tended in recent years to address technology via selected performance requirements against which industry groups could develop specific standards, and even these activities seem to have diminished over time.[7] In the turbulent wireless arena, the FCC has been changing its procedures for issuing radio licenses, from adopting auctions for allocation of spectrum to considering a systemwide rather than site-specific licensing approach.

Nonetheless, the FCC has been faulted for some of its approaches to new technologies.[8] More generally, both regulators and investors have

---

[5]Communications Assistance for Law Enforcement Act, 47 USC 1001, PL 103-414.

[6]In the 1950s, for example, advances in microwave technology (originally developed for the government during World War II) created an alternative system for transmitting telephone calls over long distances, in lieu of AT&T's embedded system of wires. In 1958, the FCC authorized large businesses to use microwave facilities to construct their own private networks. In 1969, the commission took the next step and permitted firms to compete directly with AT&T for certain types of services. And in the 1980s, with divestiture bringing the realities of competition closer, AT&T executives came to revise their own assessment of the costs of adding fiber in their long-distance network as competitor actions, such as Sprint's "pin drop" advertisements, made the case more compelling.

[7]In the case of "1+" access, for example, the FCC did not specify the particular types of modifications to existing telephone switching equipment that were required to provide "1+" access. Instead, it mandated the performance requirements that the carriers would have to satisfy and allowed the carriers, working with equipment manufacturers, to develop the specific technical modifications.

[8]Some argue that both the FCC and AT&T were slow to cultivate cellular telephony, where deployment and commercial service lagged key innovations considerably; that the granting of licenses for UHF television channels proved to be a costly diversion of resources and spectrum; and that the approach taken to standard-setting for advanced ("high-definition") television serves to slow progress in that arena. See, for example, "A Very Long Distance: A Regulatory Call Put Cell Phones on Hold," *Technology Review*, May 2001, p. 110.

guessed wrong on many technologies; it has been easy for people to both over- and underestimate the potential of new technology. This point was emphasized by many participants at the committee's June 2000 workshop, which included comments on disappointments in such technologies as Integrated Services Digital Network service and multipoint multichannel distribution service (in its video distribution incarnation), among others, for which the technology proved limited in practice, penetration never reached anticipated levels, and better alternative technology was ultimately adopted. Such experiences underscore the fundamental difficulties that regulators have in gauging the coevolution of technologies and markets—and their influence on them.[9] The problem of understanding the trends and implications of new technology seems especially acute for the Internet, since few regulatory agency staff, at least at the FCC, have been expert in Internet-related technologies.[10] The FCC has recently launched several initiatives aimed at increasing its technical capacity in this and other areas.[11]

One of the most obvious indicators of the difficulty regulators (and other policy makers) have in keeping up with technology change is the definitions they develop and use. The Telecommunications Act of 1996 refers in general terms to "advanced services." Required to report to Congress on deployment of advanced services, the FCC subsequently defined these to be at least 200 kbps in either direction.[12] As discussed in Chapter 2 in this report, this sort of definition is problematical: 200 kbps will increasingly be, at best, a lowest common denominator in an environment

---

[9]At a June 2000 workshop, Thomas Krattenmaker of Mintz, Levin (and previously the FCC and academia) observed: "I would say that any regulation or any response you propose to the FCC that is predicated on your ability to predict what technology will prevail, when, will be a useless recommendation . . . . We are just rife with suggestions, too many of which the Commission has adopted, that were based on some ability to know when technology and which technology was going to be deployed. I don't think we're capable of knowing that, and I know the commissioners are not—they're not selected on that [basis]."

[10]Casual observation shows that the FCC has engaged a single Internet-oriented individual in its Office of Plans and Policy since the mid-1990s, and beginning in the late 1990s it engaged chief technologists with Internet expertise, but there are limits to what a couple of specialists in staff positions can accomplish.

[11]Steps taken include the 1998 establishment of a Technical Advisory Council and the 2001 launch of an agencywide "Excellence in Engineering" initiative, including hiring and training measures.

[12]Broadband Second Notice of Inquiry, Federal Communications Commission (FCC, 2000, "Inquiry Concerning the Deployment of Advanced Telecommunications Capability to All Americans in a Reasonable and Timely Fashion, and Possible Steps to Accelerate Such Deployment Pursuant to Section 706 of the Telecommunications Act of 1996: Second Report," CC Docket No. 98-146, FCC, Washington, D.C., August 21).

where capabilities of many technologies are growing; it is unclear whether bandwidth demand will be symmetrical, as the requirement assumes; and, in any event, the committee believes that use of any static definition is unwise over the long run. The separation, intellectually and culturally, of those setting policy definitions from those developing the technology may be unavoidable, but it has consequences.

Thus, broadband is still a very new technology family, as is the Internet in general. The great and general potential of the technology seems clear, but how it might be effectively (and profitably) commercialized is still unclear. During this stage, one can expect to see much experimentation with different business and service models by both private and public providers. It may be wrong to assume that executives whose public remarks exude confidence have deep understanding of all dimensions of the new approaches to networking that they are developing. For example, several people at the committee's June 2000 workshop acknowledged in discussions that some of their earlier assumptions had proved wrong and that their views were evolving with experience.[13] Indeed, the years 1999-2000 saw the nation in the midst of a dot-com and telecommunications euphoria in the financial markets, while 2001 sees the reverse. All these observations, therefore, suggest caution in reading too much into the immediate situation and the importance of business strategists and policy makers staying as flexible as possible during this stage.

Asymmetrical Regulation and Achieving Technology Neutrality

The development of Internet-based services that can operate over both cable and telephone networks has accentuated convergence and technology neutrality. Cable, DSL, and wireless providers can offer relatively comparable applications and services. Not only do these alternatives each offer high-speed access to the Internet, but each also has the potential to provide services that compete directly with the traditional offerings of other networks (e.g., cable broadband facilities can be used to provide voice services, and DSL can carry streaming video).

The unsustainability of competition that may arise with asymmetrical regulation is most severe when two products or services are perfect substitutes for each other. For example, if DSL and cable modem services are

---

[13]For example, in remarks to the committee, Sprint's Jim Hannan said of his MMDS offering, "We don't have effective models . . . so we really don't understand how the network behaves. We're pushing it every day." Hannan observed that projected upstream-to-downstream traffic ratios were much higher than what was observed when Sprint deployed its network; this was attributed largely to customer use of Napster.

extremely close substitutes, disparate rule sets are likely to be a significant problem in the long run, unless bundling broadband access with other services (cable television or telephone) creates some differentiation. To the extent they are differentiated in ways that reflect demand heterogeneity, this is less of a problem. Still, even if the platforms do not provide directly compatible services, they may provide services that are nonetheless substitutable for each other.

Their convergence notwithstanding, these technologies are for historical reasons subject to separate and substantively different regulatory regimes—a situation characterized by some academics, industry representatives, and FCC officials as regulation in "stovepipes." At the FCC, stovepipes are embodied in bureaus—cable services, common carrier, mass media, and wireless telecommunications. Those bureaus, in turn, correspond to focused enabling statutes, which reinforce the traditional linkage of technologies with industries and specific services. Appendix B contrasts the regulation of telecommunications common carriers (which affects DSL provision) with that of cable operators. Terrestrial wireless and satellite are subject to yet another set of distinct regulations. Looking across the various stovepipes, the greatest constraints appear to apply to the telephone industry, where rules (retail price regulation and newer market-opening requirements) are intended to inhibit ILECs from taking unfair advantage of their historically dominant position as regulated monopolies in telephony as they enter into other market segments; but one also sees cable franchising provisions being applied to broadband delivered over cable.

The issue of asymmetrical regulation of broadband has been highlighted by the current debate over "open access," discussed in detail below. Cable operators have maintained that the Internet access service offered over their networks is a cable service and, consequently, that they are not required to offer unaffiliated ISPs that wish to reach cable subscribers access to this service. Opponents have claimed that cable operators are engaged in the provision of a telecommunications service when they offer high-speed access to an ISP and, hence, sought to have regulators require cable operators to offer that service on a nondiscriminatory basis to unaffiliated ISPs. (This argument has had traction in the courts; one response has been a move by some cable companies, which have resisted being classified as telecommunications services, to embrace the designation as a way of avoiding franchise payments, illustrating the maneuvering that goes on.) Other parties have contended that government intervention is unnecessary (and may be harmful), because marketplace forces are sufficient to cause cable operators to make access available to unaffiliated ISPs as soon as technical problems are addressed and business arrangements supporting access to multiple ISPs are put in place.

While technical development continues, successful demonstrations and availability of unaffiliated ISPs in some markets suggest that the technical problems of supporting multiple ISPs in cable systems can be overcome.[14] Business aspects—such as provisioning and troubleshooting systems— are a focus of current activity.

Further confounding the question are technology trends suggesting that fiber will be pushed ever deeper into wireline and terrestrial wireless broadband networks, meaning that provider networks will increasingly resemble each other even in terms of technology, at least in all but the last segment of the access link. As the similarity in both product (services) and delivery technology grows, the distinction between the service-producing and service-delivering industries falls, but whether or how one reconciles the associated regulatory regimes is an open question.

Regulatory legacy and convergence aside, some regulatory issues speak to inherent attributes of a technology, confounding any notion of a technology-neutral policy. Implementing local loop unbundling, for example, involves an intimate understanding of the physical environment of that plant. Policy with respect to public rights-of-way involves the details of poles and conduit access for wireline systems and tower siting for wireless. Wireless illustrates another challenge to achieving technology neutrality: with different services—including fixed terrestrial service such as MMDS and mobile services—assigned to different frequency bands, allocating scarce spectrum among these would seem to require making technology- and service-specific trade-offs. In some cases, it is entirely reasonable to make distinctions: one does not have spectrum auctions on fiber, for example. However, when obligations of any kind are imposed—performance obligations certainly—it is generally very difficult or impossible to be completely technologically neutral. How can one treat these services on an even-handed basis despite the differences in the underlying technology?

The committee's assessment of technology options (see Chapter 4) suggests that broadband will not involve a technological horse race or overall regulatory or market choice among technological options. The various access technologies will fill different niches, and multiple connections will be available in many markets (many already have two connections—phone and cable lines—capable of supporting broadband to the

---

[14]For example, in June 2001, AT&T announced that its Boulder, Colorado, open access trials were successful (Richard Williamson, "AT&T Completes First Open Access Cable Trial," *Interactive Week*. June 7). Earthlink subscriber information as of October 2001 indicates that its services are available over Time Warner Cable systems in several markets and that more markets will be added in the near future.

home). This diversity suggests that the issue of technology neutrality will be around for some time to come. To the extent that neutrality is not achieved, regulatory actions would favor or disfavor options in ways that could decrease investment incentives or otherwise distort natural market forces in ways unfavorable to consumers. Decreased choice would reduce the likelihood that facilities-based competition emerges or would deprive consumers of particular cost and performance options.

The existence of these asymmetries, as well as the looming contradictions that convergence in the access technologies themselves poses, is recognized by regulators. What is less clear is how to craft a solution that improves the situation. One problem may lie in the concept of neutrality and regulators' goals not to pick winners and losers: neutrality may not be feasible, given the tight coupling between the subjects of regulation and the details of particular technologies. In avoiding tying regulations to technology-specific considerations, one has to find some other space—some more abstract definition of broadband—in which to regulate. Here one is confounded by such factors as the dynamic nature of broadband and the two-way link between technology-specific performance characteristics such as speed and application requirements. Also, absent the specific issues that have been the source of much of telecommunications regulation, what would be the goals of regulation of "broadband"?

COMPETITION

The establishment of robust competition among multiple telecommunications providers, including broadband and other providers, is a basic premise of the Telecommunications Act of 1996 (Box 5.1). This is viewed by many as the desirable way of making broadband as affordable as possible, though the view is not universal.[15] Two principal paths toward competition are contemplated in the present policy regime—(1) unbundling and resale and (2) facilities-based competition—which are discussed in separate subsections below. Unbundling arose in the context of policies aimed at stimulating competition to the ILECs. The 1996 act mandated unbundling of local loops and other network elements. In contrast to unbundling, facilities-based competition involves new entrants using their own equipment and physical network to compete.

---

[15]For example, the National Telephone Cooperative Association (NTCA) commissioned a white paper that concluded that the entry of competitors would decrease the take-rate achievable by any single carrier, which could substantially undermine the financial case for DSL in rural areas where it is already constrained even without competition. NTCA linked the issue to its call for only incumbents to be eligible to receive universal service high-cost-area support payments (*Telecommunications Reports*, January 15, 2001, p. 6).

BOX 5.1
Key Provisions of the Telecommunications Act of 1996[1]
Related to Broadband

• *Section 251* of the Telecommunications Act of 1996 establishes a series of obligations that apply to telecommunications carriers. Some apply to all telecommunications carriers (local as well as long distance and others). Some apply only to providers of local telephone. The most detailed requirements apply to incumbent local telephone companies, such as the Bell Operating Companies. The latter—those pertaining to incumbents—consist of a variety of obligations that collectively are designed to facilitate the entry of new providers into local markets and enhance their ability to compete with the incumbents. These include, for example, a requirement that incumbents make available parts of their local networks to competing providers on just, reasonable, and nondiscriminatory terms and conditions. The procedures for implementing these requirements for incumbent telephone companies are set forth in Section 252.

• *Section 253* generally preempts, with certain limited exceptions relating to universal service and other public policy objectives, any state or local statute or regulation that prohibits or has the effect of prohibiting the ability of any entity to provide any interstate or intrastate telecommunications service.

• *Section 254* promotes access to advanced telecommunications and information services in all regions of the nation. Universal service principles to be implemented by the Federal Communications Commission include ensuring the following: quality services at reasonable and affordable rates; access to advanced services; access to such services in rural and high-cost areas; that all providers of telecommunications services make an equitable and nondiscriminatory contribution to the preservation and advancement of universal service; that specific and predictable support mechanisms are in place to carry out such preservation and advancement; that there is access to advanced telecommunications services for schools, health care, and libraries; and that other principles that the joint (federal-state) board and the FCC may determine are necessary and appropriate for the protection of the public interest are implemented.

• *Section 255* requires telecommunications products and services to be accessible to people with disabilities. This is required to the extent that access is "readily achievable," meaning easily accomplishable, without much difficulty or expense. If manufacturers cannot make their products accessible, then they must design products to be compatible with adaptive equipment used by people with disabilities, where readily achievable. What is "readily achievable" will be different for each manufacturer, depending on the costs of making products accessible or compatible and their resources.

• *Section 256* sets broad parameters to establish nondiscriminatory access for the broadest number of users and vendors of communications products and services to the public telecommunications networks that are used to provide telecommunications service through joint network planning. It defines "public telecommunications network interconnectivity" as the ability of two or more public communications networks used to provide telecommunications service to communicate and exchange information without degeneration, and to interact in concert with one another. This section also regulates coordination for interconnectivity and establishes FCC procedures for oversight. It sets out the parame-

---

[1]Formally, the Communications Act of 1934, as amended.

ters under which the FCC is to review and eliminate federal regulations that may act as market-entry barriers for entrepreneurs in providing telecommunications. The FCC was required to conduct such an initial proceeding within 15 months of the law's enactment and thereafter to conduct similar periodic reviews every 3 years.

- *Section 259* mandates that incumbent local exchange carriers (ILECs) make available to any qualifying carrier any public switched telecommunications equipment or information as should be requested by the qualifying carrier. It excepts situations under which it would be economically unreasonable or against the public interest for the ILEC to comply. It permits joint ownership and seeks to ensure that the ILEC is not treated as a "common carrier for hire" and that the carrier seeking the use of facilities will be allowed the use of these facilities on just and reasonable terms. Finally, Section 259 demands a transparent process, requiring the ILEC to report the terms and conditions of any facilities-sharing arrangements.

- *Section 271* requires that the FCC consult with the U.S. Department of Justice and the relevant state commissions before ruling on a Bell company's request to offer in-region interLATA services. Upon application by a Bell company, the FCC has 90 days to consider whether the applicant has met a 14-point "competitive checklist" of market-opening requirements contained in the section and whether the company's entry into the interLATA service market is in the public interest.

- *Section 301* stipulates that the FCC shall review any complaint submitted by a franchising authority concerning an increase in rates for cable programming services and issue a final order within 90 days after it receives such a complaint, unless the parties agree to extend the period for such review.

- *Section 302* eliminates the prohibition on local exchange carrier (LEC) provision of video programming in the LECs service area. LECs and others may offer video programming under regulations that vary according to the type of video service being provided (radio-based, common carriage, cable TV systems, or open video systems). With the law's enactment, regulation was lifted for cable programming for a basic service tier that was the only service subject to regulation on December 31, 1994, in any franchise area in which the operator serves 50,000 or fewer subscribers.

Acquisitions and joint ventures (Section 302 of the bill, Section 652 of the act) are to a large extent prohibited, though there are several exceptions for certain small and rural systems. The law also permits a LEC to acquire or joint venture under different terms and condition in cases where the subject market meets the FCC's definition of "competitive." The FCC may waive the acquisition and joint venture prohibitions if it determines that the economic viability of the market merits such or that to do so would otherwise be in the public interest, and if the local franchising authority approves.

- *Section 303* allows cable operators to provide telecommunications services without first obtaining a franchise to provide those services. Additionally, no franchising authority may interrupt a cable operator's telecommunications services based on that operator's lack of a franchise. The section also prohibits franchising authorities from requiring that any cable operator provide telecommunications services as a condition for granting a franchise.

- *Section 706* seeks to promote the deployment of "advanced telecommunications services" in a reasonable and timely fashion. It attempts to do this by means of price

continues

BOX 5.1 *(continued)*

cap regulation, regulatory forbearance, measures that promote competition in the local telecommunications market, and other regulating methods that remove barriers to infrastructure investment. This section also required the FCC to follow up with inquiries into the progress of deployment. Reports issued in August of 1999 and 2000[2] found deployment reasonable and timely based on subscribership levels, service and technology options, and infrastructure investment at the time of the inquiries. The August 2000 report observed that advanced services may be unevenly distributed owing to differences throughout the country in wealth and population concentration.

---

[2]Federal Communications Commission (FCC), 1999, "Inquiry Concerning the Deployment of Advanced Telecommunications Capability to All Americans in a Reasonable and Timely Fashion, and Possible Steps to Accelerate Such Deployment Pursuant to Section 706 of the Telecommunications Act of 1996: First Report," CC Docket No. 98-146, FCC, Washington, D.C., August; and FCC, 2000, "Inquiry Concerning the Deployment of Advanced Telecommunications Capability to All Americans in a Reasonable and Timely Fashion, and Possible Steps to Accelerate Such Deployment Pursuant to Section 706 of the Telecommunications Act of 1996: Second Report," CC Docket No. 98-146, FCC, Washington, D.C., August 21.

Unbundling and Resale Mandates

Unbundling refers to the breaking down of an incumbent's network into smaller subcomponents, which can be either technology components (e.g., a phone line) or service components (e.g., switching), so that these elements can then be sold separately to other service providers. The goal is to permit new competitors to compete with the incumbent without having to incur the costs and the risks of constructing all of these elements themselves. An important difference between resale of services and physical unbundling of network elements is how much leeway the competitor has for differentiation. With simple resale, the competitor is confined to deriving revenue from the differential between the resale and retail rates, whereas unbundling gives the competitor latitude to provide differentiated services that combine unbundled elements with elements provided by the competitor.

Most prominent in the context of broadband deployment is unbundling of the local loop. The ILEC local access facilities have been the subject of unbundling rules designed to enable CLECs to offer voice and data services without having to build their own local access facilities. The DSL competitor provides the facilities at both ends of the loop (the DSL modem and DSLAM) and connects them to the actual copper wires that make up the loop. Under present rules, the CLEC has considerable freedom to select the particular DSL technologies (and thus such parameters as speed, ratio between up- and downstream speeds, and the maximum loop length supported), including technologies not offered by the incumbent. CLECs have argued that such differentiation is critical, because the incumbents have generally not deployed the high-rate, symmetric DSL services favored by small businesses (one argument is that this reflects incumbent reluctance to cut into the more costly, profitable T1 data services offered by the incumbents). This form of unbundling, in which a passive network element—the copper loop—is made available in raw form to the competitor has the additional advantage to the competitor of helping to isolate the quality and nature of the competitor's service from potential adverse actions of the incumbent (though issues of successfully provisioning the loop in the first place and dealing with crosstalk within the cable bundles remain). As an alternative to physical unbundling of copper loops, the ILEC could also be required to provide access to its DSL at the packet level (through ATM or IP technologies).

Cable has a different context for unbundling, both legally and technically. Owing to the design of today's cable systems, most notably the shared communications medium, strict unbundling along the lines of loop unbundling for DSL is not practical. The open access arrangements contemplated by the FCC's order in the AOL Time Warner merger (and similar arrangements being explored by other cable operators) lie somewhere closer to resale than to physical-layer unbundling. The cable operator operates the cable system over which the unaffiliated Internet providers connect to customers and hands off the packets destined for the unaffiliated providers at the cable system head end. Under the terms of the AOL Time Warner merger order, the cable operator must not discriminate against the unaffiliated provider on technical quality; by the same token, the unaffiliated provider does not have latitude to compete with AOL Time Warner on the basis of the technical quality of the last mile connection.

Resale and unbundling rules raise a variety of concerns on the part of the facilities owner and the competitor. When a competitor is dependent on another for critical inputs, the facilities owner will have the incentive and perhaps the ability to use its control over the input to disadvantage the competitor in the downstream market in which the firms compete. Further, as discussed above, facilities owners express the concern that they will never be fully compensated for their costs under regulator-set access prices, and how such prices should be set is a matter of current debate. Not surprisingly, these issues have been vigorously debated since resale of telephony began, and they account for a significant fraction of telecommunications regulatory proceedings and related court cases.

When Unbundling Works

Unbundling has been playing an important role in broadband competition. CLECs have provided service in areas unserved by the incumbents, and some credit the CLECs for having stimulated deployment efforts by the ILECs. As discussed above, competitive service providers have entered the wholesale DSL business by leasing local loops and colocation space from ILECs. However, CLECs' long-term impact on the competitive landscape is in doubt. The competitive DSL industry faces an uncertain future at present, reflected in a series of major business failures. These problems reflect the difficulties inherent in forcing an incumbent monopolist to open its market to competitive entry, the effects of economies of scale and scope on smaller players, and, from the vantage point of 2001, the challenges in raising investment capital for any sort of telecommunications investment. These uncertainties raise questions about how to think about unbundling in fashioning future policy.

Unbundling creates an enforced market structure out of the assets of an incumbent. One should ask how efficient the resulting market could be—how efficient and effective are control and management with markets based on unbundled versus integrated industry structures, and what factors facilitate unbundling? The basic thrust of the literature on organizational factors is that, when technologies are easy to understand and simple, markets are likely to have a comparative advantage as coordination mechanisms owing to the incentive effects of competition.[16] In this circumstance, unbundling can be effective. But if the interfaces between players are complex, an integrated business approach will often be more effective.

The technical complexity associated with unbundling for broadband access has been seen in the case of both DSL and cable. In the case of cable video programming, there is a high-level unbundling today in the form of certain channels' being set aside for use by local broadcasters; public, educational, and government access; and leased access. These are logical unbundling variants with simple technical implications. But more recent proposals have focused on an unbundling at the Internet Protocol layer. (There were also early proposals to provide unbundling through the use of asynchronous transfer mode, or ATM, technology.) Concerns today center on the optimal technical mechanisms to support shared access and on establishing operational and management mechanisms for coordination (provisioning, troubleshooting, and the like) between the cable company and heretofore unaffiliated ISPs.

---

[16]See, for example, Oliver E. Williamson, 1975, *Markets and Hierarchies*, The Free Press, New York.

As discussed above, DSL unbundling can occur at the physical level, which permits variation in the DSL service that the competitor provides, and at the resale level. Where ILECs extend fiber closer to customers, replacing a portion of the existing copper plant, copper pairs no longer run all the way from premises to the central office, making physical unbundling very complex. Issues that must be solved include whether and how CLECs should be given access to colocation space in remotely deployed pedestals, equipment vaults, or even equipment located on pole tops. The incumbents have claimed that this level of complexity inhibits investment in new facilities and is a barrier to the progress of broadband deployment. In turn, CLECs are concerned that installation of new facilities such as fiber-fed remote terminals would complicate or preclude the physical loop unbundling on which their businesses depend. In addition to making colocation and unbundling more complex, remote terminals alter the economics of physical-layer unbundling, because competitors are able to serve far fewer customers from a single colocation point.

A specific example of this debate centers on Project Pronto, in which local exchange carrier SBC Communications has proposed a program of fiber deployment that would enable it to provide high-speed digital services to its customers that are being served by long copper loops or with loops fed from digital carrier loops, and that as a result cannot currently obtain DSL service. Because the program as originally described would have deprived the CLECs of the opportunity to select the equipment at each end of the remaining loop segments, they argued that the program would make it difficult for them to use the new infrastructure to do anything other than resell SBC's DSL service, meaning that they would be unable to differentiate their own service in order to compete with SBC. SBC argued that unbundling at a remote terminal in DSL at the physical layer is so costly and complex as to be impractical, making higher-level unbundling solutions a better alternative. The FCC preferred physical-layer unbundling, making the plan's approval contingent on SBC's agreement to increase the size of the remote terminals to permit competitors to install termination equipment there rather than simply to resell SBC's service. The issue of incumbents' unbundling obligations when they deploy remote terminals is currently the subject of a pending FCC rulemaking proceeding.

In the case of DSL, another major complication is that the individual wires connecting subscribers to central offices cannot be treated as entirely independent of each other, as physical unbundling would imply. As detailed in Chapter 4, crosstalk, the coupling of electrical signals between nearby wires, creates interference that can degrade the carrying capacity of each copper pair, decreasing the data rates supported by a given line length and decreasing the maximum line length over which

DSL can run. The interference effect depends on how the signals on the different pairs make use of the different frequencies used for transmission over the lines, which in turn depends on how the ILECs and CLECs make and coordinate decisions about provisioning customers whose twisted pairs share bundles. The problems will grow as the penetration of DSL grows and as the higher data rates contemplated in the DSL upgrade path—which are still more sensitive to interference—begin to be widely implemented. Coordination may be facilitated by technical standards, which are in development, but which would, if adopted on a mandatory basis, constitute a regulation of operational network technology. Such a standard aims to achieve the sort of clean technological interface alluded to above, thus reducing coordination problems. However, the more the coordination problems are solved, the less the flexibility of the competitor to differentiate its service, so in the end, physical-layer unbundling may be no more attractive then simple resale, though much more complex.

Implications for Investment by Incumbents

There are major incentive issues that bear on expectations for overall investment and innovation. The analytical models used to justify forcing incumbents to unbundle and sell access to network elements implicitly assume that incumbents' networks are based on a static technology and involve only facilities already deployed. In reality, networks are constantly being upgraded, and with the upgrades come new capabilities and services. Competitors argue that incumbents should unbundle new services and technologies and resell them, as they are required to do with old services and technologies. Incumbents argue that they have no incentive to invest in new facilities or otherwise innovate if they are forced to sell their innovations at cost to their competitors. In particular, where unbundling is mandated at regulated prices, the incumbent bears the risk of investment but cannot fully benefit from it.

Facilities-Based Competition

Under facilities-based competition, competitors go head-to-head, using independently built and operated local access infrastructure.[17] It is widely believed by economists, policy officials, and consumer advocates

---

[17]Facilities-based competitors may still make use of some facilities such as backhaul circuits that are owned by other telecommunications companies, including the ILECs, and all facilities-based competitors must at some point interconnect with the other ISPs that make up the Internet.

that facilities-based competition is the preferred end state (with the proviso that it also results in a reasonably efficient result, which may depend on the characteristics of the technology or market). A principal argument is that facilities-based competition is the only circumstance that will permit complete deregulation of local markets.

In this view, competition though local loop unbundling or resale is a transitional approach to be used while facilities-based competition is still developing. As new entrants grow and gain market share, they will find it economic to replace facilities leased from incumbents with facilities leased from nonincumbents or self-provided. (The cost of using an incumbent's facilities is not just the price assessed for the network elements used, but the ongoing difficulties associated with relying on a dominant competitor.) In essence, resale and unbundling rules do not remove the need for regulation, only shifting it from regulation of end customer prices to regulation of prices charged by facilities owners to reseller-competitors. As long as competitors are dependent on incumbents for some facilities, such as loops, regulation of the terms and conditions of the competitors' access to those facilities, including price, will be required. Competitors are truly independent of each other only if they have their own facilities (or access to comparable facilities that are not controlled by a dominant competitor). There is a fundamental tension between the short-run static efficiencies of unbundling or resale and the longer-run dynamic efficiencies of facilities-based competition. Forced unbundling or resale at regulator-mandated prices may permit competitors to deploy innovative new services. However, such measures also could lock in the current situation, undercutting the longer-term goal of full facilities-based competition, especially if the rule is that competitors will be granted access at controlled prices to any new facilities that an incumbent puts in place.

Structural Separation

Unbundling and resale mandates are among a range of interventions that could be invoked to address the market power of incumbent telephone companies by facilitating competitors' access to upstream inputs controlled by the incumbent. Several options would involve some sort of separation of the incumbent's lines of business. The weakest form, nonstructural separation, involves the use of accounting safeguards to separate wholesale and retail operations. The most extreme mechanism, divestiture, involves the spin-off of a unit into a separate corporate entity that is under different control. Structural separation, between these two in terms of the level of intervention, involves the separation of business units into distinct corporate entities that remain under common control. That is, an ILEC would be required to offer access to its facilities and

forces have the potential to lead to a more tiered market—or distinct markets—in which different technologies and industries are associated with different kinds of service (e.g., different bandwidths, applications, or prices).

Finally, consumers with only one or two providers may derive spill-over benefits from competition in markets with more competitors, because marketing and pricing programs often do not have sufficient granularity to discriminate in terms of price or quality between market type and because of negative public reactions to highly differential pricing.

Assessing the Degree of Competition

Precise data are limited, but the deployment numbers presented in Chapter 1 of this report suggest that facilities-based competition in broadband is beginning to occur in the United States, with ILECs and cable operators undertaking large-scale deployments in many locations across the nation, and overbuilders entering a handful of markets. Wireless is an alternative in several test markets, and satellite services offer another option. However, overall availability masks considerable variability in competition at a local level—by state, by community, or even by household.

It is a yet-unanswered but critical empirical question whether broadband local access will turn out to be a natural monopoly (as telephony was assumed to be for many years) in some or all markets. If so, it may continue to be dominated by the incumbent telephone companies and cable system operators, limiting facilities-based competition to at best two players. The fact that facilities-based competition has proved difficult to establish in the voice telephony markets that were the primary focus of the 1996 act, especially for residential service, is not encouraging, but there are differences between entry into a mature, saturated market and a new, evolving one.

At this point in time it is hard to conclude what the overall shape of the market will be. It is, however, apparent that there are some geographically defined markets that give rise to concerns about whether broadband service will be available within several years and whether there will be an adequate level of competition. In hard-to-serve areas, the sheer costs or business risks may be great enough to call into question the goal of creating a competitive market. In these areas, the key goal may be providing service at all. In deep rural areas, where costs are highest, it remains to be seen whether the performance capabilities, costs, and ability to scale up of the existing or planned satellite services will be sufficient to keep customers in deep rural areas at rough parity with others with regard to broadband access. Both the extent of coverage (in terms of geographical regions and households) and the level of competition will be the subjects of continuing scrutiny by public policy makers and other interested parties. This suggests the ongoing importance of solid data, collected on a systematic basis, to identify where and what level of competition is being created.

Open Access and Evolving Complements to
Facilities-Based Competition

When cable operators began upgrading their systems to provide cable-based broadband services, concerns were raised that they could leverage their established cable television infrastructure and franchises to exercise market power in broadband services. The position of incumbent telephone companies could inspire similar concerns, but they have been required to provide would-be competitors with access to their facilities (via unbundling or resale), and public attention has been focused on the cable system operators. The open access debate, which began in 1999, has catalyzed involvement of consumer advocates, who had had a lower profile in early- and mid-1990s debates about Internet policy, and has provided an important complement to traditional regulation in shaping broadband policy. Critical actions were the merger oversight by the FTC as well as the FCC and court decisions reviewing local efforts to require open access.

One aspect of the open access debate has been implementation—how to implement open access, what the actual extent of proposed technical difficulties is, and how much the additional costs of supporting competitive ISP access over cable facilities would be. When cable modem systems were first developed in the mid-1990s, little thought was given to providing outsiders access to the systems or technology to implement such access. The technical specifications were developed through industry standard setting, coordinated by Cable Laboratories and building on company contributions of know-how. Cable Labs has since evolved those standards, which have become more supportive of open access, but its cable industry orientation—which contrasts with the more open, broad Internet Engineering Task Force that developed many of the Internet's core standards—has caused it to be viewed with suspicion by competitors and consumer advocates. In light of the growing attention to open access, cable operators have been exploring technical options for supporting access by multiple ISPs. The goal of opening up an incumbent's facilities could, in principle, be achieved in several ways, either at a low level by unbundling the physical links of the provider, or by unbundling some higher-level service. Early on, low-level access to cable infrastructure—for example, allocation of different frequency bands to different provid-

tored by an individual (trustee) appointed to do so. This potential template for the rest of the industry was hammered out under significant pressures—above all the threat of the merger being blocked if the FTC's concerns were not addressed. Meanwhile, in 2001, AT&T—prior to a wholesale revision of its business plan—appeared to be moving toward open access through its business strategy, influenced by regulatory and legislative scrutiny as well as a larger transition in business emphasis and strategy.[22] This change in strategy, ironically, was initiated by AOL (as an ISP) prior to its cable acquisition. Other cable operators may offer similar terms to forestall the long-term threat of federal intervention in the cable broadband business. In addition, overbuilders have begun constructing hybrid fiber coaxial cable systems in some markets that ISPs will be able to use to provide high-speed services.

Whether this pattern of opening up will prove to be widespread and enduring remains to be seen. Already, similar activity has been stimulated in connection with another Internet technology, instant messaging, itself a factor in the government's approval of the AOL Time Warner merger and an emphasis in the FCC investigation into the merger. The evolving open access situation, which illustrates a government role different from regulation per se, underscores the role of political activity in the shaping of telecommunications outcomes. It raises the prospect of ISPs making appeals to federal and state regulators to seek adjustments in access terms and prices and to antitrust authorities. Under these circumstances, it is hard to ascertain what facilities operators or ISPs might do or might have done "voluntarily" as their judgments about business opportunities evolved.

Access Issues in Multidwelling Units

Much of the debate about competition and open access assumed that broadband access is arranged at the sole discretion of the actual users. In the case of multidwelling units (MDUs), the establishment of facilities-based competition also depends on installation of new in-building facilities or working out some form of shared access to this infrastructure. MDUs, in which landlords may establish partnerships (including exclusive ones) with broadband providers, have become a new battleground

---

[22]For example, AT&T launched a recently concluded open access trial in Boulder, Colorado, at the end of October 2000 that connected eight ISPs: two AT&T affiliates (Excite@Home and WorldNet), two DSL providers (Winfire, Inc., and Flashcom, Inc.), two national ISPs (EarthLink, Inc., and Juno Online Services, Inc.), and two local ISPs (RMI.net, Inc., and FriendlyWorks, Inc.) ("ISP Offers 'Open-Access' Plan; AT&T Begins Trial in Boulder," *Telecommunications Reports*, November 6, 2000, p. 17).

for competitive and incumbent providers in both the residential and commercial markets. MDUs are an increasingly attractive and important early market opportunity in university and many urban communities, which are characterized by high-density housing, high density of broadband customers, or both. The committee did not explore the multidwelling unit issue at length, but notes that it is an area of ongoing debate over competition and access, particularly because these typically high-density situations are likely most attractive to would-be overbuilders.

Landlord-provider arrangements can both improve the competitiveness of real estate through improved telecommunications services and provide an additional revenue stream through business arrangements with providers. Not surprisingly, agreements often include exclusive access provisions, raising concerns on the part of both tenants and other providers about infringements on their access. Debate relates to access to buildings by competing service providers, the latitude of building owners vis-à-vis tenants to control providers' access to their property and therefore services available to tenants, and the role of federal and state regulators. CLECs and telecommunications equipment providers, for example, have formed "The Smart Buildings Policy Project"[23] to address relevant issues via lobbying.[24] This group appears to be at odds with a new class of providers that focuses on building access, BLECs (building-focused LECs), which may receive some investment by building owners.[25] Meanwhile, building owners, with their own lobbying arms,[26] argue that the issue falls under a real estate rather than a telecommunications regulation regime. Access and service issues also fall under the purview of local governments' new municipal ordinances and cable franchising agreements. The whole area of access in MDUs awaits possible direction and clarification from the FCC and the courts.

Access to Poles, Conduit, and Rights-of-Way

Another dimension of access is access to utility poles and conduits. Facilities-based wireline entrants cannot enter a market if they cannot obtain access to the poles and conduits to install their facilities. Issues of concern include prices, terms of access, processing time for an order, and the rate at which access is provided. The situation is complex, with varied

---

[23]See <www.buildingconnections.org>.

[24] "Lawmakers Ask FCC to Hold Off on Building Access Rulemaking," *Telecommunications Reports*, September 4, 2000, pp. 9-10.

[25]"Building Owners, Carriers Spar over FCC Proposal to Block Service, Extend Ban on Exclusive Pacts," *Telecommunications Reports*, January 29, 2001, pp. 27-28.

[26]An example is the Real Access Alliance; see <www.realaccess.org>.

(age, income, education, ethnicity, and so on) are associated with lower use rates, and geographical disparities in access overlay these other factors. Density versus demand is just one possible decomposition of the problem.

"Digital divide" means different things to different people and in different situations. There are many "divides." On the technology supply side, the term may refer to unmet demand for high-capacity long-haul transport facilities, connections to the Internet backbone, as well as high-speed local access facilities (DSL, cable, or wireless). To some customers, digital divide means the time it takes to get a high-capacity T1 line installed, or the price to use existing services. To a business customer with a business-to-business Web strategy, it means the need for redundant backup facilities in case one access path is interrupted, for example by a cable cut. Supply-side problems generally require approaches that encourage building facilities, either directly through application of funds or indirectly by providing incentives or demonstrating or aggregating demand to attract provider investment.

On the demand side, digital divide may refer to having less access to computers, to Internet connections, and to training or content if one is a rural resident, senior citizen, Native American or other minority, or in a family with lower income. Demand-side strategies tend to be best addressed through a different set of strategies, including development of locally useful content that stimulates increased interest and applicability, creating community networking partnerships or providing public access points or local training in a school, library, community center, or "cyber cafe" that provides lower-cost alternatives to residential service. Such efforts may also have to face another sort of digital divide—depending on how such performance-enhancing elements as caches or content distribution systems are implemented, nonprofit groups may be at a disadvantage compared with commercial producers that are able to pay more to ensure quality of access to their content. These considerations may be incorporated in economic development programs, although even experts in rural technology deployment note that "infotainment" may be the most important driver for demand.[30]

Of course, supply-side and demand-side problems can be related. Low density makes it more expensive to build facilities. Lack of demand makes it more difficult to recover the cost of building infrastructure. Economic development programs (generally at the state and local levels) naturally treat communications infrastructure, including broadband, as an element of local economic development. Being more holistic in nature,

---

[30]Andrew Cohill at June 2000 workshop of the Committee on Broadband Last Mile Technology.

programs tend to combine cultivation of demand with provision of access, education, and opportunities; if successful, they increase willingness to pay.

Implicit Transfer Mechanisms Used for Universal Telephone Service

In contrast to programs for which support is explicit, such as the food stamps program, the support schemes in the telephone industry historically relied on implicit mechanisms. The history of the telephone industry shows that government intervention has helped to overcome actual or perceived barriers of substantial cost differences among geographical areas as well as to enable basic telephone service access among qualifying low-income individuals (e.g., through Lifeline and Linkup programs). For context, note that nationwide telephone subscribership is between 94 and 95 percent, but the penetration level for households with annual incomes under $5,000 is only 79 percent, as compared with almost 99 percent of households with incomes of at least $75,000 (a few of the high-income houses may have opted for wireless service instead).[31]

Over the years, although the goal of universal service remained a cornerstone of state, and to a lesser extent, federal regulation, the meaning of that term changed as the network evolved. In the 1920s and 1930s, universal service probably meant a single telephone in a geographic territory. In the 1940s and 1950s, universal service may have meant access to party-line service. In the 1960s and 1970s, universal service may have meant access to single-line service. And, more recently, universal service has been interpreted to mean touch-tone service and access to more advanced services.

Stated simply, business long distance customers paid more for service and residential customers paid less for connections to the public switched network. Similarly, rural customers paid substantially less than did urban customers compared to the relative cost of their lines. One view of this situation, commonly held, is that in each case, one group is subsidizing the other. Other observers argue that it is natural that different types of customers will make different contributions to the common cost of the network.[32] Whether one characterizes them as natural rate differen-

---

[31]"Phone Subscribership Holds Steady at 94.4%," *Telecommunications Reports*, December 18, 2000, p. 21, summarizing the FCC report *Telephone Subscribership in the United States*, which is available online at <www.fcc.gov/ccb/stats>.

[32]See J.C. Panzar and S.S. Wildman. 1995. "Network Competition and the Provision of Universal Service," *Industrial and Corporate Change*, vol. 4, no. 4, pp. 711-719. See also David Gabel. 1999. "Recovering Access Costs: The Debate," in B. Cherry, S. Wildman, and A. Hammond IV, eds., *Making Universal Service Policy: Enhancing the Process Through Multidisciplinary Evaluation*. Lawrence Erlbaum Associates, Mahwah, N.J.

tials or implicit transfers, the following distinctions have been the subject of telephone policy and practice:

- *Business versus residential.* Business customers typically are charged higher rates for local telephone service than residential customers, even though the cost of serving business customers frequently is lower (because they are located in areas with higher population densities). These price differentials relative to other customers are justified on a variety of grounds, including the "positive externality" produced by maximizing the number of customers connected to the telephone network. That is, the value of being connected to the telephone network increases as more subscribers are added. Also, because the existence of a business can depend on communication, businesses typically value communications more than residences do (including the value businesses attach to calls to and from residential customers), and it can therefore make sense, even in competitive markets, to set prices that reflect such different valuations.[33]
- *Long distance versus local service.* Typically, the largest single cost of providing telephone service is the cost of the loop that connects a customer to the first point of switching in the telephone network, the "local loop," the centerpiece of the last mile. The cost of a local loop is fixed (i.e., it does not vary with the number or duration of calls that are placed or received, up to its full capacity). Because the local loop is necessary to providing both long distance and local service (as well as any other telephone-delivered services), its costs are common to both. Economists are used to saying that there is no a priori appropriate way of allocating common costs among the different products that are jointly supplied by the associated assets.[34] Historically, regulators required incumbent telephone companies to recover part of the local loop costs from the flat-rated

---

[33]While the elasticities of the different customer classes are not well understood, it is likely that this results in a situation where customers with the least elastic demands pay the highest price, which is the general relationship that one gets with Ramsey pricing. An interesting question is whether this could be a competitive outcome. Historical work by Gabel and a formal model by Panzar and Wildman suggest yes, though elasticity was not an issue in the model. Furthermore, more traditional models of competition allow for price discrimination. Baumol and Willig have argued in New Zealand regulatory proceedings that competition will necessarily generate Ramsey prices. (See Panzar and Wildman, "Network Competition and the Provision of Universal Service," and Gabel, "Recovering Access Costs: The Debate," 1999.)

[34]In most economic markets, the various products produced with common assets all make contributions to the common costs. Thus, for motion pictures, the fixed cost of producing a film is covered by earnings from theaters, videocassettes, pay television, and over-the-air broadcasting, not to mention foreign markets.

monthly charges assessed to end users for local service, part from the short-haul toll rates paid by end users, and the balance from per-minute access charges paid by carriers providing interstate and intrastate long distance service. The precise manner by which the common costs are allocated will have differentiated impacts on consumers. While it has the effect of holding down the price of telephone service for those who place few long distance calls, the practice of recovering part of the fixed cost of the local loop from usage-based prices, some observe, has been inefficient and has artificially depressed demand for long distance service.

  • *Urban versus rural.* The cost of providing local telephone service to urban customers is generally lower than the cost of serving rural customers. The higher population densities enable a telephone company to serve a greater number of customers from a single switch, and the loops connecting an end user to the first point of switching generally are shorter in urban areas. At the same time, this factor may be offset owing to the greater benefit obtained from technologies that overcome distance and dispersion, and there may be more willingness to pay by rural users, other things equal, given perceived value.[35] Federal and state regulators traditionally have implemented complex cost and price averaging and other policies to maintain prices for basic telephone service in rural and other sparsely populated areas at levels comparable to and often even lower than those paid by subscribers in urban areas.[36] State regulators historically required telephone companies to average their rates over large geographic areas so that customers in densely and sparsely populated areas paid the same rates.[37] High-cost programs transfer funds for the purpose of providing service in low-density, expensive-to-serve areas. Because they support the upgrade of telephone facilities, high-cost funds can also indirectly contribute to increased DSL availability as well as increasing dial-up modem line speeds.[38]

---

[35]As noted by Richard Civille in his remarks before the committee in June 2000.

[36]Full parity is not the goal. For example, rural customers have much smaller local calling areas (the areas in which local calls are covered by the monthly flat rate) and as a result may pay much higher total bills.

[37]Some rural states adopted forms of rate deaveraging by, for example, requiring customers in some areas to pay a "zone charge" in addition to the averaged, basic rate.

[38]An area of current debate is whether the high-cost fund should be explicitly expanded to cover broadband (and, a related question, whether caps on these funds should be relaxed to support advanced services build-out). Proponents of such changes argue that they are valuable mechanisms for enhancing rural infrastructure. For example, the Federal-State Joint Board on Universal Service's Rural Task Force recommended that the FCC adopt a "no barriers to advanced services" policy that would permit high-cost funds to be used in ways supportive of providing advanced services, including reducing loop lengths, remov-

These support mechanisms have gradually been reformed in various ways following passage of the Telecommunications Act of 1996 (e.g., a shift from usage rates to flat rate recovery). But they still depend in part on one form or another of implicit transfer and still reflect assumptions about technology and the market more rooted in voice than in broadband services. The sustainability of implicit support schemes is in question when those services are not provided on an integrated basis by a regulated monopoly. Entrants will tend to target the "subsidizing" customers, since the new entrants are not required to offer service at "subsidized" rates and, consequently, the price they must offer the existing "subsidizing" customers need only be lower than the incumbent's price including the subsidy, all other things being equal. Similarly, entrants will tend to ignore the "subsidized" customers because the price they must offer those customers must be less than the incumbent's price, including the subsidy. A very substantial part of the challenge that the FCC and state regulators face in opening local markets to competition is the need to reform the historical system of implicit support to make universal service support compatible with competition. Universal service is not inconsistent with the introduction of competition, but the historical scheme for maintaining universal service is inconsistent with competitive markets for local services. The issue of which firms should contribute (and benefit from) universal service funds is, not surprisingly, a subject of ongoing political and regulatory debate. Despite these drawbacks, proponents of implicit support mechanisms note that by virtue of the internal, largely unseen transfers, these mechanisms have the advantage that they may be less-politicized and more-stable sources of funding.

Other Mechanisms for Increasing Access to Broadband

Loans and Grants

One avenue being pursued by governments, foundations, corporations, and civic groups is partnering to leverage resources and carry out programs that expand access for underserved rural and urban popula-

---

ing bridge taps, and otherwise upgrading the network to support DSL (Rural Task Force, Federal-State Joint Board on Universal Service, 2000, *Rural Task Force Recommendation to the Federal-State Joint Board on Universal Service*, submitted to the Federal Communications Commission under CC Docket 96-45, Sept. 29, available online at <http://www.wutc.wa.gov/rtf/rtfpub.nsf>). Critics question whether the program should be expanded beyond traditional telecommunications services, and the impact of any increased transfer of funds from low-cost to high-cost areas.

tions. Loans or matching grants could be considered for other instances of community-initiated efforts to develop local broadband networks.

Programs of telecommunications regulatory agencies are complemented by other kinds of programs that may also contribute to connectivity as part of a broader set of programs that support economic development and quality of life in underserved areas. The federal government has supported community access through the Department of Housing and Urban Development's Neighborhood Networks program[39] and the U.S. Department of Education's Community Technology Center grants.[40] The Rural Economic Development Act of 1990 (P.L. 101-624) created the Rural Development Administration within the U.S. Department of Agriculture (USDA), which has other relevant entities and programs, and the Rural Electrification Administration makes loans and provides technical assistance to rural telecommunications providers. For example, the USDA's Rural Utilities Service[41] supports rural electricity, water, and telecommunications infrastructure through loans, grants, and technical guidance. The Rural Utilities Service launched a 2001 pilot program to provide $100 million in 10-year loans to companies building broadband infrastructure in rural areas. The program is targeted to communities with up to 20,000 residents, and following the FCC lead, uses a 200-kbps transmission threshold to qualify for broadband status.[42] Telephone cooperatives provide telephone service and a range of data services in a number of rural areas, and rural telephone companies have been active in deploying broadband services.[43] Cooperatives can help aggregate demand across a widely distributed set of customers.[44] There are also focused cooperative

---

[39]See <http://www.hud.gov/nnw/nnwindex.html>.

[40]See <http://www.ed.gov/offices/OVAE/CTC/factsheet.html>.

[41]According to 7 CFR §1735.10 (a), "The Rural Utilities Service (RUS) makes loans to furnish and improve telephone service in rural areas. Loans made or guaranteed by the Administrator of RUS will be made in conformance with the Rural Electrification Act of 1936 (RE Act), as amended (7 U.S.C. 901 et seq.), and 7 CFR chapter XVII. RUS provides borrowers specialized and technical accounting, engineering, and other managerial assistance in the construction and operation of their facilities when necessary to aid the development of rural telephone service and to protect loan security." See <http://www.usda.gov/rus>.

[42]"RUS Sets $100M for Rural Broadband Rollout," *Telecommunications Reports*, December 11, 2000, p. 7. See also <http://www.usda.gov/rus/telecom/initiatives/initiatives.htm>.

[43]National Exchange Carrier Association (NECA). 2000. *NECA Rural Broadband Cost Study: Summary of Results.* NECA, Whippany, N.J. Available online at <http://www.neca.org/broadban.asp>.

[44]Richard Civille, Michael Gurstein, and Kenneth Pigg. 2001. "Access to What? First Mile Issues for Rural Broadband," white paper; see Appendix C. See also the National Telephone Cooperative Association <www.ntca.org>, which publishes *Rural Telecommunications*.

more evident in the decision-making process. Broadband-specific vouchers might be a useful tool for promoting broadband penetration. It is important, however, that such vouchers be targeted as narrowly as possible to specific groups of consumers (e.g., low-income consumers or those living in high-cost service areas) who are not likely to subscribe in the absence of such aid. There is little point in subsidizing purchases that would be made without the subsidy. Vouchers are especially attractive in situations in which infrastructure deployment is not an issue (service providers already have an incentive to build out an area), but to which some subset of potential customers in a built-out service area would not subscribe at prices that service providers would have to charge to cover their costs.[50] In these circumstances, a voucher can be a highly specific instrument for encouraging subscriptions that would not happen otherwise. It is less clear that vouchers have advantages over direct payments to service providers if the goal is to promote infrastructure deployment in areas that might not otherwise be served. To the extent that providers might compete to offer services to customers in such areas, there is the danger that competitive lowering of service prices would transfer some portion of the voucher to consumers' pocketbooks rather than to covering infrastructure expenses. A more efficient approach in these areas might be to let providers bid for the right to serve these territories.

Research to Develop Technology Alternatives

Finally, there is the option of supporting research as a means of promoting access. Much of the excitement associated with progress in broadband technologies and the diffusion of fiber builds on research and development that has enabled new technological approaches and/or lowered the costs or increased the performance of existing approaches. The federal government is key in supporting basic research and fostering public dissemination of the results of research. Units of the U.S. Department of Defense (notably the Defense Advanced Research Projects Agency, or DARPA), the National Science Foundation (NSF), and other federal organizations are key supporters of communications R&D. Most of that R&D recently has focused more on technologies and components that enhance network backbones or development of applications that run over high-speed networks than on local access networks. But DARPA has had a program aimed at fiber in the distribution network, and NSF and DARPA have supported a variety of wireless networking research.

---

[50]Note that, from a life-cycle or total cost perspective, decreases in the cost of equipment associated with use of broadband, "CPE," will also affect willingness to pay for service.

Looking Forward

For policy makers, the threshold issue is how to determine whether government intervention to accelerate broadband deployment is necessary or desirable. It appears that the problem is not whether most areas will ultimately have some form of broadband service, but rather that in rural areas deployment will occur well after such services are available in more densely populated areas or that the technology options and/or performance will be different in rural areas.

The leading broadband technologies today (in terms of installed base and technology maturity) are both wire-based, and it seems likely that for the near term at least, distance and population density will deter their rapid deployment in remote or sparsely settled areas. Because of the added per-passing cost of serving rural areas, different kinds of technical strategies may need to be sought there as compared with those for other (denser) areas; an example would be greater emphasis on wireless links from residences to a fiber backbone (possibly leveraging local government or electric and water utility rights-of-way).[51] With broadband satellite services—which may be able to serve these areas more cost-effectively than the wireline alternatives could—having recently been introduced to the market, one finds a situation where there is some form of broadband available in even the most remote areas of the continental United States. It is also encouraging that the initial offering prices of the Starband service suggest that the "rural penalty" may be small (recurring charges for satellite service at $60 per month versus the $30 to $50 per month typical of cable or DSL). However, it is unclear at this point whether these services will be able to achieve and maintain sufficient performance levels to serve as adequate substitutes for the functionality of wireline services, or how their cost and price will compare in the long run with wireline service in more densely populated areas.

At today's broadband penetration levels, it seems premature to make conclusions about the shape of deployment. Consumer technologies generally display an S-shaped adoption curve, which is marked by an initial period of slow adoption, followed by more rapid expansion, and, finally, a leveling off of adoption in the later stages. In the case of narrowband Internet access, NTIA data collected over the past half-decade show that overall access has expanded greatly and that some disparities—such as across sex and race/ethnicity—have narrowed over time, primarily through expansion of dial-up household access and access in the workplace or public facilities. However, this access has largely leveraged near-

---

[51]See Civille et al., "Access to What?," 2001.

ubiquitous public telephone network lines, and thus, with the exception of some instances where line quality is very poor, has not been hampered nearly as much by technological and economic constraints on where and when new facilities are deployed as broadband would be. Widespread dial-up use suggests that wide segments of the population find Internet access to be of value, and thus suggests widespread demand for broadband. In the case of residential broadband, deployment has been growing rapidly from a presently small base, from which vantage point it is hard to infer the long-term adoption rate, patterns of availability, or the ultimate level of adoption.

To the extent that policy makers are simply uncertain about the pace of broadband deployment, the benefits of government intervention to accelerate that process would have to be clear and substantial in light of the risk that such intervention may have unintended and undesirable consequences. Although government policies likely contributed to the high penetration of telephone service in rural areas, application of such policies to broadband could, in theory, deter future entry by competing broadband providers that cannot match the below-cost rates resulting from averaging and other distributional policies. Another risk is that by picking particular technologies or defining particular services, some government programs aimed at bringing a technology to all may end up freezing the technology deployed. Policy makers seeking to promote rapid, efficient broadband deployment should assess the effectiveness of strategies that help avoid these risks—including demand stimulation and aggregation, grant and loan programs, and municipal initiatives fostering market entry and competition. This analysis would require policy makers to collect and review reliable broadband data on an ongoing and timely basis. The development of a comprehensive, national universal service program may well become desirable in the future, once the pace and scope of broadband deployment become clearer.

THE LOCAL ROLE IN BROADBAND

Seeking to accelerate or enhance the delivery of telecommunications services in their communities, a number of cities, counties, and states have considered or launched initiatives aimed at facilitating, encouraging, or directly building infrastructure for broadband. Historically, the direct local role with respect to telecommunications has been limited largely to negotiating cable franchises. In addition, local governments— absent preemption from higher levels—have control over local features of the deployment environment, such as public rights-of-way, zoning, permitting, and so on. These practical issues affect decisions about special facilities, such as "carrier hotels" and data centers. Local government influence has been expressed in conflicts over siting for terrestrial wireless towers and satellite dishes. Local governments also control access to rights-of-way and proposals for local investment in conduit that can be deployed once and that contain cable or wire supporting multiple providers and services. Today, communities are exploring how to use these points of leverage as well as other mechanisms and incentives to promote broadband deployment.

Local governments have a direct interest in neighborhood, community, municipal, and regional infrastructure, and it is within the community that existing government, corporate, university, and school networks are deployed. Local governments may be in a better position than national providers are to collect and verify local marketplace information, such as discovering and/or aggregating latent demand for broadband services, and these governments involve people whose jobs involve satisfying local interests. Indeed, where local entities have moved to provide local infrastructure, it has typically been when no commercial firm was willing to invest in a given community.

Local initiatives are not without their critics, however. For instance, while local decision makers may see benefits from broadband, it can be as hard for them as for service providers to predict and elicit consumer demand[52] and design sustainable business models for municipal broadband enterprises. Telephone and cable incumbents tend to protest local efforts to serve more than government users with services procured or provided by government entities.[53] Critics also argue that locally based efforts are less likely to be commercially sustainable in the long run, suffering regularly from lack of access to capital to support upgrades. Local efforts may also have insufficient economies of scale to be viable in the long run, and risk becoming overly politicized.

Local and regional broadband initiatives cover a wide range of possibilities, from focusing on local government infrastructure to facilitating access for the community at large. Local approaches vary for obvious reasons—size, local market desirability, and whether existing providers have been introducing broadband service. This variation may ultimately

---

[52]Civille et al. ("Access to What?," 2001) argue for demand cultivation in combination with access promotion through community economic development programs. Their acknowledgment that growing demand may take work—that simple access is not sufficient—implicitly supports the view that accelerating deployment is risky.

[53]"Private-sector carriers say they shouldn't have to compete with the entities that regulate their rates, grant them operating certificates and franchises, control their access to vital rights-of-way, and tax them" ("Community Size: The Difference in Cities' Telecom Choices?" *Telecommunications Reports*, December, 4, 2000, pp. 36-38).

limit what can be learned or replicated from any specific instance, but an informal network of supporters of local efforts has fostered the exchange of relevant information, including approaches to architecture, contracting, and financing, to maximize opportunities for local officials to learn from others.[54]

The examples listed in Box 5.2 indicate the sorts of initiatives that have been undertaken at the local or regional level.[55] They include, for example, public operation of a multiservice network, where a municipal or county agency is the operator, providing retail services to the end user. Municipal service monopolies are not unusual—water or sewer authorities are the dominant model, and public power utilities are found in a number of locales—but the high level of complexity and rate of change in telecommunications technology compared with water or electricity supply pose a risk. And as noted above, this approach may raise objections from private sector providers, who see the public service as being unfairly subsidized. However, if there is no private sector provider on the horizon, it may be an attractive option.

Another option is some form of public-private partnership. Again, this raises concerns about the risk in a government body's entering into what may be a long-term relationship with a selected private sector player. If the relationship sours, it may be difficult to replace the private sector player. This sort of approach runs the same risk as that with exclusive cable franchising—communities may derive revenue or other benefits from the arrangement, but the partner may not deliver the level or quality of service desired. Additional complications arise if the public sector has contributed funding to the venture.

The drawbacks of the approaches listed above argue that local governments concentrate on taking steps to encourage and facilitate competition among private sector players rather than creating new quasi-monopolistic entities. As a public sector partner with multiple private providers, a public agency would not be competing with a private sector retail service provider. Another advantage of this strategy is that it means that private sector providers do not have to negotiate with each other to

---

[54]One ongoing effort that attracted the attention of this committee has been the work of Bill St. Arnaud as part of Canada's CANARIE program. See <http://www.canarie.ca/>.

[55]The Community Broadband Deployment Database, established by the National Regulatory Research Institute at Ohio State University for the Federal Communications Commission, lists more than 200 community broadband programs, covering a range of technologies, target user groups, and funding sources. See <http://www.nrri.ohio-state.edu/programs/telcom/broadbandquery.php>.

obtain access to facilities, which reduces the need to regulate their conduct.

Easing access to rights-of-way is the simplest step, but this may not be enough to induce new entrants. Another option is for a local or regional government agency to install fibers (or conduits through which fibers can later be pulled) and use this investment to lower the barriers to entry by private sector players by making the infrastructure available to them. This approach can be implemented in a number of ways. One is the "fiber condominium" model, in which a locality declares its intention to build out fiber along its streets and invites any interested parties to purchase some share of the fibers installed (and possibly installs additional dark fiber for future use). Typically, some provision is made to lease colocation space for service providers at the fiber termination points. Alternatively, the locality may enter into partnerships with one or more private sector companies to install (and possibly maintain) the fiber. The town itself can sign up, as can schools and municipal departments, businesses and other private sector players in the town, citizens themselves, and any interested broadband providers. The locality provides the motivation and coordination for joint action—it shares in the cost of the common construction, but it may also prohibit the digging up of streets again for some period after the construction. By avoiding the extra cost of uncoordinated overbuilding—keeping down the per-passing costs—this approach attempts to provide competition at per-passing costs comparable with those of a single provider. Local and regional government or quasi-governmental agencies can also act in effect as anchor tenants that underwrite some of the cost of installing infrastructure, reducing the costs for other government agencies, private sector firms, or even individual customers. The consequence of this action is that more providers may be motivated to enter the market in the town.

Finally, localities may choose to launch experimental pilot projects to explore new technologies, system architectures, or business models. State or federal grants can help support communities exploring options or enable them to purchase facilities that today are more costly than they will be in the future when suppliers are able to achieve scale economies in the production of such equipment. Such pilot efforts can demonstrate the viability of systems, demonstrate the extent of demand for them at the local level, and support achievement of scale in use, either by closing access gaps or increasing interest in use. The state or federal role is appropriate, given that results of the experiment can help inform future private sector or public sector initiatives using similar systems. New developments can also build in broadband infrastructure, as is beginning to happen (Box 5.3).

BOX 5.2
Some Examples of Municipal and Regional Broadband Initiatives

• *Blacksburg, Virginia.* The Blacksburg Electronic Village (BEV) initiative began in 1991 with a public-private agreement between the town of Blacksburg, Bell Atlantic (now Verizon), and Virginia Polytechnic Institute and State University. When service launched in 1993, BEV provided Blacksburg residents with dial-up access. Also, starting in 1994, integrated services digital network (ISDN) and Ethernet have been made available to an increasing number of townhomes and apartments. Because dial-up access became available from commercial providers, BEV turned over its modem pool customers to the private sector in 1995, and similarly transferred its Ethernet operations to the private sector in 1998. At present, 87 percent of Blacksburg residents are online, according to BEV information. Currently, efforts are under way to develop a townwide all-fiber network, to integrate wireless with wireline services, and to develop a broadband switch point and exchange for advanced network services. BEV was prevented from extending service to surrounding areas because, after industry lobbying, a law was passed to preclude this government service provider role.[1]

• *Abingdon, Virginia.* In December 1995, a group of citizens met to discuss the potential of providing residents of Abingdon with high-speed Internet connectivity. These activities led 'to the launch of the Electronic Village Abingdon (EVA) initiative. In addition to modem 'and ISDN connections, a fiber-optic connection from the town manager's office to the hospital and the Washington County Main Library was established as a partnership between the Town of Abingdon and Sprint. On the basis of results of early trials, the project was expanded. During Phase I, EVA's fiber-optic service was extended in the downtown area, providing high-speed connections to every building within 150 feet of the fiber backbone. Phase II, under way in 2001, is a collaborative effort with Highlands Union Bank to extend the fiber-optic cable toward the west of Abingdon. The network provides 10-Mbps connectivity within the town network and Internet connectivity at 1.54 Mbps. Subscribers need to purchase a fiber-optic transceiver (about $150) and pay a one-time installation charge of $75. Monthly access fees are $35 per month for 10 Mbps and a single Internet Protocol (IP) address. Recently, 100-Mbps service has been added for $70 per month.[2]

• *Berkshire County, Massachusetts.* Berkshire Connect was established through a 1997 grant of $250,000 from the Berkshire legislative delegation and the Berkshire Regional Planning Commission. A project task force committee, with representatives from cultural institutions, local businesses, public access organizations, and local business consultants, was established to propose a strategy for enhancing Berkshire County's infrastructure and to reduce the cost of networking government agencies. The original strategy called for Berkshire Connect to partner with the private sector and use a mix of public and private funds to build the infrastructure, but Global Crossing/Equal Access, the winning bidder, agreed to build the infrastructure without using public funds. The agreement establishing the service offers volume pricing, with prices for all members decreasing as more subscribers sign up. Berkshire Connect competes with the incumbent LEC, Verizon, in

---

[1]Blacksburg Electronic Village (BEV). 2001. "About the BEV." Available online at <http://www.bev.net/project/brochures/about.html#2>.
[2]See the Electronic Village Abingdon home page online at <http://www.eva.org/>.

both the retail and wholesale markets, though it claims more success in the wholesale market (providing backbone services to other providers). Berkshire Connect does not offer residential or last mile service at present, but is currently working to define a business strategy for last mile service. It is also exploring new business relationships with other Massachusetts regional networks.[3]

• *LaGrange, Georgia.* Through the LaGrange Internet TV initiative, the City of LaGrange, Georgia, provides Web access to all cable television subscribers in this community of 27,000 residents. In 1998, Charter Communications, Inc., and LaGrange entered into a leaseback agreement in which the city financed and constructed a two-way hybrid fiber coax network (using city funds, without state or federal support). Using WorldGate's Internet on EVERY TV Service, it allows LaGrange cable TV subscribers to have Web access at no additional cost.[4]

• *Glasgow, Kentucky.* In 1994, as Glasgow was being wired for cable, town officials decided to facilitate Internet traffic via cable as well. The 12-year-old Glasgow fiber-optic system, one of the first of its kind, provides relatively inexpensive cable and high-speed Internet services to 8,000 homes and businesses, or two-thirds of the local market for cable. According to its managers, it has broken even for the past 4 years. Proponents note that the network has been moderately successful in spurring local economic activity. For example, Franchino Mold & Engineering Co. is cited as having opened a new facility in Glasgow in 1998, in part because the city's network allowed for an easy exchange of data with engineers at the company's Lansing, Michigan, headquarters. Two-thirds of Glasgow's businesses and a quarter of its residences now pay for broadband cable. The town's network connectivity is also used for a variety of other functions including controlling traffic lights, coordinating utility repairs, and plotting school bus routes.[5]

• *Washington County, Ohio.* Seeing inadequate broadband facilities in the county, the nonprofit Washington County Community Improvement Corporation (CIC) launched a nonprofit corporation, Sequelle, to provide terrestrial wireless broadband communications to southeastern Ohio and the mid-Ohio Valley region, targeting business and educational customers. Using a mixture of state and federal startup funds, it plans to launch service in 2001.[6]

• Chicago, Illinois. Chicago's CivicNet is a citywide initiative to build a new broadband infrastructure for government, businesses, other institutions, and residents. The city plans to use the $32 million it spends each year on voice and data communications to become an "anchor tenant" for a high-speed fiber-optic network, to be constructed in partnership by one or more lead technology vendors. The city also plans to make city-owned or -controlled conduits and tunnels available to reduce installation costs. The

continues

---

[3]Sources include the Berkshire Connect home page, which is available online at <http://www.bconnect.org/>; "FCC Hearing, May 22, 2000," which is available online at <http://www.bconnect.org/FCChearing5_00.htm>; and a personal communication with Bill Ennen, Donahue Institute of the University of Massachusetts, April 19, 2001.

[4]See <http://www.lagrange-ga.org>.

[5]See David Armstrong and Dennis K. Berman, 2001, "Municipal Networks Become Rivals for Fiber-optic Telecom Companies: Dissatisfaction Spurs Competition," *CNBC and The Wall Street Journal*, August 17. Available online at <http://www.msnbc.com/news/615215.asp#BODY>.

[6]For more information, see the Sequelle home page online at <http://www.sequelle.com/>.

ultimate goal is for fiber networks to extend to every neighborhood, and ultimately down every street.[7]

• *Lane and Klamath Counties, Oregon*. The Lane Klamath Regional Fiber Consortium, formed by Lane and Klamath Counties and the cities of Coburg, Chiloquin, Klamath Falls, Lowell, Merrill, Oakridge, Springfield, and Westfir, negotiated joint agreements with Pacific Fiberlink (now Worldwide Fiber). In return for assistance with permitting and an exchange in lieu of right-of-way fees, the local governments received 12 strands of fiber installed in a contiguous strand extending approximately 200 miles from Coburg to Merrill, with points of access in the cities and significant county points along the route. Consortium members plan to use this fiber to increase communication opportunities to all the residents along the route and in communities adjacent to it.[8]

• *Marietta, Georgia*. In 1996, Marietta FiberNet became Georgia's first municipally owned company to be certified as a competitive local communications carrier. Wholly owned and operated by Marietta, it is structured as a separate business. The company began constructing its network in the spring of 1997. Today Marietta FiberNet provides high-speed voice and data services to local schools, hospitals, and businesses over 170 miles of fiber-optic cables.

• *Thomasville, Georgia*. Thomasville's Community Networks Services (CNS) operates a citywide fiber-optic network capable of supporting high-speed Internet access, cable television, and energy management services, as well as a dial-up Internet access service. CNS now has more than 3,000 customers for its Rose.Net Internet service and expects many of those customers to move up to Rose.Net express, a broadband Internet service, when it becomes available. Thomasville recently entered into an agreement with neighboring Tifton through which it will help launch Tifton's proposed Friendly City Network's Internet service.[9]

• *Grant County, Washington*. The Grant County Public Utility District (PUD) initially launched its fiber network, Zipp, in order to upgrade its electrical substation control. It later decided that the network could also be used to provide telecommunications services in the county. Through Zipp, independent service providers can provide data, voice, and video services to their customers. The PUD's fiber backbone was completed in 2000, and pilot projects aimed at commercial and residential customers are underway. In 2001, the PUD began marketing to the general public. Major residential fiber construction and build-out are slated to take place between 2001 and 2006 to reach 90,000 homes.[10]

• Muscatine, Iowa. Muscatine Power and Water (MP&W), the town's incumbent, municipally owned public utility, was first to deploy high-speed facilities in Muscatine. Following a 1996 marketing study and detailed feasibility study, the communications utility was launched following approval by public referendum in 1997. The communications utility received $18 million in initial funding from the municipal electric utility and

---

[7]See Department of General Services, Bureau of Telecommunications and Information Technology, City of Chicago. 2000. "Request for Information: Chicago CivicNet" (Specification No. B09189503), November. Available online at <http://www.cityofchicago.org/CivicNet/civicnetRFI.pdf>. See also Tom Kontzer. 2001. "Chicago's CivicNet Takes a Step Closer to Reality," *InformationWeek.com* [January 4]. Available online at <http://www.informationweek.com/story/IWK20010104S0007>.
[8]See <http://www.ruralfiber.net/lkpage.html>.
[9]See Georgia Municipal Association. 1999. "Tifton and Thomasville Enter Internet Agreement," October 7. Available online at <http://www.gmanet.com/news/1999/1007.internet.shtml>. See also Thomasville Utilities Community Network Services (CNS). 1999. "Press Releases." Available online at <http://www.tucns.com/press.html>.
[10]See the Zipp Fiber-optic Network home page online at <http://www.gcpud.org/zipp/>.

completed construction of its fiber network in the spring of 1999. MP&W provides high-speed cable modem Internet access to residential customers and a Municipal Area Network for business customers. MP&W's telecommunications network consists of a hybrid fiber coax system with 125 homes per node, which can deliver a maximum of 4 Mbps downstream and 1 Mbps upstream for connected customers. MP&W obtains its connection to the Internet backbone through a division of Iowa Network Services, Inc. (INS), a telecommunications firm formed by a consortium of 128 independent telephone companies.[11]

• *Ashland, Oregon.* Building on Ashland's earlier fiber network initiative, local Internet companies are cooperating with the city to establish a new service, dubbed "Ashland Unwired." In early 2001, the effort began with a demonstration at Ashland's Starbucks coffee shop. Using access points running the IEEE 802.11b-standard wireless local area network technology, it aims to provide wireless Internet access via the city's fiber network. Project A and Open Door Networks, city-certified Internet service providers, have offered to provide connectivity through the Ashland Fiber Network and assistance to help any business or organization wishing to provide Ashland Unwired to their customers.[12]

• *Tacoma, Washington.* The city's public utility, Tacoma Power, began its networking activities with the construction of a fiber-optic network in 1997. In 1998, it launched cable television service as a competitor to the existing franchisee (TCI, now AT&T). In 1998, it began providing Internet service over the cable television network and began full cable modem service in 1999.[13]

• *San Diego County, California.* The High Performance Wireless Research and Education Network (HPWREN) project was launched in 2000 to build, demonstrate, and evaluate a noncommercial, prototype, high-performance, wide-area, wireless network in San Diego County. Built by researchers at the University of California at San Diego under a $2.3 million grant from the National Science Foundation, the network includes backbone nodes on the UC San Diego campus and a number of rural areas in San Diego County, including the Pala and La Jolla tribes in remote San Diego County. Among HPWREN's goals are to explore how scientists can make use of the network for real-time data collection and how the network can be used by rural Native American communities for interactive computer classes and remote tutoring programs. In addition to the research and education applications, the HPWREN team is also investigating ad hoc advanced network development and experimentation in collaboration with local crisis management agencies.[14]

---

[11]See <http://www.mpw.org>. Case study reported in Federal Communications Commission. 2000. "Inquiry Concerning the Deployment of Advanced Telecommunications Capability to All Americans in a Reasonable and Timely Fashion, and Possible Steps to Accelerate Such Deployment Pursuant to Section 706 of the Telecommunications Act of 1996: Second Report," CC Docket No. 98-146, August. Available online at <http://www.fcc.gov/Bureaus/Common_Carrier/Orders/2000/fcc00290.pdf>.

[12]See Ashland Fiber Network. [Undated]. "Frequently Asked Questions." Available online at <http://www.ashlandfiber.net/index.asp?page=FAQ#1>. See also Ashland Unwired. 2001. "Open Door Networks and Project A Unveil Wireless Internet Access in Ashland" [press release], January 29. Available online at <http://www.ashlandunwired.com/news.htm>.

[13]See Tacoma Power, Click! Network. [Undated.] "Project History." Available online at <http://www.click-network.com/news/history.htm>.

[14]See the HPWREN home page at <http://hpwren.ucsd.edu/>, as well as Hans-Werner Braun's testimony before the House Science Committee's Subcommittee on Research, July 31, Washington, D.C., available online at <http://www.house.gov/science/research/jul31/braun.htm>. See also "Wireless Internet to Native American Reservations," *PopularTechnologies.com*, [undated], available online at <http://www.populartechnologies.com/news/01/02/15/0414200.shtml>.

BOX 5.3
Examples of Greenfield Developments

New community and subdivision developments are increasingly incorporating broadband fiber-to-the-curb or fiber-to-the-home with other advanced exterior and interior networking infrastructure and services. These projects are often joint ventures between building developers who own the properties and rights-of-way; convergent telecommunications providers; and real estate investors and homeowners.
Several examples follow:

• *Centennial, Indiana.* HFC Internet, phone, and cable provided to 900 homes north of Indianapolis by the builder, Estridge Company, and First Mile Technologies. The cost will be repaid through homeowners' association fees.
• *DC Ranch, Scottsdale, Arizona.* All homes are being built with structured wiring to support in-home networking.
• *Celebration, Florida.* In a Disney-built new community near Orlando, AT&T, Sprint, and Jones Communications have formed a joint venture to provide connectivity.[1]
• *Summerlin, Nevada.* In a community outside Las Vegas, fiber-to-the-curb is being installed by the Howard Hughes Corporation and Sprint.[2]
• *Valencia and Newhall Ranch, California.* In communities developed by Newhall Land & Farming, SBC Communications is providing broadband voice, video, and data to homes through a revenue-sharing venture with the developer.
• *Hatchet Ranch, Colorado.* Rye Telephone of Colorado City is installing fiber to 500 homes in an 80-square-kilometer new community.[3]

------

[1] See the Celebration, Florida, home page online at <http://www.celebrationfl.com/>.
[2] For more information, see "Summerlin: A Profile," available online at <http://www. therousecompany.com/whoweare/hughes/summprofile.html>.
[3] Information from <http://www.fone.net.soco/guide/colocity/rtc/home.html>; Robert Pease. 2000, "Rural Areas Present Better Business Case for Fiber to the Home," *Lightwave*, June, available online at <http://lw.pennnet.com/Articles/Article_Display.cfm?Section=Archives& Subsection=Display&ARTICLE_ID=73404&KEYWORD=Hatchet%20Ranch>; and Canet-3-NEWS, 2000, "Rural Areas Better Business Case for Fiber to the Home," November 2, available online at <http://www.canarie.ca/MLISTS/news2000/0185.html>.

The risk in all of these possibilities is that the local government will not be equipped with the knowledge or skills to negotiate with a large private sector provider. If the town does not act carefully, there is risk of industry capture, an outcome in which a private sector provider manipulates the situation to the point where the town becomes dependent on it and thus loses any power to negotiate or foster competition. With some notable exceptions, local governments are less likely to be familiar with the technology and business side of networking than they are with more traditional government operations, which places them at a disadvantage in planning or acquiring networking infrastructure or services than a private sector firm would be. The risk can be minimized if the town sticks to a facilitating role at the infrastructure level and encourages competition from the outset. Still, industry is not monolithic, and some companies can be expected to favor and others to resist local efforts to foster market entry. Local governments, especially in smaller communities, often have limited capabilities. Action at the higher levels of government is an important part of this local approach as well, to coordinate experiences, to catalog best practices, and to define the playing field with overarching regulation that prevents the obvious forms of mutual abuse.

Bibliography

Abramson, Norman. 1999. "Internet Access Using VSAT's." San Francisco, Calif.: ALOHA Networks, October 5.

Alvarez, Lizette. 2001. "In Capitol, AT&T and Bells Fight to Control Web Access." *New York Times*. August 29, p. C1.

American National Standard T1E1.4 Working Group on Digital Subscriber Line Access. 2001. "American National Standard for Telecommunications—Spectrum Management for Loop Transmission Systems."

Anderson, Ken, and Anne Page McClard. 1998. "Always on: Broadband Living Enabled." Broadband Innovation Group, MediaOne Labs, October.

Anderson, Ken. 1999. "Technology and Convergence of the Digerati." MediaOne Labs. June.

Andersen, William, et al. 1999. "Applying a Policy of Non-Discriminatory Access to High-Speed Internet Access Over Cable in King County, Washington." A Report to the Budget and Fiscal Management Committee, Metropolitan King County Council. October.

Andersson, Goete. 2000. "Sweden's Broad Jump: Debate Is Warming Up for Universal High-speed Service." *tele.com* (501), January 10. Available online at <http://www.teledotcom.com/article/TEL20000824S0034>.

Angwin, Julia. 2000. "Cable Alliances Prompt Some Consumers to Pay Twice for Web Access," *Wall Street Journal*, November 20, p. B1.

Angwin, Julia. 2000. "The New Media Colossus: AOL-Time Warner Megamerger Creates Behemoth That Could Dominate Web, Other Media." *Wall Street Journal*, December 15, p. B1.

Arbitron/Coleman (presented by Pierre Bouvard and Warren Kurtzman). 2000. "The Broadband Revolution: How Superfast Internet Access Changes Media Habits in American Households," October 2. Available online at <http://www.arbitron.com/downloads/broadband.pdf>.

Armstrong, David, and Dennis K. Berman. 2001. "Municipal Networks Become Rivals for Fiber-optic Telecom Companies: Dissatisfaction Spurs Competition," *CNBC and The Wall Street Journal*, August 17. Available online at <http://www.msnbc.com/news/615215.asp#BODY>.

Armstrong, David, and Dennis K. Berman. 2001. "Telecom Companies Confront New Rival: The Municipal Network." *Wall Street Journal*, August 17, p. A1.

ARC Group. 2000. *Broadband Access: Opportunities in Fixed Wireless*. Surrey, U.K.: ARC Group.

Associated Press. 1999. "IBM Offers PC with High-Speed DSL Internal Modem." August 23.

Associated Press. 1999. "Researchers Seek to Untangle Effects of Internet." June 8.

Association for Local Telecommunications Services (ALTS). 2000. *Consumer Benefits of the 1996 Telecommunications Act*. Washington, D.C.: ALTS, February 2.

Association for Local Telecommunications Services (ALTS). 2000. *The State of Competition in the U.S. Local Telecommunications Marketplace*. Washington, D.C.: ALTS, February.

AT&T. 2000. "AT&T 'Cuts The Cord' to Provide Services Into Homes; Debuts Nation's First Wireless Local Communications Company" [news release], March 22. Available online at <http://www.att.com/press/item/0,1354,2706,00.html>.

ATM Forum. 2000. "Voice and Multimedia Over ATM: Loop Emulation Service Using AAL2," AF-VMOA-0145.000, July. Available online at <http://www-comm.itsi.disa.mil/atmf/vtoa.html#af145>.

Austen, Ian. 1999. "High-Speed Lines Leave Door Ajar for Hackers: Constant Connections Through Cable or DSL Mean New Security Headaches for Home Users." *New York Times*, July 8. Available online at <http://www.nytimes.com/library/tech/99/07/circuits/articles/08hack.html>.

Aversa, Jeannine. 1999. "FCC Won't Regulate Internet. Really." *Washington Post*, March 12, p. E3.

Bagasao, Paula. 1999. "Knowing About Who Has Access: A Matter of Strategy." *iMP*, December 22. Available online at <http://www.cisp.org/imp/december_99/12_99bagasao.htm>.

Baker, Jonathan B., and Susan P. Braman. 1998. "Deployment of Wireline Services Offering Advanced Telecommunications Capability" [CC Docket No. 98-147], comment of the staff of the Bureau of Economics, Federal Trade Commission (FTC). Washington, D.C.: FTC. Available online at <http://www.ftc.gov/be/v980030.htm>.

Bar, Francois, et al. 1999. "Defending the Internet Revolution in the Broadband Era: When Doing Nothing Is Doing Harm," August. Available online at <http://e-conomy.berkeley.edu/publications/wp/ewp12.html>.

Barnett, Malcolm. 2000. "Fibre Optic Cable: Unsung Hero." *Telecommunications Online*, April. Available online at <http://www.telecoms-mag.com/issues/200004/tci/fibre.html>.

Bechtolsheim, Andreas, and David Cheriton. 2000. "Ethernet Broadband Networking" (white paper), Cisco Systems, August 11. Available online at <http://www4.nationalacademies.org/cpsma/cstb.nsf/files/wp-bb-bechtolsheim-cheriton.pdf/$file/wp-bb-bechtolsheim-cheriton.pdf>.

Belinfante, Alexander. 2001. "Telephone Penetration by Income by State (Data through 2000)." Industry Analysis Division, Common Carrier Bureau, Federal Communications Commission. Available online at <http://www.fcc.gov/Bureaus/Common_Carrier/Reports/FCC-State_Link/IAD/pntris00.pdf>

Berkowe, Kathleen Hawkins. 2000. "Open Access to Cable Systems for Internet Access Providers." *Media Law and Policy* VIII (2).

Berman, Dennis, and Shawn Young. 2001. "Bells Make a High-Speed Retreat from Broadband." *Wall Street Journal*. October 29, p. B1.

Berresford, John. 2001. "Broadband Is Not for Everyone—Extending Existing Universal Service Broadband Would Be a Mistake." *ISPWorld*, May 8. Available online at <http://www.boardwatch.com/bw/may01/Broadband_Not_Everyone.htm>.

Berst, Jesse. 1999. "Dr. Jesse's Internet Checkup: The Good and Bad News About the Health of the Web." *ZDNet*, June 25. Available online at <http://www4.zdnet.com/anchordesk/story/story_3553.html>.

Berst, Jesse. 1999. "Internet Mind Control." *ZDNet*, June 21. Available online at <http://www.zdnet.com/anchordesk/story/story_3531.html>.

Blackwell, Gerry. 1999. "Taking the VoIP Plunge." *ISP-Planet*, June 11. Available online at <http://www.isp-planet.com/services/voip-plunge1.html>.

Blankenhorn, Dana. 2001. "Clearing the Last-Mile Hurdle." *ISPWorld*, May 8. Available online at <http://www.ispworld.com/bw/apr01/Last_Mile_Hurdle.htm>.

Blumenstein, Rebecca, and Joann S. Lublin. 1999. "Amid All the Bets, One Stands Out: AT&T Ventures Into Cable." *Wall Street Journal*, November 5, p. A1.

Blumenstein, Rebecca, and Stephanie Mehta. 1999. "Qwest Makes Bid for US West, Frontier." *Wall Street Journal*, June 14, p. A3.

Blumenstein, Rebecca, Leslie Cauley, and Kara Swisher. 1999. "Inside the Tangles of AT&T's Web Strategy." *Wall Street Journal*, August 13, p. B1.

Blumenstein, Rebecca. 2000. "AT&T Filing Pledges It Won't Influence Programming of a MediaOne Venture." *Wall Street Journal*, April 21, p. B6.

Blumenstein, Rebecca. 2000. "Some Wonder if Content-less AT&T Will Rue Cable-only Plans." *Wall Street Journal*, January 14, p. B6.

Blumenstein, Rebecca, and Stephanie Mehta. 2000. "As the Telecoms Merge and Cut Costs, Service is Often a Casualty." *Wall Street Journal*, January 19, p. A1.

Blumenstein, Rebecca, Don Clark, and Leslie Cauley. 2000. "AT&T Acts to Gain Control of Excite from Cable Firms." *Wall Street Journal*, March 30, p. B6.

Blumenstein, Rebecca. 2001. "How the Fiber Barons Plunged the Nation into a Telecom Glut." *Wall Street Journal*. June 18, p. A1.

Blumenstein, Rebecca. 2001. "Reform Act Hasn't Delivered Promises to Customers." *Wall Street Journal*. May 3, p. B1.

Booth, William. 2000. "The Big Switch in Urban Renewal: Telecom Firms Bring Shine, Polish, Wires—But Few People—to Old LA Buildings." *Washington Post*, January 16, p. A20.

Borland, John. 2001. "Power Lines Stumble to Market." *CNET News.com*, March 28. Available online at <http://news.cnet.com/news/0-1004-200-5337770.html?tag=tp_pr>.

Bouvard, Pierre, and Warren Kurtzman. 2000. *The Broadband Revolution: How Superfast Internet Access Changes Media Habits in American Households*. Arbitron Company, New York. Available online at <www.arbitron.com> and <www.colemanresearch.com>.

BRDC, Ltd. 2001. "The Development of Broadband Access Platforms in Europe: Technologies, Services, Markets." Commissioned by the European Commission Information Society Directorate, August. Available online at <http://europa.eu.int/information_society/eeurope/news_library/new_documents/ broadband/index_en.htm>.

Breckheimer, Veronica, and Kevin Taglang. 1999. "Broadband and the Future of the Internet." *The Digital Beat* 1(14), August 20. Available online at <http://www.benton.org/DigitalBeat/db082099.html>.

Brewin, Bob. 2000. "Cable Creeps into the Corporation: Users of Cable for Broadband Connectivity Cite Big Savings Over Telco Offerings." *Computerworld*, October 16. Available online at <http://www.computerworld.com/cwi/story/0,1199,NAV47_STO52454_NLTam,00.html>.

Brewin, Bob. 2000. "Carriers Forge Pact to Avoid Interference in Fixed Wireless Microwave Bands." *Computerworld*, July 10. Available online at <http://www.computerworld.com/cwi/story/0,1199,NAV47_STO46911,00.html>.

Brewin, Bob. 2000. "Telcos Ante up $250 M for 'Last Mile' Connection Bidding Rights." *Computerworld*, April 10. Available online at <http://www.computerworld.com/cwi/story/0,1199,NAV47_STO43814,00.html>.

Brinkley, Joel. 1999. "Despite Agreement, Snags Remain for Digital TV." *New York Times*, November 22, p. C17.

Brinkley, Joel. 2000. "Do Viewers Even Want to Interact with TV?" *New York Times*, February 7, p. C5.

Broadband Project Office, Manitoba Innovation Network. 2000. "Accelerating the Deployment of Manitoba's Broadband Network Infrastructure" (white paper), June 6. Available online at <http://www.min.mb.ca/calendar/White_Paper.pdf>.

Burnett, Ron. 1999. "Communications Policy and the New Public Sphere: Towards a New Research Agenda." *Community Technology Review* (Summer-Fall). Available online at <http://www.civicnet.org/comtechreview/communications_policy_and_ the_ne.htm>.

Burrows, Peter. 1999. "Fred Wilson's $50 Million Bet on Info Appliances." *Business Week*, April 14. Available online at <http://www.businessweek.com/ebiz/9904/em0414.htm>.

Cable Datacom News. 2001. "Cable Modem Customer Count Tops 5.5 Million." March 1. Available online at <http://www.cabledatacomnews.com/mar01/mar01-1.html>.

Cablevision Bluebook. 2001. "High-Speed Havens of Modems & DSL." June.

Cahners In-Stat Group. 2000. *Broadband Consumers—Profiles and Strategies*, Report No. BBWIS00-05SP.

Cahners In-Stat Group. 2000. "Percentage of Internet-Connected Households Soars to 60% in 2000; In-Stat Report Reveals Results in Buying and Internet Usage Trends" [press release], March 28. Available online at <http://www.instat.com/pr/2000/is0001sp_pr.htm>.

Cahners In-Stat Group. 2000. "Many Routes to 3G Deployment—Options Depend on Starting Point" [press release], March 27. Available online at <http://www.instat.com/pr/2000/gw0003in_pr.htm>.

Canadian Radio-Television and Telecommunications Commission (CRTC). 1999. "CRTC Won't Regulate the Internet" [news release], May 17. Available online at <http://www.crtc.gc.ca/ENG/NEWS/RELEASES/1999/R990517e.htm>.

CAnet-3-News. 1999. "Glass Is Freedom: Optical Networks for the Rest of Us," June 9. Available online at <http://www.canarie.ca/MLISTS/news/1282.html>.

CAnet-3-News. 1999. "Should Fiber Infrastructure Be a Public Regulated Facility?" July 15. Available online at <http://www.canarie.ca/MLISTS/news/1298.html>.

CAnet-3-News. 2000. "No More Tearing Up of Streets to Install Optical Fiber," April 18. Available online at <http://www.canarie.ca/MLISTS/news2000/0084.html>.

Carroll, Jill. 2000. "FCC Will Determine ISP Access to Cable." *Wall Street Journal*, August 29, p. B2.

Caruso, Denise. 1999. "A New Model for the Internet: Fees for Services." *New York Times*, July 19, p. C6.

Cauley, Leslie. 1999. "Sony Enters Market for Cable-TV Boxes with $1 Billion Order from Cablevision." *Wall Street Journal*, September 17, p. B11.

Cauley, Leslie, and Nicole Harris. 1999. "Fixed Wireless Is Attracting Big Investments." *Wall Street Journal*, June 3, p. B4.

Cauley, Leslie. 2000. "AT&T Faces Challenge over Cable-Phone Goal." *Wall Street Journal*, April 28, p. A3.

Cauley, Leslie, and Nick Wingfield. 2000. "AT&T to Test Multiple ISPs on Cable Lines." *Wall Street Journal*, June 8, p. B10.

Center for Democracy and Technology (CDT). 2000. *Broadband Backgrounder: Public Policy Issues Raised by Broadband Technology*. Washington, D.C.: CDT, December. Available online at <http://www.cdt.org/digi_infra/broadband/backgrounder.shtml>.

Center for Media Education (CME). 2001. "Broadband Networks and Narrow Visions: The Internet at Risk." Washington, D.C.: CME. Available online at <http://www.cme.org/access/broadband/at_risk.html>.

Cha, Ariana Eunjung. 2000. "'Free' Wireless Networks?" *Washington Post*, December 8, p. E1.

Cha, Ariana Eunjung. 2001. "Broadband's a Nice Pace if You Can Get It." *Washington Post*, February 28, p. G4.

Chatterjee, Samir, Cherian S. Thachenkary, and Joseph L. Katz. 1998. "Modeling the Economic Impacts of Broadband Residential Services." *Computer Networks* 30(14): 1295-1310.

Chen, Kathy. 1999. "AT&T Used Carrot and Stick Lobbying Efforts in Local Debates Over Access to Cable-TV Lines." *Wall Street Journal*, November 24, p. A20.

Chen, Kathy. 1999. "FCC Backs Away from Regulating Internet Gateway." *Wall Street Journal*, January 29, p. B2.

Chen, Kathy. 1999. "FCC Chairman Calls for National Policy on High-Speed Internet Access Via Cable." *Wall Street Journal*, June 16, p. B4.

Chen, Kathy. 1999. "FCC's Kennard to Argue Against Rules on Broadband Web Access at the Local Level." *Wall Street Journal*, July 21, p. A4.

Chen, Kathy. 2000. "Comcast Hopes to Offer in 2002 Open-Access Policy." *Wall Street Journal*, March 27, p. A42.

Chen, Kathy, and Leslie Cauley. 1999. "Oregon Ruling Could Hurt AT&T Plan to Offer Internet Access on Cable Lines." *Wall Street Journal*, June 7, p. B3.

Chervokas, Jason. 1998. "The New Boys Network." *The Industry Standard*, June 12. Available online at <http://www.thestandard.com/article/0,1902,649,00.html>.

Christopher, Abby. 1999. "Opening the Door for Home Networks." *Upside* 11(6): 66-70.

Cioffi, J.M. 2001. "Unbundled DSL Evolution," T1E1.4 Contribution 2001-088, February, Los Angeles, Calif.. Available online at <http://www-isl.stanford.edu/people/cioffi/dsm/t1e1pap/1e140880.pdf>.

Cioffi, J.M., G. Ginis, W. Yu, and S. Zeng. 2000. "Spectrum Management with Advancing DSLs," ETSI TM6, Monterey TD06, November.

Cisco Systems. 1999. "Controlling Your Network—A Must for Cable Operators" (white paper). Available online at <http://www.cptech.org/ecom/openaccess/cisco1.html>.

Cisco Systems. 1999. "White Paper: Migrating to a New World Business Model." Cisco.

Civille, Richard, Michael Gurstein, and Kenneth Pigg. 2000. "Rural Regional Strategies for Broadband Demand." Center for Civic Networking and the Technical University of British Columbia, June 15.

Clark, David D. 1999. "High-Speed Data Races Home." *Scientific American*, October. Available online at <http://www.sciam.com/1999/1099issue/1099clark.html>.

Clark, David D. 1999. "Implications of Local Loop Technology for Future Industry Structure" in S. Gillette and I. Vogelsang, eds., *Competition, Regulation, and Convergence: Current Trends in Telecommunications Policy Research*. Mahwah, N.J.: Lawrence Erlbaum Associates.

Clark, David D., William Lehr, and Ian Liu. 2002. "Provisioning for Bursty Internet Traffic: Implications for Industry Structure," to appear in L. McKnight and J. Wroclawski, eds., *Internet Service Quality Economics*. Cambridge, Mass.: MIT Press.

Clark, Don. 2001. "Microsoft Advances on Game, TV Fronts." *Wall Street Journal*, January 5, p. B2.

Claymon, Deborah. 1999. "Net's Impact Revised Upward." *San Jose Mercury News*, June 9. Available online at <http://www0.mercurycenter.com/svtech/news/indepth/docs/econ061099.htm>.

CLEC News. 2000. "Competitors Made Gains, Still Face Challenges, ALTS Report Says." *CLEC News*, February 3. Available online at <http://www.clec-planet.com/news/0002/000203alts.htm>.

Cleland, Scott. 2000. "Residential Broadband Outlook—Investment Implications of a Duopoly?" Washington, D.C.: Precursor Group, August 11.

Cleland, Scott. 2001. "Datatopia—Why Data Transport Growth Stories May Disappoint." Washington, D.C.: Precursor Group, February 5.

Cleland, Scott. 2001. "How Broadband Deployment Skews Economic/Business Growth." Washington, D.C.: Precursor Group, February 22.

Cochrane, Peter. 1994. "Dark Fibre Will Transform Telecommunications." *IEEE Spectrum*, Technology 94, January.

Cohill, Andrew. 2000. "Telecommunications for Neighborhoods and Communities: Four Key Areas of Investment" (paper from Blacksburg Electronic Village). Available online at <http://www.bev.net/project/digital_library/comm_tel.pdf>.

Cohill, Andrew, and Jeffrey Crowder. 2000. "Community-based Broadband Telecommunications Infrastructure," Technical Report 2001-01v3. Virginia Tech. March. Available online at <http://www.bev.net/project/digital_library/broadbandv3.pdf>.

Cole, Jeff. 1999. "Boeing, in a Strategic Shift, to Develop Its Own Satellite Systems and Services." *Wall Street Journal*, June 14, p. A3.

Cole, Jeff. 1999. "Lockheed, Partners to Develop System of Multimedia, Internet-access Satellites." *Wall Street Journal*, May 6, p. A3.

Communications Business and Finance. 1999. "Larry Darby Asks 'How Much Broadband Capacity Enough?'" May 3.

Computer Science and Telecommunications Board (CSTB), National Research Council. 1994. *Realizing the Information Future: The Internet and Beyond*. Washington, D.C.: National Academy Press.

Computer Science and Telecommunications Board (CSTB), National Research Council. 1996. *The Unpredictable Certainty: Information Infrastructure Through 2000*. Washington, D.C.: National Academy Press.

Computer Science and Telecommunications Board (CSTB), National Research Council. 1998. *Trust in Cyberspace*. Washington, D.C.: National Academy Press.

Computer Science and Telecommunications Board (CSTB), National Research Council. 2000. *The Digital Dilemma: Intellectual Property in the Information Age*. Washington, D.C.: National Academy Press.

Computer Science and Telecommunications Board (CSTB), National Research Council. 2001. *The Internet's Coming of Age*. Washington, D.C.: National Academy Press.

Conklin, J.C. 1999. "Extension Cords." *Wall Street Journal*, September 13, p. R13.

Consumer Federation of America (CFA). 1999. "Consumers Demand Open Access to the High Speed." Washington, D.C.: CFA.

Consumer Federation of America (CFA) and Consumer Action. 1999. *Transforming the Information Superhighway Into a Private Toll Road: The Case Against Closed Access Broadband Internet Systems*. Washington, D.C.: CFA and Consumer Action, September. Available online at <http://www.consumerfed.org/bbreport.pdf>.

Consumer Federation of America (CFA). 1999. "While Federal Authorities Watch and Wait for Corporate Interests to Close the Internet, Consumers and Local Governments Should Demand Open Access." Washington, D.C.: CFA.

Federal Communications Commission (FCC). 2000. "Interim Report: Spectrum Study of the 2500-2690 MHz Band: The Potential for Accommodating Third Generation Mobile Systems." November 15.

Federal Communications Commission. 2000. "Inquiry Concerning the Deployment of Advanced Telecommunications Capability to All Americans in a Reasonable and Timely Fashion, and Possible Steps to Accelerate Such Deployment Pursuant to Section 706 of the Telecommunications Act of 1996." CC Docket No. 98-146, Second Report, FCC 0-290 (August 21). Available online at <http://www.fcc.gov/Bureaus/Common_Carrier/Orders/2000/fcc00290.pdf>.

Federal Communications Commission (FCC). 2000. "Notice of Inquiry on Deployment of Advanced Telecommunications Services." CC Docket No. 98-146. Feb. 18.

Federal Communications Commission (FCC). 2001. *High-speed Services for Internet Access: Subscribership as of December 31, 2001*. Industry Analysis Division, Common Carrier Bureau. Washington, D.C.: FCC.

Fitz, Jonathan. 2000. "Take This Bandwidth and Shove It." *Telephony*, June 5, p. 170-178.

Flint, Joe. 2000. "Broadcasters Create iBlast to Distribute Content to PCs Via Wireless Technology." *Wall Street Journal*, March 8, p. B8.

Flynn, Laurie J. 2000. "Georgia City Putting Entire Community Online." *New York Times*, March 27, p. C4.

Flynn, Laurie J. 2001. "Days of Plenty Are Over at Free Internet Services." *New York Times*, January 1, p. C1.

Forrester Research. 2000. "Broadband Misses the Mark (A Technographics Brief)," September 1.

Fowler, Thomas B. 2000. "Optical Networking: A Tutorial and Outlook." *The Telecommunications Review (2000)*. Available online at <http://www.mitretek.org/pubs/telecom/review00/article3.doc>.

Frieden, Rob. 2000. "Does a Hierarchical Internet Necessitate Multilateral Intervention?" Presentation given at the 28th Annual Telecommunications Policy Research Conference, Alexandria, Virginia, September 23-25. Available online at <http://www.personal.psu.edu/faculty/r/m/rmf5/TPRC1.ppt>.

Fulton, Keith. 1999. "Jobs, Education, Opportunity: Why Bridging the Digital Divide Through Community-based Digital Campuses Will Work." *iMP*, December.

Fusco, Patricia. 1999. "106th Congress Unleashes Internet Legislation." *Internetnews.com*, November 11.

Fusco, Patricia. 1999. "Excite@Home Cleaves Customers from Content." *Internetnews.com*, November 22.

Fusco, Patricia. 1999. "FCC/AT&T Policy Shifts Leave ISPs Out of the Game." *Internetnews.com*, October 20.

Fusco, Patricia. 1999. "ISPs Form Coalition in Bid For Open Access." *InternetNews.com*, February 2.

Fusco, Patricia. 1999. "Prodigy, GTE Offer Internet Call Waiting." *InternetNews.com*, July 19. Available online at <http://www.internetnews.com/isp-news/article/0,10878_164031,00.html>.

Fusco, Patricia. 1999. "Who Killed Reciprocal Compensation in Massachusetts?" *Internetnews.com*, May 24. Available online at <http://www.isp-planet.com/politics/whokilled.html>.

Fusco, Patricia. 2000. "High-Speed Competition Arrives in Oregon." *InternetNews.com*, February 9.

Gabel, David. 1999. "Recovering Access Costs: The Debate," in B. Cherry, S. Wildman, and A. Hammond IV, eds., *Making Universal Service Policy: Enhancing the Process Through Multidisciplinary Evaluation*. Mahwah, N.J.: Lawrence Erlbaum Associates.

Gabel, David, and Milton Mueller. (Undated). "Household Financing of the First 100 Feet?" Available online at <http://ksgwww.harvard.edu/iip/doeconf/gabel.html>.

Gantz, John. 1999. "Internet2 Is on the Way: Watch for It." *ComputerWorld*, March 1. Available online at <http://www.computerworld.com/cwi/story/0,1199,NAV47-74_STO34141,00.html>.

Garcia, John, and Jon Wilkins. 2001. "Which Broadband Technology Will Win the Race for Homes and Offices?" *The McKinsey Quarterly*, Number 1. Available online at <http://www.mckinseyquarterly.com/article_page.asp?articlename=piwa01>.

General Accounting Office (GAO). 2000. *Telecommunications: Technological and Regulatory Factors Affecting Consumer Choice of Internet Providers* (Report to the Subcommittee on Antitrust, Business Rights and Competition, Committee on the Judiciary, U.S. Senate) [GAO-01-93]. Washington, D.C.: GAO, October. Available online at <http://www.gao.gov/new.items/d0193.pdf>.

Georgia Municipal Association. 1999. «Tifton and Thomasville Enter Internet Agreement,» October 7. Available online at <http://www.gmanet.com/news/1999/1007.internet.shtml>.

Georgia Municipal Association. 2000. "LaGrange Internet TV" Initiative Provides Free Internet Access to All Cable TV Households," April. Available online at <http://www.gmanet.com/research/resources/telecomm.lagrange.shtml>.

Gerbrandt, Larry. 2001. "The Kagan Media Index." Paul Kagan Associates. January 31.

Gilder, George, and Bret Swanson. 2001. "The Broadband Economy Needs a Hero." *Wall Street Journal*. February 23.

Gillet, Sharon, and William Lehr. 1999. "Availability of Broadband Internet Access: Empirical Evidence," prepared for the Telecommunications Policy Research Conference (sponsored by MIT-ITCC), September 25.

Gillis, Justin, and Jackie Spinner. 1999. "A Nation Plugged In and Dug Up: Streets Scarred in Race to Wire Americe." *Washington Post*, July 15, p. A1.

Ginty, Maura. 1999. "Metromedia Expands in Europe." *ISP News*, Nov. 22.

Gitlin, Richard D. 2000. "Next Generation Networks: The New Public Network." Lucent Technologies.

Glassman, James K. 2001. "The FCC's Dangerous Internet Precedent." *Wall Street Journal*, January 17, p. A26.

Goldsborough, Margaret W. 2001. "Will Congressional Web Learning Report Gather Momentum or Only Gather Dust?" *New York Times*, January 3. Available online at <http://www.nytimes.com/2001/01/03/technology/03EDUCATION.html>.

Gomes, Lee, and Lisa Bransten. 2000. "Venture Capital Loves P-to-P: The Latest Technology Fad." *Wall Street Journal*, July 5, p. B1.

Goodman, David J. 2000. "The Wireless Internet: Promises and Challenges." *Computer* 33(7): 36.

Goodman, Peter S. 1999. "AT&T Plans a Big Return to Local Service." *Washington Post*, Nov. 24.

Goodman, Peter S. 1999. "Oregon Wages a Battle Over Access to Internet." *Washington Post*, Nov. 1, p. A1.

Goodman, Peter S. 2000. "Dishing Up a New Link to the Internet." *Washington Post*, November 6, p. A1.

Goodman, Peter S. 2000. "Firms Duel Over the Wired West." *Washington Post*, April 19.

Goodman, Peter S. 2000. "Rooftops Loom As a Telecom Battleground." *Washington Post*, June 12, p. A01.

Goodman, Peter S. 2000. "Teligent Expands Reach of Wireless." *Washington Post*, May 2, p. E01.

IDC. 2000. "Home Office Use of the Internet Is Growing Dramatically" (press release), July 24.

IDC. 2000. "Home Office Households Approach 37 Million in 2000 As Internet Turns 'Work Anywhere' into 'Work Everywhere'" (press release), September 1.

Isenberg, David S. 2000. "You Think It's DSL vs. Cable? Guess Again." *Fortune* 142(8): 64. (Special Issue: *The Future of the Internet*).

Isenberg, David S. 2001. "SMART Letter #56: Era of Customer-Owned Networks." *isen.com*, June 7. Available online at <http://www.isen.com/archives/010607.html>.

Ishida, T., and K. Isbister (eds.). 2000. *Digital Cities: Technologies, Experiences, and Future Perspectives*. Springer. Abstracts and chapters available online at <http://link.springer.de/link/service/series/0558/tocs/t1765.htm>.

IT Commission, Government of Sweden. 1999. *A Future-Proof IT Infrastructure for Sweden: Report by the IT Commission* (SOU 1999:134), Roger Tanner, trans. Stockholm: Ministry of Industry. Available online at <http://www.itkommissionen.se/PDF/rapp0026.pdf>.

IT Strategy Council (Japan). 2000. "Basic IT Strategy" (adopted by the IT Strategy Council on 27 November 2000). Tokyo: Ministry of Foreign Affairs of Japan. Available online at <http://www.mofa.go.jp/policy/economy/it/strategy.html>.

International Telecommunications Union (ITU). 2001. "Chair's Report," Regulatory Implications of Broadband Workshop (ITU New Initiatives Programme), Geneva, Switzerland, May 2-4. Geneva: ITU, May. Available online at <http://www.itu.int/osg/spu/ni/broadband/workshop/chairfinal.pdf>.

Jander, Mary. 2000. "Last Mile Lexicon." *Light Reading*, November 20. Available online at <http://www.lightreading.com/document.asp?doc_id=2476>.

Jayant, Nikil (ed.). 1999. *Signal Compression: Coding of Speech, Audio, Text, Image and Video*. Singapore: World Scientific.

Jesdanum, Anick. 2000. "Wiring Rural America: Just the Beginning." *Associated Press*, September 6.

Jones, Bill. 2000. "A Report on the Feasibility of Internet Voting." California Internet Voting Task Force. January.

Joyce, Amy. 1999. "Bandwidth by Demand: Telecommunications Start-up Streamlines International Networking." *Washington Post*, September 27.

Joyce, Amy. 2000. "A High-Speed Disconnection." *Washington Post*, October 5, p. E4.

Kelley, Daniel. 1999. "Deregulation of Special Access Services: Timing Is Everything." HAI Consulting. June.

Kende, Michael, and Douglas Sicker. 2000. "Real-time Services and the Fragmentation of the Internet." *Proceedings of the 28th Research Conference on Communication, Information and Internet Policy* (TPRC 2000), September 23-25, 2000. Alexandria, Va.: Telecommunications Policy Research Corporation.

Kennard, William. 1999. "The Road Not Taken: Building a Broadband Future for America." Remarks before the National Cable Television Association, Chicago, Illinois, June 15. Available online at <http://www.fcc.gov/Speeches/Kennard/spwek921.html>.

Kennard, William. 2000. "The New York Story: 'Ain't No Stopping Us Now.'" *Media Law And Policy*, New York Law School. Spring, Vol. VIII, No. 2.

Kennelly, Jim. 1994. "9 Ways Going On-Line Can Change Your Life and 6 Ways It Can't," *The Washington Post: Fast Forward*, September, pp. 9-13.

Kettler, David. 1999. "Lighting Up the Last Mile: Fiber's Future Is Brightening the Local Loop." *America's Network*, July 1. Available online at <http://www.americasnetwork.com/issues/99issues/990701/990701light.htm>.

Kirk, Don. 2001. "In Korea, Broadband Is Part of the Culture." *New York Times*, October 29, p. C3.

Kirstein, Mark, Cahners In-Stat. 2000. *Entering the Broadband Era* (Report No. BB0000CI), May. Available online at <http://www.instat.com/catalog/downloads/broadbandera8uh.pdf>.

Klein, Alec. 2000. "AOL Restrictions Alleged." *Washington Post*, October 10, p. E1.

Klein, Alec. 2001. "AOL Signs Up 3 More Internet Providers to Use Cable System." *Washington Post*, October 6, p. E8.

Klein, Alec. 2001. "FCC Clears Way for AOL Time Warner, Inc." *Washington Post*, January 12, p. A1.

Kolko, Jed. 2000. "Broadband Misses the Market." Forrester Research Brief. September 1.

Kontzer, Tom. 2001. "Chicago's CivicNet Takes a Step Closer to Reality," *InformationWeek.com*, January 4. Available online at <http://www.informationweek.com/story/IWK20010104S0007>.

Kover, Amy. 2000. "The Hot Idea of the Year [peer-to-peer]." *Fortune* 142(1), June 26.

Krause, Jason. 2000. "DSL Upstarts Can't Compete With Phone Giants." *Industry Standard*, December 22. Available online at <http://www.thestandard.com/article/display/0,1151,21043,00.html>.

Krim, Jonathan. 2001. "Gates Calls for a Cut in High-Speed Net Costs." *Washington Post*, September 6, p. E1.

Kruger, Lennard G., and Angele A. Gilroy. 2000. "IB10045: Broadband Internet Access: Background and Issues" (CRS Issue Brief for Congress), November 28. Available online at <http://www.cnie.org/nle/st-49.html>.

Kruse, Hans, William Yurcik, and Lawrence Lessig. 2000. "The InterNAT: Policy Implications of the Internet Architecture Debate." *Proceedings of the 28th Research Conference on Communication, Information and Internet Policy* (TPRC 2000), September 23-25, 2000. Alexandria, Va.: Telecommunications Policy Research Corporation. Available online at <http://www.csm.ohiou.edu/kruse/publications/InterNAT_v4.pdf>.

Labaton, Stephen. 1999. "$72 Billion Deal of Phone Giants Clears Big Hurdle: Ameritech-SBC Would Have to Expand to New Cities and Welcome Competitors." *New York Times*, June 30, p. A1.

Labaton, Stephen. 1999. "Fight for Internet Access Creates Unusual Alliances: Former Foes Find Profits in AT&T Cable Lines." *New York Times*, August 13.

Labaton, Stephen. 2000. "An Oops in Time Warner's Battle for Internet." *New York Times*, May 24, p. A1.

Labaton, Stephen. 2001. "Slew of Supreme Court Cases to Focus on '96 Telecom Law." *NewYork Times*, October 1, p. C8.

Lacter, Mark. 2000. "Click Flicks (Video-on-demand)." *Forbes.* August 7, p. 67.

Lais, Sami. 1999. "Building Industry Braces For IT, Online Onslaught." *Computerworld*, August 23, p. 14.

Landers, Peter. 2000. "NTT Intends to Link Homes To Web With High-Speed Fiber." *Wall Street Journal*, September 27.

Larson, Gary, and Jeffrey Chester. 1999. "Song of the Open Road: Building a Broadband Network for the 21st Century" (white paper). Washington, D.C.: Center for Media Education. Available online at <http://www.cme.org/access/broadband/openroad1.html>.

Lathen, Deborah. 1999. "Broadband Today." Staff Report to William Kennard, Chairman, Federal Communications Commission. October.

Lathen, Deborah. 1999. "The Emergence of Convergence" [speech], July 22. Available online at <http://www.fcc.gov/Speeches/misc/spdal901.html>.

Latour, Almar. 1999. "Standard Connecting Phones to Internet Is Fueling Service Providers in Europe." *Dow Jones Newswires*, August 9.

Latour, Almar. 2001. "How Europe Tripped Over a Wireless Phone Made for the Internet." *Wall Street Journal*, June 5, p. A1.

Laubach, Mark. 1999. "Comments on the Technical Ability to Implement Open Access Provisioning via High-Speed Data over Hybrid Fiber-Coaxial Cable Television Systems in the United States," prepared for the White House National Economic Council, May 30.

Laver, Ross. 1996. "Plugging into the Future." *Maclean's*, January 29, p. 34.

Le Blanc, Jamal. 1999. "Resolving the Digital Divide." *Digital Beat* 1(19), November 12. Available online at <http://www.benton.org/DigitalBeat/db111299.html>.

LeDuc, Daniel, and Craig Timberg. 2000. "Battle Lines Drawn Over Cable: Md., Va. Legislatures Confront Issues of Internet Access." *Washington Post*, February 7, p. A1.

Lee, Chang Hee. 2001. "State Regulatory Commission Treatment of Advanced Services: Results of a Survey." National Regulatory Research Institute, February.

Leeper, David. 2001. "A Long-term View of Short-Range Wireless." *IEEE Computer*, June, pp. 39-44.

Leibovich, Mark. 1999. "Foes Place Ads Hitting AT&T-MediaOne Deal." *Washington Post*, May 7, p. E1.

Lessig, Lawrence. 2000. "Clinton Versus the Internet: End Game." *New Republic*, June 19. Available online at <http://www.thenewrepublic.com/061900/lessig061900.html>.

Levey, Collin. 2001. "Bookshelf: Commuting by Mountain Bike and Modem." *Wall Street Journal*, January 4, p. A16.

Lewis, Michael. 2000. "Boom Box." *New York Times Magazine*, August 13, p. 36.

Li, Kenneth. 2000. "Kozmo.com, Media Company." *The Industry Standard*, May 1. Available online at <http://www.thestandard.com/article/0,1902,14545,00.html>.

Lieberman, David. 1999. "Web Growth Will Help Most Media." *USA Today*, November 10, p. 1A.

Lippman, John, and Andy Pasztor. 2001. "Hughes Electronics' DirecTV Reports a Substantial Increase in Its Subscribers." *Wall Street Journal,* January 17, p. A16.

Loftus, Peter. 2001. "Data-Equipment Firms Trim Views as Spending Slims." *Wall Street Journal*, January 16, p. B6.

Lohr, Steve. 1999. "In AT&T Deal, Microsoft Buys Itself a Stake in Post-PC Era." *New York Times*, May 7, p. C1.

Louderback, Jim. 1999. "Wireless Strikes Back." *ZDNet News*, June 25. Available online at <http://www.zdnet.com/zdnn/stories/comment/0,5859,2283013,00.html>.

Lu, Kevin. 1997. "Cost Comparisons of FTTC and FTTH for Various Demands and Densities," published at the Eighth International Workshop on Optical/Hybrid Access Networks. Paper 2.3, Atlanta, Georgia, March 2-5.

Mack, Toni, and Mary Summers. 1999. "Cheap Gamble: Sprint Enters High Stakes Game to Wire Up America With Broadband Services." *Forbes*, July 5, p. 128.

MacKie-Mason, Jeffrey K. 1999. *Investment in Cable Broadband Infrastructure: Open Access Is Not an Obstacle*. Ann Arbor, Mich.: University of Michigan, November 5. Available online at <http://www-personal.umich.edu/~jmm/papers/broadband.pdf>.

MacMillan, Robert. 2001. "As Free ISPs Fade, Others Raise Rates." *Washington Post*, January 26, p. E1.

Mannion, Patrick. 2001. "Fiber-to-the-Home Advocacy Group Formed." *EE Times*, July 3. Available online at <http://www.csdmag.com/story/OEG20010703S0028>.

Marable, Leslie. 2001. "Broadband—It's a City Thing." *The Industry Standard*, May 18. Available online at <http://www.thestandard.com/article/0,1902,24626,00.html>.

Markoff, John. 1999. "Motorola to Offer a Chip That Can Support a Variety of Cell-Phone Standards." *New York Times,* November 1, p. C4.

Markoff, John. 2000. "Ethernet Finds a New Level." *New York Times*, June 5, p. C1.

Martinez, Barbara. 2000. "An Internet Race Nets Landlords Some Rich Perks." *Wall Street Journal*, March 29, p. B1.

Masud, Abdullah, and Brenda Neidigh . 2000. "Commonwealth of Virginia Restrictions on Municipal Telecommunications." June.

Mathews, Anna Wilde. 2001. "EchoStar's Loss Narrows on Growth in Subscriptions." *Wall Street Journal*, May 4, p. B6.

May, Randolph. 1999. "On Unlevel Playing Fields: The FCC's Broadband Schizophrenia." *Progress on Point* series, Progress and Freedom Foundation, December. Available online at <http://www.pff.org/POP_6.11.htm>.

McCarthy, Bill. 1999. "Introduction to the Directory of Internet Service Providers." *Boardwatch Magazine* (Summer).

McClard, Anne. (Undated). "Unleashed: Web Tablet Integration into the Home." MediaOne Labs.

McDonald, Glenn, and Cameron Crotty. 1999. "The Digital Future." *PCWorld.com*, November 19. Available online at <http://www.pcworld.com/resource/printable/article.asp?aid=13926>.

McFarland, Henry B. 2000. "Economic Perspectives on Requiring Unbundled Access to Cable Broadband Networks." 2000 Annual Meeting Section of Antitrust Law, New York, July 11.

McGee, Art. 1999. "Culture, Class and Cyberspace Resources." *Civicnet.org*. Available online at <http://www.civicnet.org/comtechreview/culture.htm>.

McGuire, David. 2001. "Bells, Rivals Gear Up for Battle." *Washington Post*, February 28. Available online at <http://www.washtech.com/news/telecom/7915-1.html>.

McKay, Jim. 2000. "Rural Ohio Creates Its Own Wireless Connectivity." *Government Technology* (November). Available online at <http://www.govtech.net/publications/gt/2000/nov/news/index.phtml>.

McWilliams, Brian. 1999. "@Home Rolls Out Upstream Rate Limit." *InternetNews.com*, June 24. Available online at <http://www.internetnews.com/isp-news/article/0,,8_144121,00.html>.

McWilliams, Gary. 2000. "BroadJump Speeds 'Broadband' Installations." *Wall Street Journal*, February 3, p. B8.

Mehta, Stephanie. 1999. "Avici Systems Breaks Through Bandwidth Bottleneck." *Wall Street Journal*, May 13, p. B6.

Mehta, Stephanie. 2000. "U.S. Market for Broadband Is Barely Tapped." *Wall Street Journal*, January 12, p. B8.

Mehta, Stephanie, and Edward Felsenthal. 1999. "Supreme Court Restores Federal Rules Aimed at Opening Local-Phone Markets." *Wall Street Journal*, Janurary 26, p. A2.

Menendez, R.C., et al. 1997. "Cost Comparisons of FTTC and FTTH for Various Demands and Densities," Eighth International Workshop on Optical/Hybrid Access Networks, Atlanta, Georgia, March 2-5.

Metropolitan King County Council. 1999. "Oregon Decision Against AT&T/TCI Favors County Council Demand for Consumer Choice Through Open Access." June 4.

Mick, Collin, Bruce Tolley, and Willem Wery. 1999. "Running 1000BASE-Y Gigabit Ethernet over Copper Cabling." Gigabit Ethernet Alliance, March 30.

Milgrom, Paul. 1996. "Procuring Universal Service: Putting Auction Theory to Work." Lecture at the Royal Swedish Academy of Sciences, December 9.

Miller, Peter, Richard Civille, and Dirk Koning. 1999. "The Emergence of Convergence." *Community Technology Review*. Available online at <http://www.civicnet.org/comtechreview/editorintro.htm>.

Musgrove, Mike. 1999. "The Broadband Backlog." *Washington Post*, December 31, p. E1.

Namioka, Aki Helen. 1999. "Negotiating Open Access with AT&T." *Community Technology Review*. Available online at <http://www.civicnet.org/comtechreview/seattleatt.htm>.

National Association of State Information Resource Executives (NASIRE) and National Association of State Telecommunications Directors (NASTD). 2000. *Telecommunications: Closing the Digital Divide with Broadband Internet Access*. Lexington, Kentucky: NASIRE, October. Available online at <http://www.nascio.org/publications/Telecomm_Report_Oct2000.pdf>.

National Cable and Telecommunications Association (NCTA). 2001. *Industry Statistics*. Washington, D.C.: NCTA. Available online at <http://www.ncta.com/industry_overview/indStat.cfm>.

National Exchange Carrier Association (NECA). 2000. *NECA Rural Broadband Cost Study: Summary of Results*. Whippany, N.J.: NECA. Available online at <http://www.neca.org/broadban.asp>.

National Science Foundation (NSF). 1998. "Workshop on Tetherless T3 Workshop: Interim Report." Washington, D.C.: NSF, November.

National Science Foundation (NSF). 1999. "Draft/Preliminary Report: First/Last Mile Workshop." Washington, D.C.: NSF, April 26.

National Telecommunications and Information Administration (NTIA). 2000. *Falling Through the Net: Toward Digital Inclusion*. Washington, D.C.: NTIA, October. Available online at <http://www.ntia.doc.gov/ntiahome/digitaldivide/index.html>.

National Telecommunications and Information Administration (NTIA). 2000. "Federal Operations in the 1755-1850 MHz Band: The Potential for Accommodating Third Generation Mobile Systems," Interim Report (NTIA Special Publication 01-41). Washington, D.C.: NTIA, November 15. Available online at <http://www.ntia.doc.gov/osmhome/reports/imt2000/titlepage.html>.

National Telephone Cooperative Association. 1999. "Dial-tone Is Not Enough: Serving Tribal Lands." November.

New York Times. 2001. "Report Counts Computers in Majority of U.S. Homes." September 7, p. A15.

Nickell, Joe Ashbrook. 2000. "Home on the Web." *Industry Standard*, October 16. Available online at <http://www.thestandard.com/article/display/0,1151,19290,00.html>.

Nie, Norman, and Lutz Erbring. 2000. "Internet and Society: A Preliminary Report." Stanford, Calif.: Stanford Institute for the Quantitative Study of Society, February 17.

Nielsen/Netratings. 2001. "New York Local Market Dominates Broadband Usage, According to Nielsen/Netratings" (press release). New York: Nielsen/Netratings, May 15.

Norris, Floyd. 2001. "It's Not Just AT&T: How Telecom Became a Black Hole." *Wall Street Journal*, February 16, p. C1.

National Telecommunications and Information Administration (NTIA) and Rural Utilities Service (RUS). 2000. *Advanced Telecommunications in Rural America: The Challenge of Bringing Broadband Service to All Americans*. Washington, D.C.: NTIA, April. Available online at <http://www.ntia.doc.gov/reports/ruralbb42600.pdf>.

Oakes, Chris. 2000. "Napster Not at Home with Cable." *Wired*, April 7. Available online at <http://www.wired.com/news/technology/0,1282,35523,00.html>.

O'Brien, Chris. 1999. "Cable Internet Products Draw Ire of Consumer Groups." *San Jose Mercury News*, September 29.

Odlyzko, Andrew. 2000. "The Current State and Likely Evolution of the Internet." *Proc. Globecom '99*, IEEE, pp. 1869-1875.

Odlyzko, Andrew. 2001. "Content Is Not King." *First Monday* 6(2). Available online at <http://www.firstmonday.org/issues/issue6_2/odlyzko/>.

Omoigui, Sirbu, Eldering, and Himayat. 1996. "Comparing Integrated Broadband Architectures from an Economic and Public Policy Perspective." *Telecommunications and Internet Policy.*

Ortiz, Sixto. 2000. "Broadband Fixed Wireless Travels the Last Mile." *Computer* 33(7): 18.

Orwall, Bruce, and Kara Swisher. 1999. "Disney Discusses Buying All of Infoseek." *Wall Street Journal*, June 8, p. A3.

Ota, Kiyohisa. 1999. "NTT: Transforming into Information Distributor." Merrill Lynch In-Depth Report.

Owen, Bruce. 1999. "Economist Says Internet Use Is Limited." *Tech Law Journal*, July 9. Available online at <http://www.techlawjournal.com/internet/19990709b.htm>.

Pandey, Amit. 1999. "Caching 101: What's the ROI?" *ISP-Planet*, July 5. Available online at <http://www.isp-planet.com/technology/cache101-4.html>.

Papadakis, Maria C. 2000. "Complex Picture of Computer Use in the Home Emerges." Issue Brief, National Science Foundation, Directorate for Social, Behavioral, and Economic Sciences. March 31.

Parker, Edwin B. 2000. "Closing the Digital Divide in Rural America." *Telecommunications Policy* 24, May. Available online from <http://www.tpeditor.com/contents/2000/parker.htm>.

Parker, Suzi. 2000. "New Economy Recasts the Rural South." *Christian Science Monitor*, May 3, p. 3.

Pastore, Michael. 1999. "Consumer ISPs Giving Way to Business Providers." *Internetnews.com*, Nov. 11.

Pasztor, Andy. 2000. "Hughes Electronics Agrees to Provide Satellite-Based Web Service Across India." *Wall Street Journal*, March 24, p. B4.

Pasztor, Andy. 2000. "PanAmSat, Seeking a Niche, Plans Internet Video Service." *Wall Street Journal*, March 29, p. B7.

Pasztor, Andy. 2001. "Loral Scraps Plans to Be Major Operator of Two-Way Satellite Broadband Systems." *Wall Street Journal*, February 1, p. A4.

Paul Kagan Associates. 2001. *The Kagan Media Index*, January 31.

Pease, Robert. 2000. "Rural Areas Present Better Business Case for Fiber-to-the-home." *Lightwave* 17 (7): 1. June.

Peterson, Andrea. 2000. "Two Brothers Bet Everything on Free-Broadband Start-Up." *Wall Street Journal*, March 23, p. B8.

Pine, David. 1999. "Let the Feds Regulate." *iMP*, December. Available online at <http://www.cisp.org/imp/december_99/12_99pine.htm>.

Piscitello, David M. 2000. "The True Killer Application for Broadband Local Access." *CLEC-Planet.* Available online at <http://www.clecplanet.com/business/00072piscitello.htm>.

Plotnikoff, David. 2000. "Wiring the Rural West." *San Jose Mercury News.* Available online at <http://www0.mercurycenter.com/svtech/news/special/ruralwest/>.

Pollack, Andrew. 1999. "America Online to Put $1.5 Billion Into a Hughes Alliance." *New York Times*, June 22, p. C6.

Pomerantz, Dorothy. 2001. "If You Overbuild It." *Forbes*, April 16, p. 144.

Poulton, Ken. 1999. "The Palo Alto Fiber to Home Trial" (slide presentation), November 24. Available online at <http://alcatraz.labs.agilent.com/Ken_Poulton/ftth/poulton-v10e/>.

Raik-Allen, Georgie. 2000. "ISky Shoots for the Stars." *Red Herring*, January 19. Available online at <http://www.redherring.com/vc/2000/0119/vc-isky.html>.

Ramstand, Evan, and Dean Takahashi. 1999. "Sony, TiVo Set Deal on TV-Recording Device." *Wall Street Journal*, September 9, p. B6.

Schwartz, John. 1999. "Open-Access Online Fight Escalates." *Washington Post,* July 28, p. E1.

Schwartz, John. 2001. "Wiring the City: Humans Won't Do." *New York Times,* March 8, p. G1.

Semon, D. 2001. "A Brief History of Data Over Cable." Time Warner. January.

Shannon, Victoria. 1999. "Why It's Slow Going on the Net," *Washington Post,* May 24, p. F20.

Shin Luh, Shu. 1999. "AOL Sees Future in Palms." *Washington Post,* June 23, p. E1.

Shin Luh, Shu. 1999. "Phone Companies Reach Pact." *Washington Post,* August 3, p. E3.

Shishkin, Philip. 2000. "AOL, Time Warner Offer Open Access for Five Years." *Wall Street Journal,* September 25, p. A28.

Shishkin, Philip. 2000. "EC Scrutinizes Microsoft's Telewest Plan." *Wall Street Journal,* June 13, p. A22.

Shumate, Paul W. 1998. "Comparing the Latest High-Speed Access Technologies: FTTx, HFC, xDSL, and Wireless," presented at IEEE Lasers and Electro-optics Annual Meeting, December 3, Orlando, Fla.

Sicker, Douglas, et al. 2000. "The Internet Interconnection Conundrum." Draft OPP working paper. April.

Siembab, Walter. 1999. "Public Transit for the Information Highway." Available online at <http://www.civicnet.org/comtechreview/public_transit.htm>.

Simon, Greg, and Rich Bond. 1999. "Freedom of Choice: Why Local Control Protects Consumers' Choices." *iMP,* December. Available online at <http://www.cisp.org/imp/december_99/12_99simon.htm>.

Sliwa, C. 1999. "Jini: Promising Technology, But Will It Catch On?," *Computerworld,* March 15, p. 76.

Smart, Tim. 1999. "Lockheed, Partners Plan System of Satellites." *Washington Post,* May 7, p. E10.

SMART Winnipeg. 2000. "The Case for Municipal Fiber White Paper" (white paper). Winnipeg, Manitoba: SMART Winnipeg, August 15. Available online at <http://www.smartwinnipeg.mb.ca/Municipal_Fibre.htm>.

Solomon, Deborah. 2000. "Amid Steep Business Declines, Phone Giant Calls It Splits; Cutting the Prized Dividend." *Wall Street Journal,* October 26, p. B1.

Speta, James. 2000. "Handicapping the Race for the Last Mile?: A Critique of Open Access Rules for Broadband Platforms." *Yale Journal on Regulation,* Winter.

Speta, James. 2000. "The Vertical Dimension of Cable Open Access." *University of Colorado Law Review* 71(4), Fall.

Sprint. 2000. "MMDS—Better Than Sliced Bread" (white paper). Available online at <http://www.sprintbroadband.com/prsite/articles/MMDS.html>.

Staff Report. 1999. "Panel Rejects Ordinance in Internet/Cable-TV Case." *Wall Street Journal,* October 20, p. B11.

St. Arnaud, Bill. 2000. "Gigabit Internet to Every Canadian School by 2005," discussion paper. Ottawa: CAnet-3, February 4. Available online at <http://www.canet3.net/library/papers/GigabittoHomeby2005.html>.

Stern, Christopher. 2000. "Broadband Market Growth Slows." *Washington Post,* August 28, p. E01.

Stern, Christopher. 2000. "Broadcaster's Promise of a Digital TV Age Has Not Been Met, and Now Congress Is Having Second Thoughts About Its Role." *Washington Post,* December 17, p. H1.

Stevenson, Ted. 1999. "ISP Valuation: From the Horse's Mouth." *ISP-Planet.com,* November 10. Available online at <http://www.isp-planet.com/business/ispcon_valuation.html>.

St. Sauver, Joe. 2000. "A Fiber Optic Primer and Tutorial: Designing Networks for Optimum Performance." *Computing News* [University of Oregon]. Available online at <http://cc.uoregon.edu/cnews/summer2000/fiber.html>.

Swisher, Kara, and Khanh Tran. 1999. "High-Stakes Internet Battle Erupts in San Francisco." *Wall Street Journal*, July 26, p. A24.

Taglang, Kevin. 1999. "Community Technology Centers: Closing the Digital Divide." *OMB Watch*, September 29.

Taschdjian, Martin. 2000. "From Open Networks to Open Markets: How Public Policy Affects Infrastructure Investment Decisions." Center for Information Policy Research, Harvard University, Cambridge, Mass. November.

Tech Law Journal. (Undated). "Summary of Bills Affecting Broadband in the 106th Congress." Available online at <http://techlawjournal.com/cong106/broadband/Default.htm>.

Technology Review. 2001. "Special Issue: Wired and Wireless." June.

Technology Review. 2001. "A Very Long Distance: A Regulatory Call Put Cell Phones on Hold." May, p. 110.

Tedeschi, Bob. 2000. "E-Commerce Report: Sites Not Yet Pitching at Full Speed." *New York Times*, December 4.

Telecommunications Reports. 1999. "AIG Telecom's Bandwidth 'Forwards Market' Looks Toward Rapid Growth in Telecom Minutes." August 2.

Telecommunications Reports. 1999. "ALTS Eyes Strong Enforcement, Service Integration; Kennard Urges Carriers to Go into Residential Markets." May 10.

Telecommunications Reports. 1999. "AT&T's Plans Are Focus of Senate Hearing." February 19.

Telecommunications Reports. 1999. "Bell Atlantic, IBM Set Home Networking Venture." February 8.

Telecommunications Reports. 1999. "Bell Atlantic, SBC Form New Broadband Coalition." July 5.

Telecommunications Reports. 1999. "Canada's Teleglobe Unveils $5 Billion Global Broadband Network." May 17.

Telecommunications Reports. 1999. "Canada Takes Hard Line on Cable Modem Access; U.S. Court Adjusts Schedule for Portland Review." July 12.

Telecommunications Reports. 1999. "C & W USA to Invest $670 M In Fiber Internet Backbone." April 19.

Telecommunications Reports. 1999. "Competitive Carriers Set to Unveil Broadband Coalition." March 29.

Telecommunications Reports. 1999. "CRTC Renounces 'New Media Services' Regulation, Reaffirms Internet Access Rules." May 24.

Telecommunications Reports. 1999. "Debate over Reallocated DTV Spectrum Exposes Ruts in Information Superhighway." July 26.

Telecommunications Reports. 1999. "FCC's Decision Against Cable Modem Probe Fails to Hinder Push for Opening Networks." February 8.

Telecommunications Reports. 1999. "Goodlatte Pledges Persistence in Pushing Broadband Bills." May 24.

Telecommuncations Reports. 1999. "Home Networking Alliance Eyes Broadband Synergies." August 2.

Telecommunications Reports. 1999. "Long Distance Group Opposes Broadband Service Measures." June 28.

Telecommunications Reports. 1999. "NTIA Wants Few Changes to FCC Unbundling Rules." August 9.

Weller, Dennis. 1996. "Transition Strategies for Regulation," IDATE, *Communications & Strategies*, No. 23, 3rd Quarter, pp. 99-115.

Weller, Dennis. 1999. "Obligations for Universal Service Obligations." GTE, November. Available online at <http://www.comslaw.org.au/research/Universal/19991101_Weller.html>.

Wigfield, Mark. 2000. "Schools' Spectrum Rights Promise a Bonanza, But Can They Cash In?" *Wall Street Journal*, September 6, p. B1.

Wigfield, Mark. 2001. "Rural Virginia Town Fights for Broadband Access." *Wall Street Journal*, June 7, p. B6.

Wilke, John R. 2000. "AOL, Time Warner Pledge Cable Access." *Wall Street Journal*, December 14, p. A3.

Williamson, Oliver E. 1975. *Markets and Hierarchies*. New York: The Free Press.

Williamson, Richard. 2000. "Satellite Net Service Launches." *Interactive Week*, November 12. Available online at <http://www.zdnet.com/zdnn/stories/news/0,4586,2652654,00.html>.

Williamson, Richard. 2001. "AT&T Completes First Open Access Cable Trial." *ZDNet*, June 8. Available online at <http://www.zdnet.com/filters/printerfriendly/0,6061,2770807-3500.html>.

Wingfield, Nick. 1999. "Free Web Services Challenge AOL's Dominance." *Wall Street Journal*, September 23, p. B8.

Wingfield, Nick. 1999. "Sandpiper Aims to Prevent Event-Driven Web Pileups." *Wall Street Journal*, June 17, p. B10.

Wirbel, Laura. 2000. "New Carriers Follow Alternate Broadband Route." *EE Times*, February 8. Available online at <http://www.eetimes.com/story/OEG20000208S0008>.

Witt, Sarah. 1999. "Broadband's First Beachhead: High-Speed Internet Service for Multi-Tenant Buildings Leads a Gradual Move to Providing Fast Access for All." *Internet World*, June 14.

Wolcott, David A. 2001. "An ALTS Analysis: Local Competition Policy & The New Economy." ALTS, February 2.

Wolverton, Troy, and Wylie Wong. 2000. "Internet World Showcases Broadband Moves." *CNET News.com*, April 7. Available online at <http://news.cnet.com/news/0-1004-200-1661401.html>.

Woolley, Scott. 2000. "Fast Glass." *Forbes*, November 13, p. 322.

Working Group on Digital Subscriber Line Access (T1E1.4). 2001. *American National Standard for Telecommunications—Spectrum Management for Loop Transmission Systems (T1.417-2001)*. Standards Committee T1. Washington, D.C.: Alliance for Telecommunications Industry Solutions.

Working Party on Telecommunications and Information Services Policies; Committee for Information, Computer and Communications Policy. 2001. *The Development of Broadband Access in OECD Countries*. Paris: OECD, October.

World Wide Packets. 2000. "Last Mile Broadband Technologies" (white paper). Available online at <http://www.worldwidepackets.com/solutions/papers/wp_lastmile.jsp>.

World Wide Packets. 2000. "World Wide Packets Deploys First Gigabit Ethernet Broadband Solution with Grant County Washington PUD" (press release), August 7. Available online at <http://www.wwp.com/news/pressRelease.jsp?id=17>.

Woroch, Glenn A. 1998. "Facilities Competition and Local Network Investment: Theory, Evidence and Policy Implications." June. Available online at <http://elsa.berkeley.edu/~woroch/faccomp.pdf>.

XDSL Today. 2000. "US West and Consortium of 13 Competitive Local Exchange Carriers Sign Nation's First Region-Wide 'Line-Sharing' Agreement." May 1. Available online at <http://www.xdsl.com/newsreleases/xdsl/11151.asp>.

Young, Shawn. 2001. "Covad, One of Last DSL Competitors, Blames Troubles on Bell Tactics." *Wall Street Journal*, August 9, p. B1.

Young, Shawn. 2001. "Northpoint Communications Files for Chapter 11 Creditor Protection." *Wall Street Journal*, January 17, p. B10.

Young, Shawn. 2001. "Rhythms Tells Customers It Will Close." *Wall Street Journal*, August 13, p. B3.

Zelnick, Nate. 2000. "Packets from Heaven." *Internet World*, March 30. Available online at <http://www.internetworld.com/news/archive/03302000.jsp#3.30sat>.

Zerega, Blaise, and Scott Lajoie. 1999. "Will They Come? Builders of High-Bandwidth Networks May Be Overestimating Their Potential Market." *Forbes*, November 29.

Zerega, Blaise. 2000. "Carriers Shift from Voice and Data Transmission to New High-Bandwidth Services." *Red Herring*, December 4.

Zigmont, Jason. 1999. "Pricing Your Services." *ISP-Planet.com*, June 25. Available online at <http://www.isp-planet.com/business/pricing3a.html>.

Zona Research. 1999. "The Economic Impacts of Unacceptable Web Site Download Speeds." Available online at <http://www.zonaresearch.com/deliverables/white_papers/wp17/>.

Appendixes

A

Broadband Technologies

In the course of its work, the Committee on Broadband Last Mile Technology developed highly detailed material related to various broadband technologies. The committee decided that this level of detail was not appropriate for the main text of its report, but provides the material, which is not intended to be comprehensive, in this appendix for the reader interested in learning more about broadband technologies.

HYBRID FIBER COAX TECHNOLOGY[1]

Coaxial Cable

The foundation upon which hybrid fiber coax (HFC) broadband communications networks are based is coaxial cable (Figure A.1), a radio frequency (RF) transmission line capable of transporting a large number of carriers (channels). At the head end, or central signal-processing center, each carrier is modulated with baseband analog or digital information, and all carriers are multiplexed together in the frequency domain (Figure A.2). Spectral separation is accomplished through the use of frequency-selective diplex filters to allow simultaneous transmission of information in opposite directions (Figure A.3), commonly called "reverse" (i.e., from the home to the head end) and "forward" (from the head end to the

---

[1]Adapted from James Chiddix. 1999. "The Evolution of the U.S. Telecommunications Infrastructure Over the Next Decade. TTG2: Hybrid-Fiber-Coax Technology" (IEEE workshop paper).

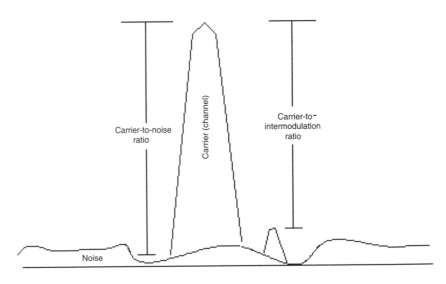

FIGURE A.5   Carrier-to-noise and carrier-to-intermodulation distortion.

nals to every customer within a particular community. This design served the cable industry well, but it did have limitations. The most significant restriction imposed by this topology was the accumulation of noise and distortions (Figure A.5) through the extended cascades of broadband RF amplifiers needed to compensate for transmission losses. This architectural facet affected plant reliability and signal quality at the customer's home. Additionally, for a given design bandwidth, there were practical and theoretical limits to the number of amplifiers that could be cascaded. In order to maintain acceptable performance levels, it was necessary to limit the operational bandwidth of such cable systems to a few hundred megahertz, far below the potential of the cable alone.

Another limitation was imposed by this topology: every customer receives the same complement of signals. This is generally acceptable for TV services, but makes the delivery of individually switched or routed services difficult.

Fiber-Optic Transmission Technology

By the late 1980s, optical lasers were successfully adapted for use in a broadband environment. Optical transmission had been practical for some time through the mechanism of turning the transmitting laser "on" and "off" in synchronization with the ones and zeros of a digital signal. A breakthrough came when it was determined that a laser could be left "on" and intensity-modulated with the highly complex analog signal representing the broadband RF spectrum (Figure A.6).

Lasers used in this way required characteristics different from their digital counterparts. The most critical were very low internal noise and an extremely linear transfer function. Such devices had been in development for the digital market in an effort to achieve higher data-transmission speeds over optical fibers (in contrast to coaxial cable), but further optimization was required for broadband applications.

At the receiving end of an optical link, a relatively simple photodetector was used to convert the optical signals back into an RF spectrum essentially identical to the one presented at the input (transmitting) end. The cable industry quickly adopted this technology for a portion of its transmission plant, and continues to use it as a way to cost-effectively transform coaxial tree-and-branch systems into something much more powerful—hybrid fiber coax (HFC) architecture (Figure A.7). In essence, this approach transforms large systems into highly concentrated collections of smaller systems. This is a very important characteristic, as discussed below.

Current HFC designs are now providing transmission to and from neighborhood clusters of a few hundred homes or fewer (Figure A.8). This arrangement of fiber and coaxial cables allows segmentation of the traditional coax-only transmission plant into many localized areas (called nodes), each of which is capable of providing a unique assortment of information to end users (Figure A.8). The coaxial network that connects to homes from each optical node remains a small version of the original tree-and-branch system (more of a bush than a tree).

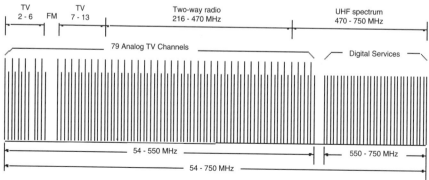

FIGURE A.6   750-MHz forward spectrum.

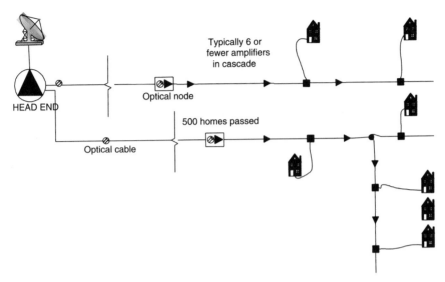

FIGURE A.7   HFC networks allow smaller serving areas.

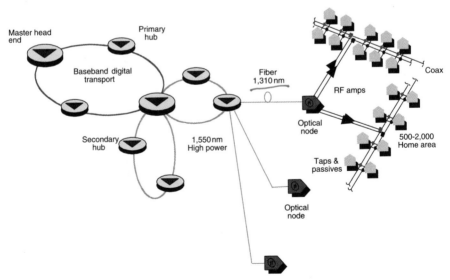

FIGURE A.8   HFC networks allow narrowcasting of content to the customer.

Design Considerations

Current HFC designs call for fiber nodes serving about 500 homes on average, but these nodes can be further segmented into arbitrarily small coaxial serving areas. Figure A.9 illustrates one way that the spectrum available within one node may be used.

The ability to assign and reassign spectrum to different uses is an important benefit of HFC architecture, because it allows for advances in digital services and technologies while continuing to support existing services. Thus, the architecture can simultaneously support many separate virtual networks. This makes the investment to upgrade to HFC a sustainable one for most cable companies. At least some cable operators plan to build as many as five separate (virtual) networks on the foundation of their upgraded fiber transport plant (Figure A.10).

The HFC architecture enables great flexibility to segment the service area. Step-by-step segmentation can match investment with revenues from new, high-bandwidth services; in the extreme case, fiber can be extended to the property lines of homes and businesses (not shown in

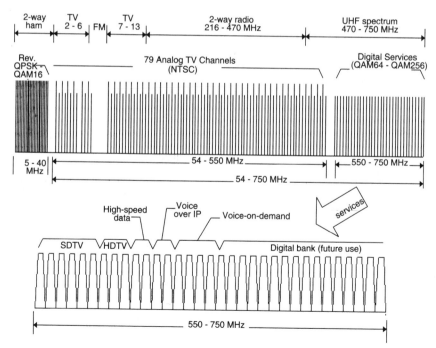

FIGURE A.9   Forward and reverse spectra at node.

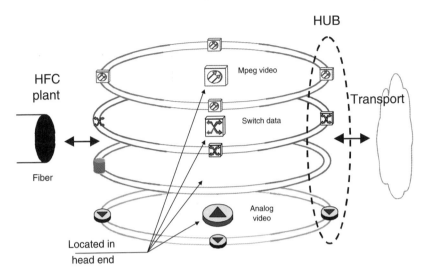

FIGURE A.10   Capability to support multiple networks within HFC.

Figure A.10), or at least to those with the need for services requiring hundreds of megabits per second of connectivity. Only those nodes that have need of greater data capacity (and the potential for greater revenue) have to be divided; the rest can remain undisturbed.

As nodes are divided and fiber is deployed closer to the customer, the total amount of usable bandwidth becomes greater; this makes it possible for every node division to more than double the available data capacity while reducing the number of users who share it.[2] Similarly, breaking a 500-home node into four parts, each passing an average of 125 homes, increases the available reverse and forward capacities significantly more than fourfold and provides more than four times the bandwidth per user.

Trials within the industry have made use of the spectrum from 900 MHz to 1 GHz (as compared with the traditional use of the 5- to 50-MHz region) for reverse signals. Because of reduced RF interference at these higher frequencies and the resulting higher-modulation efficiencies, it is possible to provide an additional 200 Mbps of transmission capability. Again, this number can be multiplied through segmentation, as outlined above.

---

[2]The accompanying reduction in noise over the coaxial portion of the network—in accord with Shannon's law—means that the *usable* bandwidth within each subloop also increases significantly.

It is possible to push these numbers even farther. If very high speed, truly symmetric capacity is required, frequencies above 1 GHz can be used. Some cable plants being constructed today use fiber to feed neighborhoods of 60 homes or fewer with a more-than-commensurate increase in the per-user capacity for both switched and routed digital services.

In 2001, the latest version of the industry standard, DOCSIS 2.0, embraced two optional refinements that can substantially increase upstream throughput by using improved modulation in situations where the noise level permits. One is the use of advanced time-division multiple access (TDMA), which allows modulations up to 256 quadrature amplitude modulation (QAM) in upstream bursts (theoretically 8 bits per hertz, real-world about 6.5), compared with the 16 QAM (4 bits per hertz theoretically) of the current version. The other is synchronous code-division multiple access (CDMA), which permits much more robust transmissions in the presence of certain kinds of interference.

Providing Services in Year 2010

Information and entertainment services can be classified in two broad categories—common and dedicated. Common services include such programming as off-air broadcast, PEG (public, educational, and government) channels, basic networks (such as ESPN and CNN), and subscription services (such as HBO, Cinemax, and Starz). Dedicated services include any number of specialized programs that are delivered to the end user on an individual basis; video-on-demand (VOD) and high-speed Internet access are examples of this type of service.

The cable television (CATV) industry in the United States typically thinks of a channel as being represented by a contiguous 6-MHz portion of the available spectrum—thus, a standard 750-MHz HFC plant has approximately 112 such "channels" within a total usable spectrum of 672 MHz. Table A.1 provides some details regarding a hypothetical 750-MHz HFC plant's ability to provide almost unlimited service options for customers, including the following:

- *Standard analog television.* The cable television industry will probably always carry some amount of NTSC signals, perhaps 20 or so RF channels; but it is anticipated that the number of these signals will decrease as most of them are incorporated into compressed digital formats.
- *Digital standard definition television (SDTV).* This will become the "standard" signal as 256-QAM channels are used to distribute some 200 simultaneous networks (HBO, ESPN, CNN, and so on), including most of the subscription services.

TABLE A.1   Potential Services That a 750-MHz HFC Cable System
Could Provide

Services Provided	Channels and/or Bandwidth Required	Channels Remaining
Common signals		
Standard analog television	20 channels (120 MHz) for NTSC signals	92
Digital SDTV	20 channels (120 MHz) for 200+ programs of compressed digital video format	72
Digital HDTV	10 channels for 20 programs (60 MHz)	62
Dedicated services		
Telephony	1 channel (6 MHz) for 300 DSOs (voice channels)	61
IP data—standard service	20 channels (120 MHz)— 10-Mbps data rates	41
IP data—very high speed	3 channels (18 MHz)— 100-Mbps data rates	38
Video-on-demand	20 channels (120 MHz) for 200+ programs of compressed digital video	18
Future	18 channels, services as needed (108 MHz)	0

• *Digital HDTV.* These networks will be capable of providing adequate bandwidth to support as many as 20 RF channels (each 6 MHz wide) as the transition to broadcast HDTV services continues.

• *Telephony.* More than 300 voice channels can be provided within a typical 6-MHz segment of the spectrum, if needed.

• *IP data services.* This class of service includes voice over IP (VoIP), video telephony over IP (VTIP), streaming video, and high-speed data services. Higher-data-rate services (100 Mbps) can be provided, as needed, for work-at-home or commercial uses.

• *Video-on-demand.* Even with all of the services listed above, enough bandwidth remains to handle VOD applications in both SDTV and HDTV formats.

Security Considerations

Since cable operators have built their plant to provide video and other services, and many of those services are available at lower cost, albeit with lower quality or lacking some other feature, cable operators have had to find ways to secure their services from unauthorized access. The typical solution has been to provide a decoder in the customer's home, then to send commands from a head-end controller to the decoder in order to identify the services for which each subscriber is authorized; this strategy also permits the operator to capitalize on its economies of scale and scope by broadcasting all signals simultaneously over the entire tree-and-branch cable plant.

The deployment of HFC networks has complicated the traditional controller-to-decoder scenario. That is, the network architecture and capacity have both changed, enabling the head-end controller to send a discrete broadband signal—custom-tailored to the consumer's requirements, preferences, or purchases—to each home. In many parts of the network, the signals for all customers may pass over the bus and to the home of each customer, so the set-top box would be employed to cull out for delivery only those signals that are to be received by a specific consumer. When the services are broadcast video programs, there is no interactivity and consequently little need for security beyond the remote scrambling of the video signal. However, when interactivity is a significant portion of the services, the consumer now has access to devices for both receiving and transmitting—particularly with the PC connected to a cable modem connected to the bus network. The potential exists for both intentional and accidental spillage of signals, onto and off of the network.

Conclusion

The existence of ubiquitous, broadband cable television networks in this country affords an opportunity to see the rapid realization of extremely powerful digital networks. The hybrid fiber coax network offers an excellent high-speed data network solution today and combines that with a high degree of scalability to adapt to new technologies or services that may be introduced in the future. The key to the provision of this capacity is the ability to increase the penetration of optical distribution equipment as the need arises. This path to progress will eventually lead to fiber-to-the-curb (FTTC), and even fiber-to-the-home (FTTH). Leading HFC suppliers drive this technology development and deployment in response to the cable operators' customer demand and sustaining revenue sources.

DIGITAL SUBSCRIBER LINE

Introduction

Digital subscriber line (DSL) service provides high-bit-rate digital service over ordinary phone lines, allowing from 100 kbps to tens of megabits per second to reach a telephone company customer. DSL service may implement digital telephone service, fast Internet or other data services, and/or digital video and entertainment services. DSL is the phone company's alternative for broadband access. This section summarizes the basic concept and architectures of DSL service, provides an overview and projection of standards and equipment, and envisions DSL's future and ultimate broadband-access capabilities of telephone companies.

There are 500 million voiceband modems in existence today, most of which are used at speeds to 56 kbps to provide digital connection between various service providers and customers or to transfer data and facsimiles. Voiceband modems are limited in speed because the signals must traverse telephone company switches that allocate only 64 kbps maximum (of which 56 kbps are available) to any voice signal, as shown in Figure A.11. These switches can allow aggregation to higher data rates of several voice channels, but not over a single voice channel through the switch. These digital high-speed data must follow an alternative path through the switch. An additional modem at the telephone company side of the loop differentiates a DSL connection from a voiceband modem connection, as in Figure A.12. DSL's placement of the extra modem at the telecommunications company (telco) switch enables the much higher speeds of DSL to be switched because the switch can now accept that modem's digital output into higher-digital-bandwidth routes through the switch. Thus, the DSL signal returns to digital format when it enters the central office, while the voiceband modem signal is effectively embedded in analog throughout the switch network. The bandwidth of the twisted pair alone is potentially very high, much higher than the 64/56 kbps

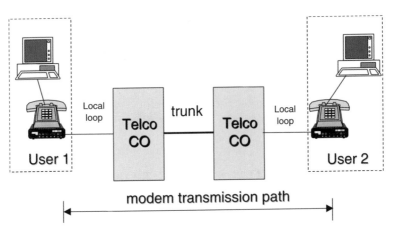

FIGURE A.11   Voiceband modem reference model.

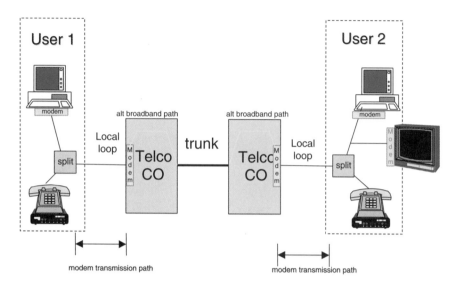

FIGURE A.12   DSL modem reference model.

allowed for digitized voice paths through the switch. However, high digital speed on the copper loop requires sophistication in the design of the DSL modems that attach to the loop. Telephone companies originally did not appreciate the value of their copper asset and considered replacement with fiber or coaxial systems, but release of DSL standards and availability of low-cost DSL equipment have provided phone companies with an opportunity to leverage their existing plant.

Below are summarized some of the technical challenges of the DSL modem and the use of existing phone lines for high-speed digital service, as well as some of the challenges for network design and support of DSL. Generally, higher DSL data rates occur on shorter phone lines. As phone companies can afford the time and money to install fiber into more of their network, copper phone lines reduce in length. Thus, an incremental migration over the next 50 years to fiber, allowing increasing data rates for customers and greater and greater connectivity and information age service, can occur without need for whole-scale network replacement.

Figure A.13 depicts the growth to date in digital transmission speeds on phone lines. Several types of digital transmission on phone lines are shown for comparison. Generally, DSL today often really means ADSL, an asymmetric DSL service that can carry up to 8 Mbps *downstream* from a telephone company central office to a customer and up to 1.5 Mbps back *upstream*. Approximately 1 million ADSL lines are now deployed, and the numbers are growing rapidly as early problems and delays with service

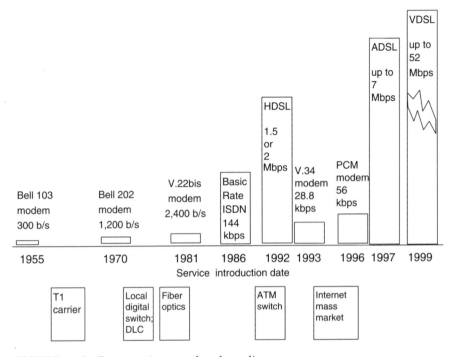

FIGURE A.13   Data rate increase for phone lines.

introduction have begun to abate, and telephone company personnel are increasingly trained and fluent in this new service. In a short time, tens of millions of customers will be connected. ADSL service can now be ordered in nearly one-third of the United States, and telephone companies plan ubiquitous coverage in the near future. VDSL, the latest of the DSLs, can carry up to 60 Mbps on a single phone line and is in early trial and standardization phases. VDSL presumes some use of fiber to shorten phone-line lengths, consistent with eventual migration to fiber by phone companies. These are clearly much faster than voiceband modems. ISDN and high-bit-rate DSL (HDSL), some phone company early DSL alternatives, are also shown in Figure A.13 for perspective. ADSL deployment, though, will soon eclipse the number of ISDN and HDSL circuits in service.

As fiber penetrates and very large scale integrated circuit (VLSI) technology allows yet further sophistication in the design of copper-pair modems, eventually 100 Mbps plus symmetric connection to individual customers is possible with DSL, making it by far the broadband access technology of greatest potential individual bandwidth to the customer.

DSL Standards

To establish a DSL connection, two modems—one owned and operated by a telephone company and the other owned by the customer—must interoperate, thus mandating standardization of the interface. As described in Cioffi et al.,[3] standards committees have charted the course of DSL technology and the architecture for the associated networks. The International Telecommunication Union (ITU) has headquarters in Geneva, Switzerland, and has a major role in standardization. However, the fundamental DSL standards work has largely been conducted in the T1E1.4 committee of the American National Standards Institute (ANSI),[4] the European Telecommunications Standards Institute (ETSI), and the ADSL Forum. The earliest DSL standards, all adopted internationally after minor modification, originated in the American group. These standards groups maintain close cooperation with each other and the ITU. ITU Study Group 15 (SG15) has recently taken the lead in developing an offspring of ADSL called G.lite (also known as Universal ADSL) for consumer-oriented use at bit rates of 1.5 Mbps and below. The G.lite standard was released in 1999 as G.992.2 along with an international version of the ADSL standard called G.dmt (G.992.1). The main difference in the two standards is speed, with G.lite at 1.5 Mbps and G.dmt allowing in excess of 8 Mbps. The industry appears to have turned to use of the latter G.dmt modems at the lower speeds of G.lite with imbedded potential for future speed increase as service providers condition and shorten phone lines. (For more on standards bodies and the relationship of the groups for DSLs, see Chapter 16 in Cioffi et al.[5])

DSL Architectures

There are almost 1 billion phone lines worldwide. The telephone lines are twisted pairs of copper wires, with the twisting invented by A.G. Bell himself, in 1887, along with the phones (1876) to which they are attached.[6]

---

[3]J. Cioffi, T. Starr, and P. Silverman. 1998. *Digital Subscriber Lines.* Prentice-Hall, Upper Saddle River, N.J.

[4]See American National Standard T1.601-1992, "Integrated Services Digital Network (ISDN) – Basic Access Interface for Use on Metallic Loops for Application on the Network Side of the NT (Layer 1 Specification)," 1992, New York, N.Y., and "VDSL System Requirements Report," ANSI Document T1E1.4/98-043R2, June 1998, Huntsville, Ala., Rev 14a. See also ETSI technical specification TS101-270-1 (1998-04), European Telecommunications Standards Institute, Sophia Antipolis, France.

[5]Cioffi et al., *Digital Subscriber Lines*, 1998.

[6]R.B. Bruce. 1973. *A.G. Bell, and the Conquest of Solitude.* Cornell University Press, Ithaca, N.Y.

The phone lines are varied in a great many respects, but the topology of the loop plant of a phone company usually follows that of Figure A.14.

The phone lines are terminated on central office equipment, where the DSL modem can reside. The central office (CO) equipment is connected to phone lines at a main distribution frame (MDF) that essentially allows physical connection ("jumpering") of switch/DSL-modem lines to customer lines—as many as 160,000 of which may enter a single central office. The first segment of the loop plant is typically called the "feeder plant," where hundreds of phone lines may be bundled in a cable that runs to a smaller distribution point, labeled as SAI in Figure A.14. This feeder segment is the first that phone companies upgrade to fiber, with approximately 10 percent of the United States now so upgraded and smaller percentages in other countries. Such fiber is expensive, but the cost of labor, digging, and so on can be shared over a greater number of customers in the feeder segment, making certain upgrades economical. At the distribution point, splicing and connection to smaller cables containing fewer phone lines occurs, and those cables run through the "distribution plant" to pedestals or cabinets within a neighborhood where

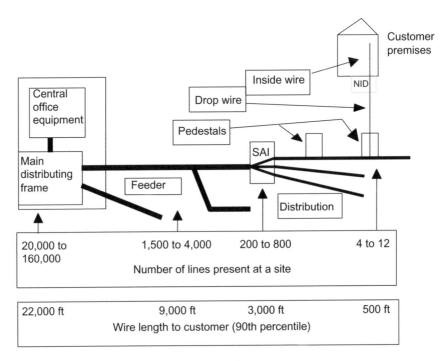

FIGURE A.14   Telephone loop plant topology.

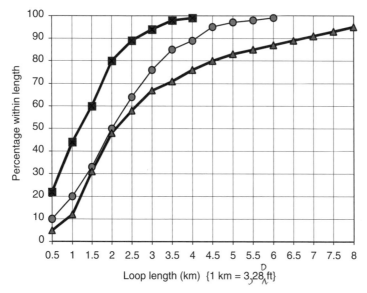

FIGURE A.15 Cumulative loop distribution for Italy (solid squares), the United Kingdom (solid circles), and the United States (solid triangles).

connection to the actual twisted pair in a specific customer site (home or business) occurs. Phone lines may thus be several miles in length. Eventually, fiber can run to the pedestal as demand for high bandwidth becomes very high, and ultimately to the customer's premises as economics allow.

Figure A.15 illustrates the distribution of lengths of twisted pairs for three countries: Italy, the United Kingdom, and the United States. Clearly the United States has the longest loops, simply because its network was deployed the earliest, when phone company practice was to use longer loops. The United Kingdom is intermediate in terms of loop demographics, while countries that lagged the United States by several decades, such as Italy, have the shortest loop demographics. One can thus expect the achievable data rates to be the lowest for DSLs in the United States. Italy, Germany, and Sweden, for instance, are excellent candidates for higher-speed DSL service because a large fraction of their loops are within a kilometer or two of the central office. However, fiber deployment is occurring faster and sooner in the United States in the feeder segment, which will ultimately reverse the relative lengths shown in Figure A.15. For instance, the largest U.S. telephone company, Southwest Bell Corporation, recently announced a $6 billion DSL loop renovation program, known as Project Pronto, that will bring many loops to less than 4 km within a few years. Project Pronto is an example of reversing the trend in Figure A.15. Deregulation and aggressive DSL and Internet use in the United States have motivated SBC to move quickly, unlike international operators who still have far less competition because unbundling deregulation has lagged that of the United States by a few years at least.

Central Office

Figure A.16 illustrates the network architecture of DSL. A DSL access multiplexer (DSLAM) resides at the telephone company side of the twisted pair. A splitter circuit may precede the DSLAM termination so that analog POTS signals can be passively separated from the DSL signals and conveyed to the voice telephone switches. Splitters are 3-port devices that ensure that DSL signals above 30 kHz and POTS signals below 4 kHz are simultaneously passed over the telephone wire without mutual disruption. The DSLAM houses the modem and processes the customer bit streams into larger rate fiber transported data streams that usually use ATM formatting. Various gateway devices can accept the fiber inputs and

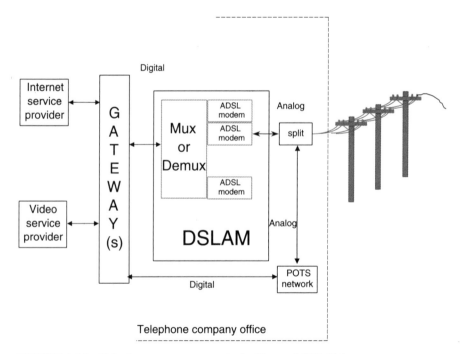

FIGURE A.16   Telephone company central office and DSLAM.

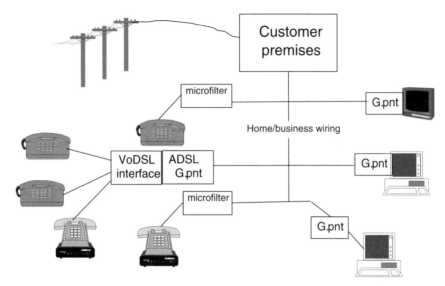

FIGURE A.17   Customer premises (residence or small business) DSL interface.

separate the signals into individual applications' provider networks, such as Internet service providers, video and entertainment providers, or voice service providers. Colocation today involves separate DSLAMs for each service provider. An alternate service provider must be given fair and equal access to the phone lines of the service provider's customers.

Customer Premises

Figure A.17 illustrates the customer premises end of a DSL connection. The customer can be a residential user or a business user. While a splitter can be used at the customer premises also, the cost of installation is often perceived as excessive, and so DSL signals typically enter the customer's premises and terminate on application devices. Existing phones often are augmented by a passive lowpass filter known as a microfilter, which protects the phone from DSL signals and protects DSL from ring-voltage transients that otherwise would be disruptive to DSL service. The DSL modem may be part of a residential or small-business gateway that either connects to another network in the home or redistributes digital signals to all application devices at frequencies above 5 MHz. (ADSL and its latest protégé, very-high-data-rate asymmetric DSL [VADSL or VDSL-lite], exist only below 5 MHz.) The ITU SG15/Q4 group also standardizes this redistribution system, which is known currently as

G.pnt. Customer premises wiring alone can carry huge data rates above 5 MHz, and sophisticated modem design is less necessary because the actual redistributed data rates are well below fundamental limits. However, the DSL signals that traverse the much longer path from central office to customer need a high degree of sophistication to achieve the data rates desired in DSL.

DSL Transmission Environment

The DSL transmission environment is challenging, and should not be underestimated. This challenge was the first that had to be addressed in developing an opportunity for DSL. In fact, in the early days of DSL, there was little phone company support or interest because it was believed that this challenge would be insurmountable. Fortunately, an initially small (but now very large) group of transmission experts worked together through standards groups to derive practical, high-speed DSL modems. Challenges continue for yet further increases in DSL speed and capability. This section discusses the salient characteristics of telephone lines for digital transmission, with the intent of conveying the difficulty of the transmission problem for DSLs.

The journey of a bit over a phone line is analogous to a long, arduous trip with several borders to cross, potentially dangerous trip segments, with various difficulties and costumes imposed upon the traveler, potentially disguising that person's appearance to all but those who know well how to recognize the traveler at the destination. Only the best prepared travelers (bits) can successfully complete the journey, if the receiver also knows well how and what to look for. The shorter the journey, the more successful travelers/bits conveyed to the final destination. Phone lines typically comprise several segments of wire, characterized by gauges (19, 22, 24, or 26 in the United States and equivalent 0.8-, 0.6-, 0.5-, and 0.4-millimeter [mm] diameters in the metric system internationally). The higher the gauge, or more narrow the wire, the more arduous the journey. At the borders between phone line segments, some energy is reflected, meaning that a bit may be harder to recognize as a 1 or 0 by the time it reaches its destination. This energy loss may be equated to an aggressive customs officer confiscating some identifying documents from the traveler. Some bit energy may also be diverted to unused open-circuited phone branches (for extension phones or extension phone jacks), further marring the appearance of the bit; these branches are known as bridged-taps. The effect of bridged-taps is analogous to unnecessary dead-end side trips by a traveler to a port that the traveler did not know was closed, but draining their energy with the wasted round trip, making the exhausted traveler yet more difficult to recognize. Some standardized phone line characteristics and behavior appear in the subsection on loop-transfer characteristics.

Phone lines endure a lot of noise, which obscures or disguises the bit. The noise is typically electromagnetically coupled into phone lines. The external sources of energy that contribute to noise can include signals on other phone lines (known as crosstalk), radio, and ham broadcasts, and virtually any type of electrical or mechanical equipment within close proxmity to the phone line. Such noise can be severely disguising, and transmitted bits need to be adequately prepared to avert complete loss of identity if they are to negotiate their journey successfully. The subsection entitled "Sources of Noise in DSL Systems" below, overviews several types of noises.

The energy from a bit may also radiate from a phone line, potentially disturbing radios within the vicinity of any portion of the phone line. This is analogous to a boisterous traveler upsetting all the other travelers, thus running the risk of retribution of some sort. The subsection below entitled "Emission Constraints and PSD Masks" describes this problem and the level of concern.

Characterization of Twisted-Pair Telephone Lines

Chapter 4 of Cioffi et al.[7] details the calculation of the frequency-response of phone lines, which are often described by their "insertion loss." The insertion loss is measured in decibels (10 times the base-10-logarithm) of the ratio of the power injected into a phone line at any given frequency to the power emanating at the end of the phone line at that same frequency. The injected power may be measured without the phone line present, and then measured again after the phone line is "inserted," whence the name "insertion loss." Some insertion loss plots versus frequency for American standardized 3- and 4-mile phone lines appear in Figure A.18. These loops were chosen by ANSI to represent the top 10 percent of worst-case lines in the United States. Loops 1-4 in the left plot represent simple gauge changes. The usable bandwidth over the lines, where signals are still distinguishable from noise, may extend to about 600 kHz. Note the large range from as high as –20 dB to –100 dB in insertion loss for usable frequencies. This means that the largest signals on the line may be 100 million times more powerful than the smallest signals of interest. By contrast, voiceband modems see a range of only a factor of 100, making DSL transmission a million times more sensitive!

---

[7]Cioffi et al., *Digital Subscriber Lines*, 1998.

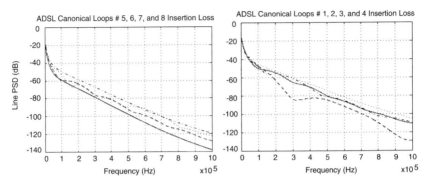

FIGURE A.18   ANSI loops 1-4 (at the left) and 5-8 (at the right), insertion loss.

Loops 5-8 on the right have bridged-taps. Notice the rippling of the insertion loss, corresponding to signal energy reflecting from the open-circuited extensions and returning later in time to the main line to add to the current signals there. At some frequencies, the reflected signals are 180 degrees out of phase and destroy the current signals, corresponding to the dips. At other frequencies, energies add, essentially returning the signal closer to its original unreflected signal level. (A good discussion of bridged-tap and other effects appears in an article by J.J. Werner.[8])

Figure A.19 shows insertion loss characteristics of some shorter standardized loops,[9] indicative of what might be used with VDSL over a yet wider bandwidth of 30 MHz. The left plot shows insertion loss for 300-m and 500-m loops of 26-gauge (TP1) and 24-gauge (TP2) wire, respectively. As the length increases, the slope also increases. On the right, a short loop VDSL5 with a bridged-tap has very noticeable rippling, but otherwise is similar in slope to the insertion loss characteristics on the left. As the length is increased to 1 km and then to about 1.5 km for VDSL6 and VDSL7, respectively, the insertion loss decays much more rapidly with frequency and still exhibits significant rippling because of the bridged-taps. The same large dynamic range (now because a greater range of frequencies is used at shorter lengths) is again evident for VDSL.

The bridged-tap in VDSL5, 6, and 7 is 10 meters in length, a reasonable and typical number. Thus, the notches are an often-encountered phenomena.

---

[8]Werner, J.J. 1991. "The HDSL Environment." *IEEE Journal on Selected Areas in Communication* 9(6):785-800, August.

[9]"VDSL System Requirements Report," ANSI Document T1E1.4/98-043R2, June 1998, Huntsville, Ala., Rev. 14a. See also ETSI technical specification TS101-270-1 (1998-04), European Telecommunication Standards Institute, Sophia Antipolis, France.

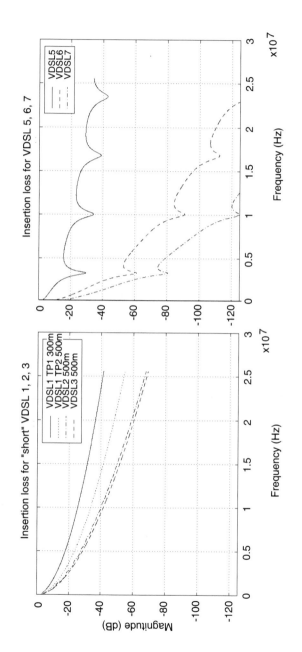

FIGURE A.19   Shorter loops for VDSL systems (TP1 = 26 gauge and TP2 = 24 gauge).

Sources of Noise in DSL Systems

Noise on a twisted-pair transmission system arises from three mechanisms:

1. The thermal noise of the twisted pair itself,
2. The noise generated internally by the receiving modem, and
3. Signals electromagnetically coupled into the phone line.

Thermal or actual medium noise on a twisted pair is extremely small, near the Boltzman limit of –174 decibels per millihertz (db/mHz) at room temperature, and essentially can be ignored. The noise generated by terminating equipment depends on the design of the receiver electronics. Standards groups often suggest that this noise level should be about –140 dBm/Hz,[10] but well-designed modems often generate less, to as low as –160 dBm/Hz. This noise is usually flat in spectrum (i.e., "white") and determines the ultimate frequency limits of a DSL. The insertion loss of a DSL, as discussed above, and the transmit power-spectral density in dBm/Hz determine the line output power-spectral density (PSD). For instance, an ADSL system transmitting at the maximum PSD of –40 dBm/Hz can tolerate up to about 85 to 90 dB of insertion loss before resulting in a channel output PSD of –125 to –130 dBm/Hz, 10 dB above –140 dBm/Hz (10-dB signal-to-noise ratio) necessary for adequate detection even in well-coded and designed DSLs). Thus if –140 dBm/Hz is the receiver noise floor, then a DSL using one of the lines on the right in Figure A.19 would use bandwidths of up to 600 to 700 kHz. ADSL systems actually allow use of bandwidths up to 1,104 kHz, which would thus occur on lines that are shorter than those displayed in Figure A.19, thus having less insertion loss at 1 MHz.

Electromagnetically coupled noise occurs because the twisted pair is often bathed in radiation from a number of electronic sources. The twisted pair has imperfections that cause this radiation to induce noise voltages into the differential signal carried between the two wires of a twisted pair. Figure A.20 shows the twisting of a twisted pair and the opposite spatial polarity of the voltage at adjacent twists. Theoretically, this twisting introduced by A.G. Bell himself in his 1887 patent should almost cause cancelation of induced voltages. This is because impinging radiation would have different polarities in the adjacent segments and thus cancel itself, the reason for the twisting. Of course, the twisting is never perfect, nor is the cancelation, but twisting is better than no twisting. Many phone cus-

---

[10]American National Standard T1.413-1995, "ADSL Metallic Interface Specification," 1995, New York, NY. Please see Issue 2, if available, T1.413-1999.

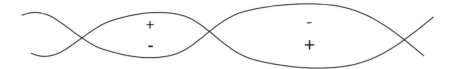

FIGURE A.20   Twisted-pair voltage polarities.

tomers are familiar with the "flat pair" they purchase for extending phone lines within their home. This wire is not twisted, and is much more susceptible to noise pickup; nonetheless, fortunately, this flat pair represents only a small segment of the total length of the phone line. Category 3 twisted pair, typically used by phone companies, has a few twists per inch. Category 5 twisted pair is a higher grade, with tighter twisting and about 100 times better rejection of noise. Category 5 twisted pair finds increasing use in new buildings (which almost always still use twisted-pair wiring) and in local area network connection. Flat pair is, of course, the worst for noise pickup.

Crosstalk Noise

Figure A.21 illustrates crosstalk noise, which is the noise produced by signals on other phone lines. As discussed above, several phone lines share the same cable. Typically, 25 to 50 twisted pairs are wrapped tightly in a binder group. Different twisted pairs within the binder group have different numbers of twists per inch (to prevent radiation patterns from exactly matching and offsetting the twisting pattern on other twisted

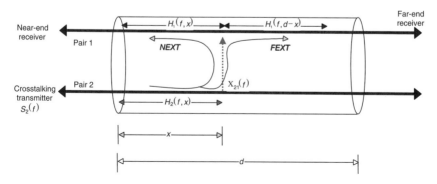

FIGURE A.21   Crosstalk illustration.

pairs), and there is some level of rejection caused by twisting. Nonetheless, a signal launched from a near-end transmitter on the right in Figure A.21 will enter the cable and begin to couple into the reverse direction on another twisted pair. This type of opposite-direction crosstalk-noise coupling is known as NEXT, or Near-End CROSSTalk. When the insertion loss of the segment of wire between the coupling point in both directions is considered and the noise problem integrated over the total length of wire, basic physics leads to the standardized crosstalk coupling function for DSLs of

$$PSD_{NEXT}(f) = \left[\frac{N}{49}\right]^6 \cdot 10^{-13} \cdot f^{1.5} \cdot PSD_{near-end,xmit}(f), \tag{1}$$

which not coincidentally increases with the 1.5 power of frequency matching the decrease in balance of the twisted pair as frequency increases. The factor of N represents the number of twisted pairs in the binder expected to carry crosstalking signals. This type of noise often dominates receiver noise when it exists. For instance, the PSDs of several DSL signals appear in Figure A.22, where it is clear that the PSD often exceeds −140 dBm/Hz, especially over the frequency range of operation of the offending DSL.

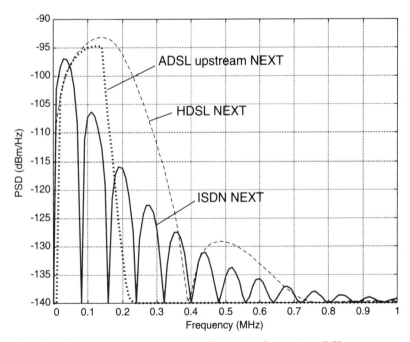

FIGURE A.22   Some worst-case crosstalk spectra for various DSL types.

The reader should note that while the crosstalk coupling increases with frequency, the noises plotted in Figure A.22 combine the coupling with the transmit power spectral of each of the signals, and if there is no signal at higher frequencies, then there is no crosstalk. The actual crosstalk into an individual twisted pair from one of its neighbors is not as bad as the model at all frequencies. Clearly the coupling is heavily frequency dependent and only at worst case exhibits the behavior of the standards model above in Equation (1). Nonetheless, this model is heavily used for conservative DSL design.

Also in Figure A.21 is the coupling of signals from one phone line to another in the same direction, which is often called FEXT, for Far-End CROSSTalk. An exercise similar to the one for NEXT finds a standardized FEXT coupling function of

$$PSD_{FEXT}(f) = \left[\frac{N}{49}\right]^{.6} \cdot 9 \times 10^{-20} \cdot d \cdot f^2 \cdot |H(f,d)|^2 \cdot PSD_{xmit}(f), \qquad (2)$$

where d is the length of the line in feet and H is the insertion loss of the twisted pair. The FEXT model is similarly pessimistic and does not include the highly frequency-dependent nature of real crosstalk when only one or at best a few other lines interfere in any given frequency band. The level of FEXT is usually well below NEXT and even below −140 dBm/Hz often, but at higher frequencies above 500 kHz begins to become significant and indeed dominant at yet higher frequencies because of the dependency on the square of the frequency. FEXT is usually of strong concern only in VDSL.

Radio Noise

As Figure A.23 implies, telephone lines are great radio receivers, especially for AM radio broadcasts. Indeed, AM radio signals are delivered to customers on phone lines in some countries (e.g., Switzerland). AM radio signals exist in the internationally recognized band from 560 kHz to 1,600 kHz. The double-sideband-with-carrier-modulated AM signals are 10 kHz wide and likely to have PSD levels of −100 to −120 dBm/Hz on phone lines, comparable to crosstalk signals and much larger than internal modem noises. It is common, if not the norm, to see 2 or 3 large AM radio signals on a phone line in the metropolitan area of any city. Thus, only a small percentage of the transmit band is disturbed, but in those bands, the disturbance cannot be ignored. The problem is particularly evident on elevated phone lines (telephone poles), but not insignificant even on buried phone lines.

AM radio interference is of concern for both ADSL and VDSL but does not overlap the transmission bands for high-bit-rate DSL (HDSL) or ISDN.

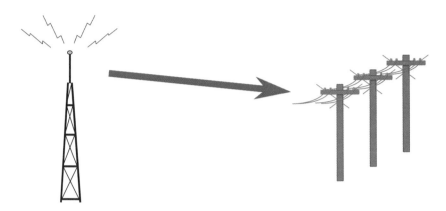

FIGURE A.23   Radio interference.

Ham radio signals are an even greater problem. While smaller power is transmitted by ham radio operators, the ham antennae are distributed massively through residential environments, often being only 10 to 100m away from a phone line. The level of interference is sometimes as large as –35 dBm/Hz, and typically on the order of –50 to –60 dBm/Hz, well above the levels of any other noise type. Fortunately, ham radio signals are typically only 2.5 kHz wide, and there may likely only be one of them when such interference occurs. Ham radio signals may be transmitted in internationally recognized narrowbands from 1.8 to 2 MHz, 3.5 to 4 MHz, 7 to 7.1 MHz, 10.1 to 10.15 MHz, 14 to 14.35 MHz, and 18.068 to 18.168 MHz that overlap VDSL transmission, but not other DSLs.

Impulse Noise

Impulse noise is nonstationary crosstalk from temporary electromagnetic events in the vicinity of phone lines. Examples of impulse generators are as diverse as the opening of a refrigerator door (the motor turns on/off), control voltages to elevators (phone lines in apartment buildings often run through the elevator shafts), and ringing of phones on lines sharing the same binder. Each of these effects is temporary and results in injection of noise into the phone line through the same basic mechanism as RF noise ingress, but typically at much lower frequencies.

Differential (metallic) induced voltages are typically a few millivolts (mV) but can be as high as 100 mV, corresponding to levels of –50 to –70 dBm/Hz. Typical impulses last tens to hundreds of microseconds (µs) but can span time intervals as long as 3 µs.

Emission Constraints and PSD Masks

DSLs need not only be concerned with noises generated by other electronic signals, but also with the radiation they create. The concern for such emission exceeds that normally associated with electronic equipment, where the FCC (in the United States) mandates certain maximum levels of radiation in various frequency bands. In the case of DSL modems, the telephone line itself, while not inside the modem, does radiate, and so this type of radiation is typically limited by limiting the power spectral density of signals transmitted on phone lines.

Unbundling and Standards Solutions

The American National Standards Institute's T1E1.4 group has taken a lead role in discerning problems with crosstalk between various types of DSLs, standardized and nonstandard. The idea is that if all services comply with defined spectrum masks, coexistence of different service providers' equipment in the same cable of twisted pairs is possible without the transmission technique itself having to be standardized. A voluntary ANSI spectrum management standard was issued in 2001 and offered to the FCC for possible use in future rulemaking.

Evolution Possibilities for DSL Technology

An enabling event for DSL transmission at high speeds occurred on March 10, 1993,[11] when ANSI selected the discrete multitone transmission (DMT) technology for ADSL. The technology offered greater adaptivity than previous conventional technologies for transmission. The essential ingredient was an ability of the receiver and transmitter to communicate through a low-speed overhead back-channel that allowed the transmitter's DSL spectrum and information content to adjust to each and every phone line in an individually optimized manner. The technology outperformed even the best-optimized nonadaptive methods in several independent tests (sometimes showing more than a thousandfold improvement in noise immunity), and was selected. While early modems were expensive, the standards groups successfully bet on VLSI improvements eventually making most of the gains of the DMT technology cost-effective, which has now happened, and DMT is the basis of all ADSL standards, including the recently released ITU standards "G.lite" (G.992.2) and "G.dmt DSL" (G.992.1). The additional benefit of standardization allowed economies of

---

[11]Curiously, the 100th anniversary of the invention of the telephone.

competition, as multiple suppliers are assured of interoperable products through the use of and adherence to standards.

Good DMT designs gain outstanding performance on telephone lines, and this section enumerates both present performance levels and future performance levels. This particular technology will allow a number of solutions to the unbundling and crosstalk problems mentioned above; these solutions have yet to be implemented but are simulated here to allow an understanding of future research directions in this DSL area.

As phone companies increasingly deploy fiber, telephone line lengths become shorter. It is thus of interest to know the possible data rates versus line length. Three such plots are presented in the following subsections. In each, the current state-of-the-art methods are plotted, as well as a number of potential enhancements that researchers have suggested will further DSL performance.

ADSL and Projections

Figure A.24 lists the first set of curves for DMT ADSL. The vertical axis plots data rate, while the horizontal axis plots line length in feet. As line length increases, all data rates decrease. The lowest curve shown is the performance of a good design that meets current ADSL standardized performance levels. Most current ADSL modems will not allow more than 10 Mbps maximum speed, which occurs at about 2,000 feet in the lowest curve. At about 3 miles, 1.5-Mbps speed is attainable, while a few hundred kilobits per second are possible beyond that range. ADSL uses only the lower 1.1 MHz of bandwidth on a twisted pair.

A first step in improving these curves is to allow the modems to use sophisticated multiuser information-theory-based detection methods to eliminate crosstalk effects between lines. The next two curves eliminate NEXT and NEXT/FEXT, respectively. Note that when crosstalk is removed, a huge jump in data rate is attained—by a factor of about 3. Suddenly, 10 Mbps is possible even to a 2-mile range. A 2-mile range is a target of projects such as SBC's Project Pronto. The so-called bit-cap is related to ADC (analog-to-digital converter) performance levels, and with improvements in such technology beyond today's state-of-the-art conversion devices, additional improvement is possible. Finally, a last curve shows the improvement in performance with some of the most powerful coding methods yet found (i.e., turbo codes).

VADSL and VDSL Projections

Figure A.25 lists the first set of curves for what is known recently as DMT VADSL. This extension of ADSL allows up to 5 MHz of bandwidth

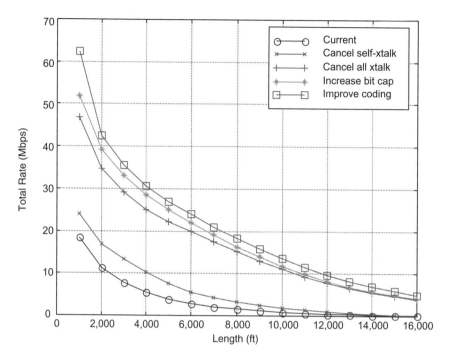

FIGURE A.24   Current ADSL and projections.

to be used on a twisted pair, which allows considerably higher data rates on shorter lines.

Data rates jump on lines of a few thousand feet, with 20 Mbps plus possible on 3,000-ft lines (which characterize the second of the fiber termination points—the so-called distribution node) with current methods. Again, with use of more sophisticated methods, another doubling in the data rate is feasible.

Figure A.26 is for so-called VDSL, which uses up to 20 MHz of bandwidth on a twisted pair. Here, data rates on 1,000-ft loops, so-called pedestal drops, can exceed 250 Mbps with all possible and/or known improvements included. A last curve, "Ultra DSL," allows an increase of transmit power to 400 milliwatts, perceived as an analog limit for phone lines with VDSL parameters.

Network and Application Interfaces for DSL

As discussed in the introduction to the major section "Digital Subscriber Line," DSL technologies are able to achieve their high bandwidths

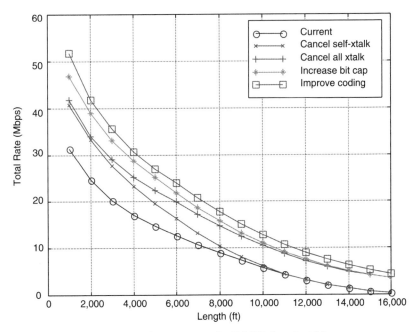

FIGURE A.25   VADSL and projections for 5 MHz bandwidth use.

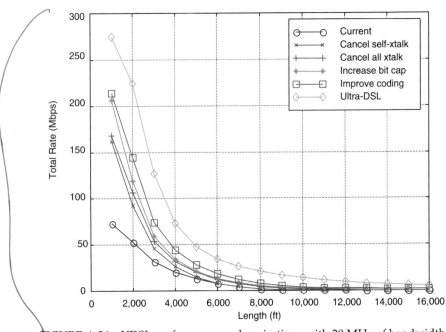

FIGURE A.26   VDSL performance and projections with 20 MHz of bandwidth.

over the copper loop because they avoid the existing telephony network of switches and transmission channels optimized for voice traffic. In a sense, the existing non-DSL modem technology "creatively abuses" the physical path that is established from point to point for carrying voice traffic by placing the data on a path designed to carry voice. This has the advantage of allowing for worldwide switched connectivity of data. However, it also limits the bandwidth of the connection to, at most, 64 kbps. This is the rate supported by the digital voice channels within and between the switches of the worldwide transmission network.

Providing a DSL-based physical path on a copper loop will allow a user to transmit at high data rates over that loop. However, DSL will get the data only to the end of the copper in the central office. To reach destinations desired by the DSL user, a high-bandwidth data network must be provided from the CO to these remote sites. Telecommunications carriers thus face new problems in constructing and managing a network that is intimately involved in data networking issues.

In the current environment, they need only provide the physical-layer connectivity (using either the switched network or a private dedicated line for higher-bandwidth connections). They are isolated from the details of their users' data networks. In the case of the voice network, it is as if the telco provides trains from place to place and does not care what type of car is placed on the trains or what is in the boxcars. In providing DSL services, the telephone companies must provide a network that interacts directly with their users' networks and protocols. The telco now needs not only to operate the tracks and trains but also to provide boxcars, tank cars, and transshipment between trains, ships, and planes.

The carrier needs to address the following issues if it is to provide DSL services to its customers:

- It must provide a data network connecting the ADSL terminated copper loops to the service providers desired by customers. Examples of service providers include the public Internet, private corporate networks, interactive video services, or highly interactive games.
- It must provide cost-effective interfaces between its network and the service providers.
- The data protocols that connect the customer to service providers over the ADSL network must be compatible with existing technologies and procedures used by both customers and service providers and must also support the high-bandwidth services provided by ADSL.
- The carrier must develop methods to manage this new network. The carrier must be able to add new customers, repair problems, and bill for the services provided.

Although there are many potential implementations that can address these issues, a discussion of two contrasting environments and potential solutions can illustrate the current direction of ADSL end-to-end architectures:

1. The large common carrier environment in which a telecommunications provider offers services to masses of customers and supports many different service providers;
2. Use of DSL in very specialized environments such as college campuses, military bases, or condominium apartments.

The Large Common Carrier

A large local exchange telephone company may support more than 2 million telephone lines in a major metropolitan area. Even a 10 percent penetration of ADSL results in 200,000 ADSL customers in the area. For both regulatory and business reasons, the carrier will need to provide common-carrier access between users and any service provider who pays to connect to the access network. A user of the ADSL service may wish to connect to any service provider it chooses. Simultaneous connections from a user to multiple service providers are likely to be required. Other users may connect to only one service provider but require that the connection be physically secure. For example, a remote office might use the ADSL service to connect to a central corporate LAN.

Although large-scale ADSL service has yet to be deployed by any carrier, many carriers are converging toward a common architecture. Each central office is served by one or more DSLAMs,[12] which terminate the ADSL line in the central office. POTS voice traffic is also carried on each loop. Splitters groom the POTS traffic, carried at frequencies below 4 kHz, before the loop is terminated on a port on the DSLAM. The POTS traffic is placed on a voice switch in the carrier's legacy voice network.

The ADSL connection only provides a physical layer between the customer's ADSL modem and the modem in the CO within the DSLAM. In this architecture, ATM provides a data link layer end-to-end between the users' computing environment and the service provider's network. An ATM virtual circuit is established between the user's ADSL modem and the interface between the carrier's ATM network and the service provider's network.

---

[12]DSLAM is an acronym for Digital Subscriber Line Access Multiplexer. The term is now never translated but has become a generic term for CO-based devices that terminate DSL loops.

The DSLAM in the CO terminates many ADSL lines (typically in the range of 200 to 600 ADSL ports per DSLAM) and concentrates the traffic to and from the customers over DS3 (48-Mbps) or OC3 (155-Mbps) trunks that connect to ATM switches in the carrier's ATM data network. The service providers are also connected to the carrier's ATM network via similar high-speed trunks. The use of ATM allows for scalability of the service to support hundreds of thousands of users in a metropolitan area and a wide range of potential future ADSL services.

If the service provider and customer communicate using IP, the use of PPP (point-to-point protocol) over ATM, as defined in Kwok et al.,[13] will allow both the user and the service provider to operate in an environment that is similar to that provided by dial-up modems today. In that environment, the IP is placed in PPP that is carried over the voice network between the users' and service providers' modems. By using PPP over ATM, the carrier can isolate both the service provider and user from the complexities of both ADSL and ATM.

The Specialized Carrier

In contrast to the large public carrier, many specialized deployments of ADSL are possible. Any organization that has access to copper loop can deploy ADSL. For example, the owner of a large rental apartment building may install an ADSL service to provide high-speed Internet access to the tenants. A competitive local exchange carrier (CLEC) can, under the terms of the Telecommunications Act of 1996, lease copper loops from the incumbent phone company (the incumbent local exchange carrier, or ILEC) and serve customers with ADSL.

The largest CLECs may end up resembling ILECs in both scale and architecture of their ADSL services. However, in many cases the deployment will be small and will have similar requirements to the small ADSL implementation in the apartment building. Other examples of small ADSL deployments could include college campuses (which typically own their own copper loop plant), hotels, or military bases.

The requirements for these "niche" deployments of ADSL include these: small scale, that is, from 100 to 1,000 users total; limited need to support multiple providers; and the service provider and carrier may be identical. In the case of an ADSL-equipped apartment building, the customers are connected directly to the ISP contracted to provide service to

---

[13]Timothy Kwok et al. 1997. "An Interoperable End-to-End Broadband Service Architecture over ADSL Systems (Version 3.0)," ADSL Forum Contribution 97-215.

the building. In the case of a CLEC, the CLEC may itself be an ISP. In the case of a campus, the users will be connected directly to the university or company's data network.

The DSLAM containing the ATU-Cs is either in close proximity to or integrated with an IP router. The router is connected directly to the IP network of the ISP or corporate network. It is managed as an integral part of that network. The ADSL connections to the user support IP over HDLC directly on the ADSL physical layer.[14] The ADSL user appears as host directly on the service provider's IP network.

WIRELESS

Introduction

Broadband wireless access is frequently mentioned as an important alternative to wired technologies, namely, to DSL, cable, and fiber. Wireless has always played an important role in telecommunications networks because of its inherent advantages of modest infrastructure investment (no wires!), rapid service deployment, and end-user mobility support. The strategic significance of wireless communication services has increased over the past decade as cellular-telephony subscriber growth continues to outpace all earlier projections. It is now clear that wireless will continue to play an important role in emerging telecommunications services, including narrowband data and broadband services because of the same intrinsic advantages. For both Internet and broadband services, wireless services have experienced a larger-than-expected gestation period owing to a combination of factors such as technology cost and performance problems, spectrum regulation barriers, and weak standards. However, wireless data and broadband Internet services seem poised for technical and market breakthroughs over the next 3 to 5 years, and should thus provide an important alternative for facilitation of broadband services in the United States and other parts of the world.

Service Concept

The concept of a wireless broadband access network is shown in Figure A.27. The basic idea is to provide a high-speed wireless link between subscriber devices such as PCs, Internet appliances, PDAs, and new per-

---

[14]ADSL Forum. 1997. *Framing and Encapsulation Standards for ADSL: Packet Mode.* ADSL Forum Technical Recommendation-003, June.

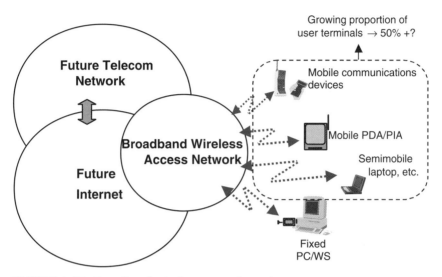

FIGURE A.27   Broadband wireless network service concept.

sonal multimedia devices (both fixed and mobile). It is expected that initial applications of broadband wireless access will start with fixed devices such as home PCs connecting to an ISP, with a gradual migration toward mobile applications as end-user devices become more and more portable. Thus, the initial impetus for wireless access comes from the need to rapidly deploy networks capable of supporting high-speed Internet access. With increasing investment in next-generation wired networks, it may be expected that (at least in developed countries), the focus for wireless systems will shift toward semimobile or mobile services, given that an increasing percentage of computing platforms will become inherently portable. It is noted that the wireless access network shown in Figure A.27 may be expected to interface with both the future public telephony network and the Internet, which are themselves experiencing some degree of convergence as they migrate toward broadband services. This means that wireless access networks for future broadband systems are likely to be architecturally aligned with protocols used in fixed networks, rather than being designed as custom overlay solutions (as is the case with today's cellular networks). In the long term, this may be expected to drive convergence between fixed and wireless networks further, where the same service is offered to both wired and wireless devices in a seamless manner.

Technology Overview

As mentioned above, adoption of wireless data services has been inhibited by a rather slow improvement in wireless technology cost and performance during the past decade or so. The previous generation of wireless data technologies (including cellular modems, wide-area data, satellite data, and wireless LANs) fell far behind Moore's law improvements experienced by most computing and telecommunications technologies. While wireless does pose important technical challenges, there appears to be no fundamental reason for this discrepancy, which was probably caused by insufficient R&D and/or venture funding needed to drive this area. The situation has been largely corrected during the last 2 or 3 years, during which various new broadband wireless technologies have emerged as competitive options to wired solutions. This is illustrated in Figure A.28, which shows the evolution of wireless technology performance over the last decade. As shown in the figure, newer commercial or precommercial wireless technologies have reached the Mbps+ bitrate levels necessary for viable broadband services, either fixed or mobile.

Figure A.29 shows the typical bit-rate and mobility regimes for various broadband wireless networks currently under consideration. The figure shows the relative roles of fixed wireless access, high-speed wireless LAN, semimobile broadband PCS, and wideband cellular (IMT-2000). Although these services are generally viewed as distinct (and may be worked on by different technical and business communities), changes in technology are likely to result in new service models that merge one or more of the existing categories. In the United States, broadband wireless services are likely to start out with fixed access to residences and gradually evolve towards portability and mobility. The reverse is likely to happen in Europe and Japan, where so-called 3G mobile services are expected to appear on the market within the next few years, and may later be applied to broadband wireless local loop (WLL) scenarios.

The generic architecture of a broadband wireless network consists of the following major components: radio modem (physical layer), radio link protocol (RLP), and fixed infrastructure network with capabilities for supporting wireless/mobile services. The following subsections summarize key technology issues related to each of these major subsystems.

Physical Layer

Broadband wireless networks require physical-layer bit rates that are orders of magnitude higher than those for current digital cellular or WLL systems, i.e., 10 to 100 Mbps versus the current 10 to 100 kbps. The higher bit rates must be achieved without introducing line-of-sight (LOS) con-

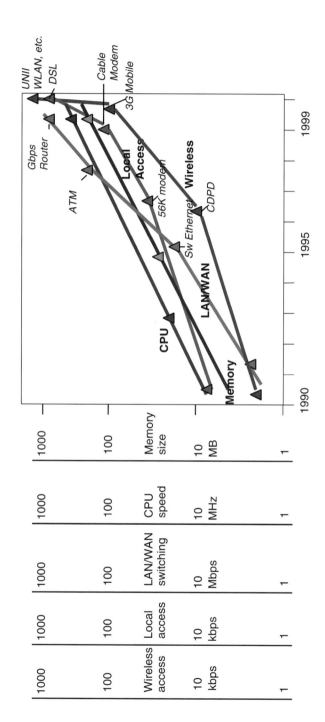

FIGURE A.28 Evolution of wireless technology performance, 1990-1999.

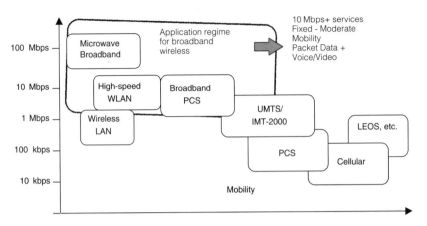

FIGURE A.29   Broadband wireless service scenarios in terms of mobility versus bit rate.

straints, thus indicating a need for robust modulation techniques that work well for non-LOS channels with fading. At the same time, spectrum limitations imply the need for significantly higher spectrum usage efficiency (bps/Hz/unit area), that is, 5 to 10 bps/Hz/cell versus the current 0.5 to 1 bps/Hz/cell. Clearly, if broadband wireless services are to reach significant penetration, cell sizes will have to be relatively small (~1- to 5-km radius), capable of providing, say, 100 Mbps to 1 Gbps of data throughput per square kilometer for frequency allocations of a few hundred megahertz.

The above order-of-magnitude improvements can indeed be achieved via a combination of technology improvements, including these:

• *High-speed (Mbps+) radio modems based on advanced signal-processing techniques, such as equalization, spread spectrum, multicarrier modulation, spatial processing, and smart antennas.* Examples include equalized QAM, used in several first-generation fixed wireless systems; equalized VSB in the U.S. terrestrial HDTV standard; wideband direct-sequence CDMA, under consideration for the 3G mobile (IMT-2000) standard; and OFDM, proposed for various fixed and semimobile scenarios (including ETSI Hiperlan II and several proprietary WLL systems, such as Clarity Wireless/Cisco). Spatial processing with multiple antennas, mentioned above, is a new dimension for improving modem performance, and has recently been proposed by several independent groups (Bell Labs, Stanford University, Iospan) as a means for dramatically improving both non-LOS coverage and spectral efficiency. All of these technologies are maturing rapidly, and it may be expected that commercial products will soon deliver 10 Mps+ services with cellular reuse and spectral efficiency on the order of 5 bps/Hz/sector. With continuing advances in signal processing, achievable bit rates should increase to 100 Mbps+ with spectral efficiency of 10 bps/Hz over the next 5 years.

 • *Cellular technology capable of scaling to small cells and multiple sectors necessary for effective coverage of areas with higher population density.* Scaling of broadband wireless services to small cells is inevitable in areas with higher population density, where throughputs on the order of 100 Mbps to 1 Gbps/km² must be achieved in order to serve even a modest fraction of the population. Efficient cellular reuse implies the need for modem technology that can operate at relatively low carrier-to-interference (C/I) ratios. This can be achieved by a suitable combination of time/frequency/ space processing. For example, spread spectrum achieves high spatial reuse via time-frequency processing, while multiple antenna spatial processing OFDM modems do so using frequency-space processing. Wideband CDMA adopted for IMT-2000 radio access achieves a spatial reuse factor of 1:1 using spread spectrum and interference cancellation techniques. However, net throughput per square kilometer is limited by the relatively low ~0.5-bps/Hz efficiency of spread spectrum modulation. Spatial processing techniques mentioned earlier have the potential for achieving spectral efficiencies on the order of 5 to 10 bps/Hz/cell with ~1:3 spatial reuse. Further gains can be achieved for both CDMA and spatial processing OFDM with directional remote antennas and base station sectorization.

 • *Spectrum regulation and management policies that facilitate rapid deployment of broadband services, while promoting efficient use.* The pace of wireless network deployment is critically dependent on spectrum regulation policies, both international and domestic. Historically, the process of frequency allocation has been rather slow, with the United States and to some extent the European Union taking the lead in introducing both spectrum auctions and unlicensed bands in order to stimulate efficient economic usage. While one-time spectrum auctions in the United States have had their intended effect (e.g., PCS and MMDS bands), it may be time to consider introducing more dynamic market mechanisms that allow spectrum to change hands in time-constants of minutes or hours rather than months or years. For example, it may be possible to establish an online commodity trading system for spectrum that would permit operators with higher economic utility to bid for their peak usage needs without having to go through a lengthy procurement process.

Rapid deployment of wireless services would be further facilitated by streamlined approval processes for a wider range of customer equipment, including those with higher-powered directive antennas. This would probably require further advances in antenna beam and power control, but should be technically feasible in the near term. The broadband WLL business model depends to a large extent on user-installable or self-configuring customer premises equipment (CPE), something that would require some relaxation of current rules in MMDS and other fixed access bands. In addition, it may be expected that fixed access will gradually migrate toward semimobile services as cell sizes become smaller, further increasing the need for simple approval policies.

Unlicensed spectrum, such as the 5-GHz unlicensed national information infrastructure (U-NII) band in the United States, is an important facilitator for broadband access. FCC's allocation of the U-NII spectrum has stimulated considerable commercial activity in the high-speed wireless LAN area. It is recognized that the same type of technology (perhaps with somewhat higher power levels and larger coverage areas) could be used as a broadband PCS access network for public semimobile services in urban and suburban communities. There is, however, one remaining technical problem—that of spectrum etiquette—a decision on which was deferred by the FCC in its initial U-NII ruling. The problem is that existing unlicensed band etiquettes such as listen-before-talk (LBT) do not work well for stream services with quality-of-service (QoS) requirements. In such cases, the etiquette must be designed for equitable sharing among contending stream users, without reducing all of them to an unacceptable QoS level. The FCC has invited the industry to propose a suitable etiquette, but a specific scheme has yet to be identified. A possible technical solution is to introduce a common spectrum coordination channel at the edge of each unlicensed band and require users to execute mutually agreed sharing procedures (priority, dynamic auction, and so on) using a standardized etiquette protocol.

Radio Link Protocol

Broadband wireless access requires a new type of radio link protocol (RLP) capable of reliably transporting both packets and media streams with specified QoS. The broadband RLP itself may be decomposed into a medium access control (MAC) layer for channel sharing among multiple subscribers, and a data link control (DLC) protocol for error recovery. Broadband wireless networks tend to use either a packet CDMA, dynamic TDMA type, or an extended 802.11 carrier sense, multiple access/collision avoidance (CSMA/CA) MAC protocol. CDMA is the basis for the emerging IMT-2000 wideband CDMA standard for 3G mobile, and is associated with the choice of spread spectrum modulation believed to be appropriate for vehicular mobile systems. Dynamic TDMA has generally been adopted for broadband applications, as well as for some high-speed LANs (such as wireless ATM and the European Telecommunications Standards Institute's broadband radio access networks) in view of its ability to support a combination of packet data and constant bit-rate streams (voice and video). Extended 802.11 protocols provide streaming extensions for QoS support, and may be suitable for Ethernet-equivalent WLAN scenarios. DOCSIS MAC protocols used in cable networks have also been modified for WLL applications, but will generally incur a performance penalty owing to large packet sizes.

Data-link-layer retransmission for error recovery is an essential feature for broadband wireless service, since higher-layer protocols are critically dependent on low packet error rates on each link of the end-to-end connections. DLC involves fragmentation of data packets into relatively small units, the optimum for which is typically between 40 and 200 bytes, depending on the channel and traffic model. Many current implementations have adopted the ATM cell payload of 48 bytes as the basic unit of fragmentation on the radio link. This has the advantage of simplifying the interface to ATM backhaul networks, which are often used in carrier broadband and DSL networks. Error control on the radio link involves the addition of a wireless link header containing a sequence number used for identifying data units to be retransmitted. Implementation results have shown that significant improvements in end-to-end protocol performance (typically 2 orders of magnitude in packet error rate) can be achieved with fragmentation and retransmission on the radio link. This in turn permits wireless systems to operate in a higher C/I environment, thus increasing overall capacity of cellular networks.

Infrastructure Network

Broadband wireless access links are being designed as "plug-ins" to existing fixed network architectures based on IP and/or ATM. In order to facilitate ubiquitous deployment, it is important that both fixed WLL and mobile access be easily integrated with broadband DSL and cable networks currently being deployed. This means that the radio air application programming interface should be harmonized with both IP and ATM to the extent possible, particularly in terms of providing generic parameters for service establishment and QoS control. For fixed wireless access, interface functions specific to the radio link are performed by the base station, which puts out standard IP and/or ATM data and control into the infrastructure network.

For mobile scenarios, services (such as location management and handoff) specific to mobile users may be provided either with a mobility overlay, used in current cellular systems, or by integrating mobility support into the core network protocols, such as IP or ATM. The latter method (i.e., support integrated mobility in IP or ATM) is the preferred method for broadband in view of performance and scalability requirements. Moreover, as an increasing proportion of user devices becomes portable, the distinction between fixed and mobile user addresses will become more difficult to administer (the integrated approach does not require a priori partitioning of mobile and fixed addresses). Protocol specification work aimed at integrating mobility support into IP and ATM has been done in both the Internet Engineering Task Force (IETF) (mobile IP) and the ATM Forum. While much further work remains (3G.IP and so on), it may be expected that mobility will increasingly be integrated as a standard feature into fixed network infrastructures. Ultimately, this technical direction will further accelerate fixed and wireless network convergence, which has been predicted for some time.

MEDIA COMPRESSION

Media signals include (digital) data as well as analog information and entertainment signals: speech, audio, image, video, graphics, and other audiovisual signals such as hand gestures and handwriting. These signal classes are universal and are representative of most if not all information that needs to traverse the first mile, in either direction.

Complementary Roles of Modems and Compression Systems (Codecs)

Modem and access technologies have evolved to expand the transmission pipe for conveying digital information. In parallel, compression technology has evolved to compact the amount of digital information that is needed to convey the information in a signal with a specified level of fidelity. Access speeds have generally advanced on a faster track than has compression technology. That said, it is the combination of faster modems and greater levels of compression that has enabled advances and revolutions in digital communication. This section focuses on the impact of media compression as a direct enabler of digital communication over channels and networks with limited capacity.

Computing is an overarching enabler of multimedia communications, whether one is implementing coders or decoders (codecs for short) or is implementing modulators or demodulators (modems for short). Moore's law has direct implications on the rate at which computing technology (memory and arithmetic capability) advances as a function of time. In this view, advances in computing are much more rapid than are advances in access technologies. That said, advances in computing will only help speed up advances in access, but these advances are strictly knowledge-or algorithm-limited, as are the advances in compression.

The Dimensions of Performance in Media Compression

There are four dimensions of performance in a compression system: (1) quality, (2) bit rate, (3) delay, and (4) complexity. "Quality" refers to the quality of the signal after compression, measured in absolute terms or in terms of closeness to the original version of it. The "bit rate" is the data rate after compression. The "delay" is the sum of delays in the encoding and decoding parts of the system: the compression and decompression algorithms. (This does not include delay components resulting from specific implementation details or specific transmission latencies in the communication of the encoder bit stream.) Finally, "complexity" refers to the computational effort needed to perform the compression and decompression algorithms, measured for example, in millions of instructions per second (mips) and kilobytes (the read-only and random-access memories used in the codec [coder-decoder]). As processing technology improves, the importance of the complexity parameter tends to diminish, but delay remains as a fundamental performance metric. Delay is particularly important in interactive, or two-way, communications.

The Fuzzy Fifth Dimension: Richness of Content

In studies of compression efficiency, where one measures quality degradation as a function of increasing levels of compression, one assumes that the bandwidth, or frequency content in the signal, is a prespecified characteristic. For example, telephony is always associated with a speech signal of 4-kHz bandwidth, and television with a signal whose effective horizontal and vertical resolutions are on the order of a few hundred pixels in each case (a total number of pixels per frame on the order of 100,000).

In Table A.2, the notation of pps refers to pixels per second. It is the product [H × V × F] of horizontal resolution (H pixels per row), vertical resolution (V pixels per column), and temporal resolution (F frames per second).

With the evolution of flexible and scalable communications technology, one often has the option of considering input signals of higher bandwidth, as long as the compression is strong enough to delimit the output data rate to a specified number. Examples are high-bandwidth audio (such as FM-grade speech with 12- to 15-kHz bandwidth or CD-grade music with 20-kHz bandwidth, or multichannel sound) and high-definition television (a total number of pixels on the order of 2 million, 60 frames per second).

TABLE A.2   Multimedia Formats

Format	Sampling Rate	Frequency Band
Telephone	8 kHz	200-3,400 Hz
Teleconference	16 kHz	50-7,000 Hz
Compact disk	44.1 kHz	20-20,000 Hz
Digital audio tape	48 kHz	20-20,000 Hz
CIF Video	3 Mpps [360 × 288 × 30]	
CCIR Video	12 Mpps [720 × 576 × 30]	
HDTV	60 Mpps [1,280 × 720 × 60]	

NOTE: Mpps = megapixels per second.

SOURCE: Nikil Jayant, 1993, "High Quality Networking of Audio-Visual Information," *IEEE Communications Magazine* 31(9).

Scalability in bandwidth is a somewhat fuzzy situation in that users are often not conditioned to the continuum in this parameter between, or beyond, well-established anchors. For example, wideband speech is a fuzzy term that implies any bandwidth in the range between well-defined telephone and CD grades (4 and 20 kHz), and first-generation Internet video often is understood to mean anything that is usable, albeit below TV quality (such as 10,000 to 100,000 pixels per frame). The video situation has the additional dimensions of viewing distance, physical picture size, and fractional-screen displays, which further control user appreciation of picture quality or user perception of picture degradation.

The Algorithms of Media Compression

The description of compression algorithms is beyond the scope of this appendix. It is also not needed for the purposes of this report. What is important, however, is to note that all compression algorithms are based on only two basic principles: removal of redundancy in the input signal, and the reduction of irrelevancy in it. "Redundancy" is usually characterized in a statistical fashion, while "irrelevancy" is best linked to a perceptual criterion. Compression techniques are also usefully classified into three types: (1) lossy, (2) lossless, and (3) perceptually lossless. Mathematically lossless compression is used in some archival, legal, and medical applications, while perceptual losslessness is a pragmatic criterion for a large class of applications in transmission and storage. Most compression standards tend to address this criterion. Other characteristics to keep in mind are the delay and complexity of the algorithms, and how they are distributed between the compression and decompression parts of the system. For example, interactive and two-way applications look for low-delay compression, servers can typically afford high complexity, and client systems need to be relatively simple to implement. Implementation platforms can be ASIC (application-specific integrated circuit), DSP (digital signal processor), or NSP (native signal processor, as on a Pentium). As a matter of calibration, a Pentium II (400-MHz) processor can decode MPEG1 video streams in real time, and a pocket PC in 2001 has a processor that works at half the speed (about 200 MHz).

Compression Standards

Tables A.3 and A.4 provide nonexhaustive lists of compression standards for audiovisual signals. In general, results refer to lossy compression, although these standards include special functions for lossless compression. For example, in JPEG image compression, there is a lossy (perceptually lossless) version with typical bit rates of 0.5 to 2 bits per pixel (bpp), while a mathematically lossless version may use a bit rate of 5 to 6 bpp.

In Figure A.30, the horizontal axis displays bit rates after compression for classes of applications that are arranged in clusters that represent speech, audio, and image applications. The bit rates range from 1 kbps to 100 Mbps. Interestingly, the geometric mean of this range is 300 kbps, a number typical of conservative ADSL and cable modem rates in the year 2000. The data rates in Figure A.30 are strict lower bounds in the sense that in most applications, the compressed information needs to be supplemented with ancillary data.

Bit Error Protection

In a rate k/n error correction code, k information bits are protected for transmission over an error-prone channel by adding $(n-k)$ redundant bits. The fractional overhead is $1-k/n$.

Sophisticated methods of error protection include these:

- *Unequal error protection*, in which different parts of the compressor output receive different levels of error protection, depending on models of their relative perceptual importance;
- *Joint source and channel coding*, in which, for example, the total bit rate available is shared dynamically between source bits and error protection bits, depending on the model or knowledge of the channel state.

TABLE A.3   Standards for Speech Compression

Standard (year)	Algorithm	Bit Rate	Application
G.722 (1988)	Subband ADPCM	64, 56, 48 kbps	Teleconferencing
MPEG-1 (1992)	Musicam ASPEC	384, 256, 128 kbps	Two-channel audio w/video on CD
MPEG-2 (1996)	PAC	320 kbps	Five-channel surround sound for multimedia recording
DAB (1996)	PAC	160 kbps	Two-channel audio for terrestrial broadcast
JBIG (1991)	Run length coding	0.05-0.1 bpp	Binary coded images (half-tone)
JPEG (1991)	DCT	0.25-8 bpp	Still continuous-tone images
MPEG-1/2 (1991, 1994)	MD-DCT	1-8 Mbps	Addressable video on CD
P × 64 (1991)	MC-DCT	64-1,536 kbps	Videoconferencing
HDTV (1996)	MD-DCT	17 Mbps	Advanced TV
G.711 (1972)	Mu-Law and A-Law PCM	56-64 kbps	Network transmission
G.721 (1984, 1987)	ADPCM	32 kbps	Bit-rate multiplexers, undersea cable
G.723 (1988)	ADPCM	24, 40 kbps	Overload on undersea cable, data modem
G.726/G.727	ADPCM	16, 24, 32, 40 kbps	High overload rate for undersea cable
G.728 (1992)	LD-CELP	16 kbps	Transmission at low delay
G.729 (1995)	ACELP	8 kbps	Second-generation digital cellular
G.723 (1995)	ACELP	6.3, 5.3 kbps	Low-bit-rate videophone
GSM (1987)	RPE-TLP	13 kbps	European digital cellular full-rate
IS-54 (1989)	VSELP	8 kbps	North American digital cellular-TDMA
IS-96 (1993)	QCELP	8.5, 4, 2, 0.8 kbps	North American digital cellular-CDMA
GSM-1/2 (1994)	VSELP	5.6 kbps	European digital cellular half-rate
EVRC (1996)	RCELP	8.5, 4, 0.8 kbps	NA CDMA, 2nd generation
IS-136 (1995)	CELP	8 kbps	NA TDMA, 2nd generation
JDC (1989, 1992)	VSELP	8, 4 kbps	Japanese digital cellular— full and half rates
FS-1016 (1975)	CELP	4.8 kbps	Secure telephony—full rate
FS-1015 (1975)	LPC-10E	2.4 kbps	Secure telephony—half rate
FS-1015 (1996)		2.4 kbps	Secure telephony—half rate, 2nd generation

SOURCE: After R.V. Cox. 1999. "Current Methods of Speech Coding," in N. Jayant (ed.), 1999, *Signal Compression: Coding of Speech, Audio, Image and Video*, World Scientific, Singapore.

TABLE A.4 Standards for Audio, Image, and Video Compression

Standard (Year)	Algorithm	Bit Rate	Application
G.722 (1988)	Subband ADPCM	64, 56, 48 kbps	Teleconferencing
MPEG-1 (1992)	Musicam/ASPEC	384, 256, 128 kbps	Two-channel audio w/ video on CD
MPEG-2 (1996)	PAC	320 kbps	Five-channel surround sound for MM recording
DAB (1996)	PAC	160 kbps	Two-channel audio for terrestrial broadcast
JBIG (1991)	Run length coding	0.05-0.1 bpp	Binary coded images (half-tone)
JPEG (1991)	DCT	0.25-8 bpp	Still continuous-tone images
MPEG-1/2 (1991, 1994)	MC-DCT	1-8 Mbps	Addressable video on CD
P × 64 (1991)	MC-DCT	64-1,536 kbps	Videoconferencing
HDTV (1996)	MC-DCT	17 Mbps	Advanced TV

NOTES: kbps = kilobits per second; bpp = bits per pixel.

SOURCE: After R.V. Cox. 1999. "Current Methods of Speech Coding," in N. Jayant (ed.), 1999, *Signal Compression: Coding of Speech, Audio, Image and Video*, World Scientific, Singapore.

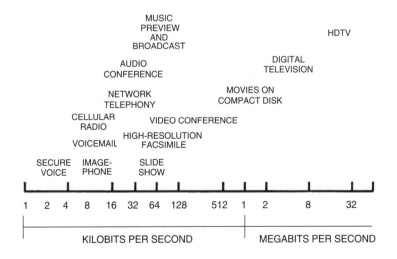

FIGURE A.30 Data rates in digital representations of signals. Rates are numbers after compression. SOURCE: After R.V. Cox. 1999. "Current Methods of Speech Coding," in N. Jayant (ed.), 1999, *Signal Compression: Coding of Speech, Audio, Image and Video*, World Scientific, Singapore.

Resiliency to Packet Losses

Packet networks are often limited by packet losses rather than bit errors. Packet losses can be addressed by retransmission in delay-insensitive applications. In delay-sensitive communications, packet losses can be anticipated by redundancy in the packet generator.

In sophisticated algorithms, such as embedded coding and multiple description coding, this redundancy is contained by unequal protection of subpackets, depending on models of perceptual importance of these subpackets, as in unequal bit error protection.

Information Hiding, Steganography, Watermarking, and Multimedia Annotations

Increasingly, digital communications will include ancillary information that may convey a variety of information to the end user that is related to authentication (information about sender and intended receiver, for example), and such information is embedded in the main message in an unobtrusive and imperceptible form. These are the techniques of information hiding, with subclasses called steganography and watermarking. Multimedia annotations also involve additional data, but not necessarily in imperceptible or hidden form.

The overall effect of all of the above processes is that the data rate for digital communication is strictly higher than the data rates at the output of the signal compression stage. While there is no rigorous way of measuring the resulting overhead in data rate without regard to the application and the needs of it, it is useful to use the following guideline:

Typical overall overheads are in the range of 10 to 100 percent, and the rates on the horizontal axis of the compression chart in Table A.4 need to be increased by factors as high as 2.0, especially in the case of unfriendly access methods such as wireless links that are power- and interference-limited and/or in networks that are operating in situations of overload.

In scalable media communications, the inherent excursions in data rate in the compression algorithm can well exceed the factor of 2 referred to above. In these cases, the metrics of importance are the average data rate in the scalable compression algorithm, and, where available and usable, more detailed descriptions of the data rate histogram. In fact, assessments of traffic and channel loading depend directly on these difficult and highly variable characterizations of the information source. The least complex nontrivial measure of overall data rate is the average data rate after compression, multiplied by the overhead mentioned in the guideline above.

Media-Specific Examples: Access Implications and Questions

- *Toll-quality telephony versus Internet or cable modem telephony.* What are the quality and delay targets in IP-telephony and cable telephony? What are the consumer expectations? Is there a business case for AM-radio-grade telephony? What is the competitive landscape?
- *Audio/video streaming at lite-ADSL, cable modem, and wireless speeds.* Are user expectations going to be tied to television quality? What is the longevity of partial-screen solutions? What is the competitive landscape?
- *Uploading of information from a home.* What are the primary cases for upload-speed on demand? What are the demands of such applications as telemedicine, teleworking, home publishing? Is there a case for symmetric uplink and downlink?

Definitive answers to these questions do not exist, but as applications mature, it will be possible to understand and quantify them at least implicitly and qualitatively.

Research and Technology Outlook

At this time, compression technologies are mature. Although it is difficult to define the fundamental limits in the game, typical data rates for specified levels of quality are generally known. Increasing compression ratios will become the preoccupation of specialists. Likewise, decoders and clients will become pervasive and affordable. New advances in first mile and first meters multimedia communications will depend increasingly on advances in access speed and on innovations in networking.

B

A Brief History of Telecommunications Regulation

A large legacy from past policy, dominated by telecommunications regulation, shapes the context for broadband policy. That legacy principally concerns regulation of wireline communications through common carriers, but it also includes regulation of cable, broadcasting, other wireless communications, and regulations applied to the Internet. The legacy's salient features are briefly reviewed in this appendix.

THE LEGACY FROM PAST POLICY

Common Carriers (Telephony)

Local and long distance telephone companies operate as common carriers, which historically have had close regulatory scrutiny by both federal and state agencies. The history of common carriage is fundamental to the baseline for broadband deployment, because it shaped what exists today in the telephone infrastructure as well as expectations in numerous industries and locales about the nature of investment and competition in communications and information infrastructure.

A telecommunications "common carrier" is the term used to describe a provider of telecommunications transmission service that offers its service to the public for a fee and, in contrast to, for example, a television station owner or a cable television operator for most of its channels, does not control the content of the information transmitted by its facilities or services. Rather, the carrier's customer controls the content and the destination of the transmission. Criminal or civil responsibility for the content rests (for the most part) with the sender, not the carrier. For most of the 20^{t}h century, federal and state regulation of common carriers has been considered necessary because telecommunications services in any geographic area have been provided by a single carrier.[1] Similar thinking and tactics have been applied to providers of other kinds of infrastructure regarded as utilities, such as electric power or water, and historically to transportation, including rail, toll roads, ferries, and the like.

While policy goals are established through laws, regulatory agencies implement the laws through rulemaking, The Federal Communications Commission (FCC) regulates the interstate activities of such carriers,[2] and state commissions regulate their intrastate activities.[3] Rulemaking and other administrative proceedings follow a set of practices that involve issuing a notice of intent to act, solicitation of comments, and other formalities. These processes have given rise to a cadre of in-house and private-practice lawyers, economists, and lobbyists seeking to promote or discourage certain kinds of decisions by regulators. Depending on one's perspective, these processes may reflect an open, fair process for implementing regulations or a drag on the telecommunications marketplace.

Regulators were persuaded that local and long distance services were natural monopolies and, consequently, could be provided at the lowest cost through a single firm. Economic regulation, not competition, would constrain the prices and practices of the monopoly carriers. Under this regulatory regime, the Bell System provided local telephone service in virtually all urban areas and gradually extended its reach to many rural areas. Its long distance network interconnected Bell as well as subscribers of the remaining thousand-plus independent telephone companies (each a monopoly in its franchise territory), enabling any subscriber to call any other telephone subscriber. Over time, the Bell System became the envy of the world because of the breadth, price, and quality of its service offerings.

---

[1]These monopolies were created initially by AT&T's aggressive acquisition of independent telephone companies in the early 20th century. The regime emerged in the wake of the 1913 agreement between the Bell Telephone system and the U.S. Department of Justice, known as the Kingsbury Commitment. In return for certain concessions, Bell Telephone was permitted to retain the local telephone companies it had acquired since the turn of the century and to maintain its monopoly control over long distance.

[2]Under Title II of the Communications Act of 1934, as amended.

[3]Because AT&T and the independent local telephone companies were permitted to operate as government-protected monopolies, the prices and other terms and conditions of their service offerings were subject to close scrutiny by federal and state regulators to prevent the telephone companies from exercising their market power. If a call originates in one state and terminates in another state or foreign country, that service is subject to the FCC's jurisdiction. If a call originates and terminates within the same city or within the same state, that service is subject to the state commission's jurisdiction.

In the last third of the 20th century, however, technological advances cast increasing doubt on the premise that telephone service, or at least certain aspects of it, should be provided on a monopoly basis. In the 1960s and 1970s, the FCC gradually relaxed regulation of telephone terminal equipment (e.g., telephone handsets, private branch exchanges), known as customer premises equipment (CPE).[4] These actions spawned the emergence of an intensely competitive market for handsets, fax machines, private branch exchanges (PBXs), and other terminal equipment.[5] In the 1970s and 1980s, the FCC followed a similar pattern of phased regulatory relaxation in the long distance market. The most significant event in the introduction of long distance competition involved an antitrust case spawned by such competition and AT&T's response to it. In 1982, AT&T and the U.S. Department of Justice entered into a consent decree, known as the "Modified Final Judgment" (MFJ), that required AT&T to divest its local operating companies.[6] By separating AT&T's monopoly segments from its more competitive long distance operations, the decree went a long way toward opening the latter to facilities-based competition, because it eliminated the incentive of the local telephone companies to discriminate against MCI and other would-be AT&T competitors through their monopoly control over the local network.

The decree removed one of AT&T's most substantial competitive advantages by requiring the Bell Operating Companies to provide equal access to other long distance companies.[7] As competition in the long distance industry matured, additional technical impediments were eliminated (such as the introduction of 800-number portability across long distance carriers) and new entrants began to make inroads into AT&T's

----

[4]Prior to the FCC's action, telephone equipment was part of the service that the local telephone company provided to its customers. Indeed, customers were prohibited by the companies' tariffs from attaching other equipment to the network.

[5]In deregulating CPE, the FCC also preempted state commissions from continued regulation of that equipment. The FCC's jurisdiction under the Communications Act of 1934, as amended, in the 1970s was limited to interstate services. The commission recognized, however, that, as a practical matter, it could not deregulate "interstate" CPE, since such equipment is used to place and receive both interstate and intrastate communications. Hence, it barred state agencies from continuing to regulate the provision of CPE in order to prevent such policies from frustrating the FCC's national deregulation policy. *See North Carolina Utils. Comm. v. FCC I.*

[6]*See United States v. American Tel. & Tel. Co.*, 552 F. Supp. 131 (D.D.C. 1982), *aff'd,* 460 U.S. 1001 (1983).

[7]The operating companies were required to modify their networks to enable a subscriber to these other providers also to use the "1+" prefix to obtain access. Prior to the implementation of this "equal access" requirement, subscribers of long distance companies other than AT&T were required to dial a seven-digit local number, then dial a multidigit personal identification number, and then dial the long distance number they were calling.

market share, the FCC gradually relaxed price regulation of AT&T on a service-by-service basis.[8]

The latter half of the 1980s and first half of the 1990s were marked by the continued erosion of AT&T's long distance dominance, as MCI, Sprint, and scores of other competitors gained significant inroads (although AT&T remains the largest provider). In light of these changes in the marketplace, the FCC gradually loosened its controls over different segments of AT&T's long distance business, culminating in a 1995 decision that eliminated the remaining FCC price controls of AT&T's basic residential services.[9] Although AT&T remained subject to price regulation for more than a decade after it divested its Bell Operating Company subsidiaries, the prices of interstate services offered by new (and accordingly much smaller) providers of long distance, such as MCI, were not regulated.[10] By the end of the 1990s, AT&T's share of the long-distance market had slipped below 50 percent

In the late 1980s, federal and state regulators also began to take the first steps toward opening local telecommunications markets to competition. Following several states such as New York and Illinois, the FCC adopted its Expanded Interconnection rules, which required incumbent telephone companies to interconnect their networks with new firms that wished to provide competing local transport services. These developments raise the possibility of shifts in state regulatory emphasis from retail rate regulation to wholesale enforcement.[11]

The enactment of the Telecommunications Act of 1996 marked the commencement of the most concerted effort by state and federal regula-

---

[8]For example, when 800-number portability made it possible for an 800-number customer to switch long-distance carriers and retain its 800 number (e.g., 1-800-FLOWERS), the FCC removed its price regulation of AT&T's 800 service offerings.

[9]Because the FCC's jurisdiction is limited to interstate services, it does not regulate the rates that local telephone companies charge for local and intrastate services (such as calls from Los Angeles to San Francisco). Local telephone companies, however, provide origination and termination service to interstate long distance companies. That is, the local telephone companies carry an interstate call from the originating end user to the interstate carrier's switch, where it is placed on the long distance carrier's network. Local telephone companies also carry calls from the long distance company's switch to the called party's premises. This origination and termination service is known as interstate access service and is subject to the FCC's jurisdiction.

[10]The FCC's theory was that since the new entrants did not possess market power, there was no need to regulate their rates. If consumers were dissatisfied with an MCI offering, they could always take service from AT&T, whose rates were regulated.

[11]Bob Rowe. 2000. "Implementing a Cooperative Federalist Approach to Telecom Policy." Speech presented at Federalist Society, Washington, D.C., September 27.

tors to dismantle the monopoly control over local telecommunications markets exercised by the Bell Operating Companies and other incumbent telephone companies. The results have yet fallen short of the quick movement to "deregulation" that some had hoped for. Armed with new statutory authority, the FCC and state regulatory commissions moved aggressively to require local incumbents to open their markets. Incumbent telephone companies, called ILECs (incumbent local exchange carriers) continue to have overwhelming market shares, particularly among residential customers, thanks to their initial monopoly position and scale and scope economies that are difficult to overcome. To help overcome these incumbent advantages, the Telecommunications Act of 1996 mandated that incumbents offer competitors (CLECs) access to unbundled network elements at reasonable rates. Because ILECs continue to control well over 90 percent of local market revenues and customers, they remain subject to comprehensive price regulation at both the federal and state level. CLECs, lacking market power, generally are not.

In 1999, the FCC adopted rules for the gradual deregulation of the incumbent telephone companies' provision of local service used for interstate communications. Prices should be deregulated when there was evidence that the incumbent could not exercise market power.[12] Meanwhile, there has been horizontal consolidation among telephone companies plus vertical integration of such companies (e.g., Qwest acquired USWest; NYNEX merged with Bell Atlantic, which merged with GTE to become Verizon; SBC acquired Pacific Telesis and Ameritech; MCI merged with WorldCom, which also merged with UUNet; and AT&T acquired TCI and other cable interests). Thus, although the 1996 act eliminated legal barriers to entry in those states where they persisted, economic and technical barriers are eroding more slowly. Nevertheless, competitors have made inroads among business customers in urban markets. Against this backdrop, issues posed by open access in broadband have prompted FCC initiatives.

Cable

The regulatory regime governing cable television systems is entirely different from the common carrier scheme. It has a much shorter history,

---

[12]What criteria should be applied remains a controversial subject. The incumbents have chafed at delays to their entry into long distance. Competitors to the ILECs have maintained that the criteria used by the FCC do not provide an accurate picture of the availability of alternative providers of local telecommunications services, and that the FCC blueprint would permit the incumbents to preserve their monopoly control over local markets by granting them substantial pricing flexibility when they continue to wield market power.

and it reflects the fact that following its earliest days, when cable was used to provide television service in regions not reached by broadcast television, cable grew by providing an alternative to an existing entertainment and information service (broadcast television) and faced initial deployment challenges. Cable operators do not have to offer their transmission service to the public on a nondiscriminatory basis, unlike common carriers. Most important for understanding how regulation was approached, cable systems maintain considerable control over the content that is transmitted over their distribution facilities. Unlike common carriers, they have asserted First Amendment rights with regard to the content they carry, a status upheld by the courts. Cable operators generally are not required to offer access to their distribution system to enable other (unaffiliated) content providers to deliver their products to cable subscribers (major multiple system operators that vertically integrate content production and cable service are required to devote a portion of their system capacity to unaffiliated networks). Even without any mandate to do so, however, operators offer unaffiliated content channels for two reasons: (1) no single operator has enough high-quality content to fill all of its capacity, and (2) operators generally find that customer demand for these channels exists. Thus, almost every system carries CNN, which is an AOL Time Warner service, and ESPN, which is owned by Disney-ABC. In addition, cable operators, under certain circumstances, are required to offer access to providers of traditional video services under the so-called leased access provisions of Title VI of the Communications Act of 1934 (as amended). Also, there have been local content requirements through public, education, and government channel provisions of franchises. Nonetheless, the contrast between the relative freedom to control content and the obligations placed on common carriers—which gives rise to expectations of similar behavior in the future—is one genesis of today's "open access" debate,[13] discussed below.

Cable television is subject to limited federal regulation. Under Title VI of the Communications Act of 1934 (as amended), the "basic tier" of services, encompassing mostly local television signals, is subject to rate regulation. Local authorities could regulate the price of the basic tier, pursuant to formulas prescribed by the FCC, unless "effective competition" existed, as defined by the Cable Act of 1992 (such price regulation expired in 1999). Cable television operators also are limited in their ability to expand horizontally and vertically with content providers. Devising,

---

[13]Proponents of open access have argued, among other things, that when a cable system furnishes access to an Internet service provider, it is engaged in the provision of a common carrier service and, consequently, should be required with the same access obligations that characterize common carriage provided by telephone companies.

implementing, and enforcing regulations for the cable industry under the 1992 act was difficult and time-consuming. A major complication was that cable service, like broadband, is multifaceted and varies in capability from one service area to the next. In the end, it is not clear that the regulation accomplished much in the long run, with the exception of the rules that made cable network programming available to overbuild competitors and satellite services at "reasonable" prices, which spurred competition in video delivery.

Cable systems are also subject to local regulation—through the franchise agreements that they execute with municipal, county, or, in a few cases, state authorities. These agreements typically run one or more decades and are a source of revenue for the municipalities that issue them.

As franchise agreements have come up for renewal, the new capabilities of cable systems to deliver advanced video and data services have dominated the negotiations. As discussed in Chapter 4 in the report, a key development beginning in the 1990s was the progressive upgrading of cable plant to incorporate fiber (hybrid fiber coax), which increased system quality and capacity and more recently facilitated use of cable infrastructure for Internet access. However, cable operators are not under a legal obligation to upgrade their plant to be able to offer broadband, cable modem services. Further, if operators complete such an upgrade, they currently are not (as a class) required to make access to that transmission service available to unaffiliated providers of broadband services. Open access requirements (discussed in Chapter 5) have figured heavily in several franchise negotiations. Other elements arising in contemporary franchise negotiations include establishment of minimum data bandwidth and rights-of-way (such as joint trenching rules where there are multiple entrants). New considerations analogous to the traditional public, educational, and government (PEG) requirements include extensions to non-video services and making fiber available to local governments (and possibly for other customers).

Internet

Fear of regulation has always haunted the Internet, although it is considered "unregulated." Popular misunderstanding has even motivated the FCC to issue a fact sheet (last revised in January 1998) to dispel myths about charges and taxes it was alleged to have imposed or to be considering imposing on the Internet or its use.[14] Since the late 1990s, FCC com-

---

[14]Federal Communications Commission. 1998. "The FCC, Internet Service Providers, and Access Charges." Available online at <http://www.fcc.gov/Bureaus/Common_Carrier/Factsheets/ispfact.html>.

missioners and staff have written and spoken publicly about the benefits of the commission's hands-off approach to the Internet.[15] But the growth in public interest in the Internet and the businesses behind it continues to raise questions about prospects for government intervention, including regulation, whether direct or indirect.

The historic interaction of regulation with the Internet was ad hoc, even unintended. Anecdotal evidence suggests that the Internet was not recognized as a phenomenon or concern by most regulators until the 1990s, when it became commercial, and those circumstances or actions that can be identified do not seem to have been framed with the Internet in mind.[16] For example, a key enabler, in retrospect, was a series of FCC decisions that gave customers the right to attach approved devices directly to the network, which has allowed both ISPs and users to attach modems to their phone lines—a necessary precondition for dial-up access.[17] Some observers also point to common carriage regulation as an important Internet enabler. Entry by ISPs has been facilitated by common carrier rules which mandate nondiscriminatory access and reasonable rates apply to both the dial-up lines used by individual customers and the telephone network dedicated lines used by many ISPs to connect points of presence to the Internet.

Another enabler came in the 1980 second Computer Inquiry, when the FCC ruled that firms that use basic telecommunications services to provide an enhanced service of some kind (such as information delivery) are not engaged in the provision of a "basic" common carrier, telecommunications service (such as local telephone service). Rather, they are providing an "enhanced" service and, accordingly, are not subject to the direct jurisdiction of the FCC or state regulatory commissions. That decision served to nurture commercial value-added networks, bulletin boards, database services, and other data communications services in the 1970s

---

[15]See, for example, Jason Oxman. 1999. "The FCC and the Unregulation of the Internet." Office of Plans and Policy, Federal Communications Commission, Washington, D.C., July. Available online at <www.fcc.gov/bureaus/opp/working_papers/oppwp31.pdf>.

[16]The early development of the Internet was motivated in part by a desire to find relief from the high costs of dedicated leased line services available from the regulated telecommunications industry of the 1960s, which constrained early applications of data communications for government and the research community. The prevailing telecommunications environment fed the interest and efforts of the researchers supported by the Defense Advanced Research Projects Agency, who both developed the early technology and were the first to benefit from the economies provided through packet-switching.

[17]The certification scheme in 47 C.F.R. Part 68, adopted in the 1970s, enables firms to obtain FCC approval for devices that are attached to the network, permitting third parties to develop innovative communications equipment while ensuring that attachment of this equipment does not threaten the integrity of the network.

and 1980s. These proved, in retrospect, to be training grounds for the more open Internet, as well as ISPs, in the 1990s.

More recently, through Section 271 of the Telecommunications Act of 1996, the former Regional Bell Operating Companies are prohibited from offering interLATA services—which include both long distance telephony and Internet transmission services—in states in which they provide local telephone service, until they have satisfied certain market-opening requirements. As a result, while these companies may operate dial-up and broadband ISPs, customers must obtain connectivity to the rest of the Internet through a regional or national ISP operated by another company. Also, although virtually all Internet communications cross state lines, in 1997 the FCC affirmed[18] an earlier ruling that the transmission between an end user's premises and an enhanced service provider's location in the same calling area would be treated as a local call, rather than as an interstate call, regardless of whether that transmission carries data, an e-mail message, or even (at least under certain circumstances) a voice call over the Internet.[19] Finally, differences in inter-network traffic flows have fed debate over so-called reciprocal compensation, a subject of FCC inquiry in 2000-2001.[20]

The Telecommunications Act of 1966 had another consequence that has been important for the deployment of broadband Internet access. Because the act required the ILECs to unbundle their circuits to CLECs, a class of CLECs came into existence that offered data rather than voice over these circuits, by means of DSL technology. This investment in DSL by competitive providers seems to have spurred investment in DSL by ILECs, and thus to have driven the overall rate of DSL deployment. At the present time, the market downturn has put many of these competitive DSL providers in peril, but this should not cause one to dismiss the contribution of competition in this case.

When incumbent telecommunications providers offer DSL, this service comes under the purview of the historical legacy of telecommunica-

---

[18]Access Reform Order, FCC 97-158, adopted on May 7, 1997.

[19]Precisely which voice transmissions might be subject to access charges is a delicate area. For example, the Federal Communications Commission indicated in a 1998 report to Congress that a handset call to an ISP that terminated at a handset in another state may be classified as a basic telecommunication service and hence be subject to access charges.

[20]The concern is that different kinds of providers may terminate traffic out of proportion to that which they hand off—especially the relative burdens of dial-up Internet traffic. At present, more may be terminated on CLEC than ILEC networks, implying (at least to the ILECs) significant reciprocal compensation payments by ILECs to CLECs, but the nature of potential funds flows depends on actual dial-up use in the future, a subject of disagreement ("In 'Recip Comp' Debate, CLECs, Telcos Rely on Varying Projects for Dial-up Internet Traffic," *Telecommunications Reports*, January 8, 2001, pp. 9-10).

tions regulation. When an incumbent telecommunications provider sells an enhanced service (which is not regulated) over a "basic" service, the incumbent provider must provide the basic service to others. DSL is seen as a basic service. Thus, at the present time, the ILECs must unbundle their data services at two levels. They unbundle their physical loops so competitive DSL providers can implement DSL, and they unbundle their DSL service so competitive ISPs can sell Internet access over the incumbent's DSL service.

The history presented here, which illustrates indirect regulatory support for the Internet that has been largely inadvertent (at least until the late 1990s), unfolded without consideration of broadband. It focuses on the presence or absence of regulatory intervention into pricing and market entry. Broadband expands the potential space for intervention in at least two ways: First, it involves different kinds of industries and technologies providing Internet access under different regulatory regimes (e.g., some have expressed concern about the implications for ISP support of cable-based Internet access in contrast to common carriers). Second, distinguishing between information services and telecommunications carriers blurs when facilities owners integrate carrier and information service functions, as is being seen in at least cable- and satellite-based broadband offerings.

PRESENT: THE 1996 ACT

Much of the current policy framework relates to the Telecommunications Act of 1996, which was framed as a reform effort. Since its enactment and the unfolding of derivative activities, there is increasing awareness of what it does and does not accomplish. This piece of legislation, a major modification to the Communications Act of 1934, was shaped during the early to mid-1990s. The language of the act indicates that its primary goals are to promote competition and reduce regulation as a means of increasing growth in telecommunications services and reducing prices.[21] It was enacted shortly after the 1995 commercialization of the Internet backbone and introduction of the browsers that helped to popularize the World Wide Web and before such technologies were widely used. Even though many of the key actors understood that sweeping change was on the horizon, full appreciation of the key role of the Internet did not exist, in society or in Washington.

---

[21]The preamble calls it "An Act to promote competition and reduce regulation in order to secure lower prices and higher quality services for American telecommunications consumers and encourage the rapid growth of new telecommunications technologies." Telecommunications Act of 1996, P.L. 104-104, 110 Stat. 56 (1996), Preamble.

The Telecommunications Act of 1996 adjusted the relative roles of federal and state regulators, increasing that of the states. Whereas the Communications Act of 1934 preserved state authority over intrastate rates and services, the 1996 Act specified state roles in interconnection, incumbent telephone company long distance market entry, and promotion of advanced services. It sent mixed signals on federal preemption of state regulators, and it reinforced a kind of cooperative federalism.[22]

Most directly relevant to broadband, the Telecommunications Act of 1996 calls for the FCC and states to encourage deployment of advanced technologies for telecommunications to all Americans on a reasonable and timely basis. But what satisfies "advanced," "all," "reasonable," and "timely"? The act, in support of service to "all" Americans, calls for access to advanced telecommunications and information services in rural and high-cost areas to be "reasonably comparable" to that in urban areas in terms of price and quality. This formulation is interesting because it joins unregulated information services with regulated telecommunications services; what that implies for policy approaches and their targets is unclear. Specific provisions of the act related to broadband are summarized in Box 5.1, Chapter 5.

p. 178

---

[24]Rowe, "Implementing a Cooperative Federalist Approach to Telecom Policy," 2000.

C

List of White Papers Received

As input to its ongoing study of broadband last mile technology issues and options, the Computer Science and Telecommunications Board issued a call for white papers in summer 2000. The papers (arranged alphabetically by authors' last names) are available for download at CSTB's Web site, <www.cstb.org>. Please note that circulation of these white papers does not constitute endorsement of them by the Committee on Broadband Last Mile Technology, the Computer Science and Telecommunications Board, or the National Academies.

"Factors Influencing Investment in Residential Broadband Equipment and Services—A Venture Capital Perspective"
George Abe, Palomar Ventures

"Broadband Satellite Networks for Last Mile Technology"
Ian F. Akyildiz, Georgia Institute of Technology

"Ethernet Broadband Networking"
Andreas Bechtolsheim and David Cheriton, Cisco Systems

"Broadband Services to Rural Western Massachusetts"
Edward Ciesla, Flack & Kurtz Consulting Engineers

"Access to What? First Mile Issues for Rural Broadband"
Richard Civille, Richard Civille and Associates; Michael Gurstein, Michael Gurstein and Associates; Kenneth Pigg, University of Missouri at Columbia

"Last Mile Connectivity Utilizing Fiber Satellite Solutions"
Tom Dennett, Harmonic Data Systems

"High Bandwidth, Applications, and Economic Development: Let's Tie It Together!"
Sylvie Doucet, Planned Approach, Inc.

"Broadband Access Over Inverse Multiplexed Copper"
Einar Edvardsen, Telenor R&D

"Getting Tele/Tech on Local Government Radar"
Richard Esposto, Western Integrated Networks

"Technology Developments for Quality Multimedia Delivery for Residences: Coupling of the Broadband and Home Network Technologies"
Aura Ganz, University of Massachusetts

"Regulatory Issues, Pricing, and Access to Public Utility Right-of-Way"
Henry Kilpatrick and Paul Baker, Georgia Institute of Technology

"The Use of Satellite Technology for Last Mile Broadband Access"
Jose-Marie Montpetit and R. Deininger

"Deployment of Multimedia Services to Residential Customers"
Jose A. Pozas, Telefonica I+D

"Residential Internet Ready Buildings (IRBs)"
Amnon Ptashek, EDSL Networks, Inc.

D

Biographies of
Committee Members

Nikil Jayant, *Chair*, is the John Pippin Chair in Wireless Systems in the Electrical and Computer Engineering Department at Georgia Institute of Technology, founding director of the Georgia Tech Broadband Institute, and executive director of GCATT, the Georgia Centers for Advanced Telecommunications Technology. Earlier at Bell Laboratories, Dr. Jayant created and managed the Signal Processing Research Department, the Advanced Audio Technology Department, and the Multimedia Communications Research Laboratory. Contributions from these organizations include the definition of unified structures for signal processing and computing, the invention of new technology for high-density magnetic recording, the creation of the 16-kbps CCITT (Consultative Committee on International Telephony and Telegraphy) international standard for network telephony, channel equalization and data coding technologies for the IS54 North American Digital Cellular standard, coding and transmission methodologies for voiceband videotelephony and high-definition television, the establishment of perceptual coding as a definitive criterion for low-bit-rate coding of audiovisual signals, and the development of a digital audio broadcast system as potential future technology for CD-quality radio broadcasting in the United States. More recent contributions include software for text-to-speech synthesis, automatic speech recognition, and natural language dialog; software for Internet communication of speech, music, and video signals; and multimedia systems for messaging and the human-computer interface. Dr. Jayant has published more than 100 papers, written a number of books, and has been granted more than

20 patents. Businesses created by Dr. Jayant's research and leadership span several segments in audiovisual and data communications. Dr. Jayant has received several honors, including the Alfred Hay Gold Medal (for the best student in communication engineering, Indian Institute of Science, 1965), the IEEE Browder J. Thompson Memorial Prize Award (for the best IEEE publication by an author under thirty years of age, 1974), the Industry Paper Award from the Institution of Electrical and Telecommunication Engineers (India, 1990), the IEEE Donald G. Fink Prize Paper Award (for the best tutorial paper in an IEEE publication, 1995), and the 1997 Lucent Patent Recognition Award. Dr. Jayant was inducted into the New Jersey Inventors Hall of Fame for his contributions to the reduction of noise in communication systems and is a fellow of the IEEE and a member of the National Academy of Engineering. Dr. Jayant serves on the advisory board of NTT-DoCoMo-USA and is a co-founder and chief scientist of EGTechnology, which creates software solutions for last-mile multimedia. Dr. Jayant received his PhD in Electrical Communication Engineering from the Indian Institute of Science, Bangalore, India, in 1970.

James A. Chiddix is president of the Interactive Personal Video Group at AOL Time Warner. The IPV Group is headquartered in New York City and is chartered with the development of a new broadband video service to be delivered to the company's millions of digital cable subscribers. The service will provide an array of server-based products, ranging from access to a large library of video on an on-demand basis, to personal video recorder access and storage of live programming. It also will provide highly targeted advertising delivery. For the last 15 years, Mr. Chiddix has served as senior vice president and chief technical officer for Time Warner Cable, headquartered in Stamford, Connecticut, and its predecessor companies. Mr. Chiddix has been deeply involved in the introduction of virtually every new cable technology since the mid-seventies. He played a pioneering role in exploring the use of broadband optical fiber technology in cable television systems, which led to the universally adopted Hybrid Fiber Coax network architecture for cable systems. In 1994, he accepted, on behalf of Time Warner Cable, an Engineering Emmy Award for this work. He led the upgrade of Time Warner's Queens, New York, system to 150 channels (1-GHz bandwidth), and was the architect of Time Warner's Full Service Network interactive television trial in Orlando, Florida. Mr. Chiddix has been in the cable television business for 30 years. He spent 15 years in a variety of operating positions with two cable companies in Hawaii. He was also founder and president of CRC Electronics, Inc., in Honolulu, which manufactured videotape playback, automated delay, and random-access commercial insertion systems. CRC was sold to Texscan in 1981. In 1986, he joined Time Warner Cable's corporate office. He also served for 8 years on the board of directors of CV-21, a cable television company in Fukuoka, Japan. Mr. Chiddix is a senior member and former director of the Society of Cable Television Engineers, a senior member of the Institute of Electrical and Electronics Engineers, and a member of the Cable Pioneers. Mr. Chiddix is a member of the Computer Science and Telecommunications Board. Mr. Chiddix currently serves on the committee studying broadband access and helped produce the CSTB report *The Unpredictable Certainty: Information Infrastructure Through 2000*.

John M. Cioffi, BSEE, 1978, Illinois; PhDEE, 1984, Stanford; Bell Laboratories, 1978-1984; IBM Research, 1984-1986; EE prof., Stanford, 1986-present. Cioffi founded Amati Com. Corp. in 1991 (purchased by TI in 1997) and was officer/director from 1991 to 1997. He currently is on the boards or advisory boards of BigBand Networks, Coppercom, GoDigital, Ikanos, Ionospan, Ishoni, IteX, Jubilant, Marvell, Kestrel, Charter Ventures, and Portview Ventures and is a member of the U.S. National Research Council's CSTB. Cioffi's specific interests are in the area of high-performance digital transmission. He has received various awards: member, National Academy of Engineering 2001; IEEE Kobayashi Medal (2001), IEEE Millennium Medal (2000), IEEE fellow (1996), IEE JJ Tomson Medal (2000), 1999 University of Illinois Oustanding Alumnus, 1991 IEEE Comm. Mag. best paper; 1995 ANSI T1 Outstanding Achievement Award; and NSF Presidential Investigator (1987-1992). Cioffi has published over 200 papers and holds over 40 patents, most of which are widely licensed, including basic patents on DMT, VDSL, and vectored transmission.

David D. Clark is a senior research scientist at MIT's Laboratory for Computer Science, where he is currently in charge of the Advanced Network Architecture group. Dr. Clark's research interests include networks, network protocols, operating systems, distributed systems, and computer and communications security. After receiving his Ph.D., he worked on the early stages of the ARPANET and on the development of token ring local area network technology. Since the mid-1970s, Dr. Clark has been involved in the development of the Internet. In the period 1981 to 1989, he acted as chief protocol architect for this development and chaired the Internet Activities Board. His current research area is protocols and architectures for very large and very high speed networks. Specific activities include extensions to the Internet to support real-time traffic, explicit allocation of service, pricing and new network technologies. In the security area, Dr. Clark participated in the early development of the multilevel secure Multics operating system. He developed an information security model that stresses integrity of data rather than disclosure control.

Dr. Clark is a fellow of the ACM and the IEEE and a member of the National Academy of Engineering. He received the ACM SIGCOMM award, the IEEE award in international communications, and the IEEE Hamming Award for his work on the Internet. He is a consultant to a number of companies and serves on a number of technical advisory boards. Dr. Clark is currently the chair of the Computer Science and Telecommunications Board. He chaired the committee that produced the CSTB report *Computers at Risk: Safe Computing in the Information Age*. He also served on the committees that produced the CSTB reports *Toward a National Research Network*, *Realizing the Information Future: The Internet and Beyond*, and *The Unpredictable Certainty: Information Infrastructure Through 2000*. Dr. Clark graduated from Swarthmore College in 1966 and received his Ph.D. from the Massachusetts Institute of Technology (MIT) in 1973.

Paul Green recently retired as director of Optical Networking Technology at Tellabs in Hawthorne, New York. He joined Tellabs in January 1997 after many years at IBM Research, and before that, at MIT Lincoln Laboratory. At Lincoln he developed the first operational spread spectrum system (1953), coinvented the first channel-adaptive receiver (Rake, 1958), invented planetary range-doppler mapping (1960), and worked on large digital seismic arrays for computerized discrimination between earthquakes and nuclear explosions. At IBM, his team pioneered peer networking, which later became standard in IBM's System Network Architecture. He initiated the WDM optical networking program there, which is credited with the first operational all-optical network (Rainbow-1 of 1991) and the first commercial WDM product, the IBM Muxmaster (1995). At Tellabs, his interests center on all-optical crossconnects, the key building block of all-optical networking. Dr. Green received the IEEE Simon Ramo Medal in 1991, the Association of Computing Machinery's Annual Communication Award in 1994, and a number of IBM patent awards. He is a member of the National Academy of Engineering. He has been president of both the IEEE Information Theory Society and the IEEE Communication Society.

Kevin Kahn is an Intel Fellow, the corporation's highest technical position, and currently the director of the Wireless Technology Lab, a corporate advanced development and research lab in Intel's Corporate Technology Group. Additionally, he helps drive communications strategies and policy for the corporation and coordinates a variety of cross-corporate networking research. Some of his primary current focuses are broadband access to the home, home networking, wireless LANs, and Internet issues bearing on these topics. Throughout his 25-year career with Intel, he has worked in system software development, operating systems, processor architecture, and various strategic planning roles on programs involving most of the processors Intel has developed during the period. He has held both management and senior individual contributor roles. He was the co-chair of the Universal ADSL Working Group, an industry alliance dedicated to accelerating the deployment of consumer ADSL services for higher speed Internet access, and served as a member of the Board of Directors of the DSL Forum. He serves on a variety of NSF and NAS committees and panels, and is a member of the FCC Technical Advisory Committee. He holds a B.Sc. in mathematics from Manhattan College, and M.S. and Ph.D. degrees in computer science from Purdue University.

Richard Lowenberg is a tele-community planner, environmental designer, media artist, and cultural activist. He has been executive director of the Davis Community Network and Yolo Area Regional Network in California since 1996. In this position he has been a consultant to the California Smart Communities Project and was principal coordinator of "WaterWorks," an online civic decision-support project, funded by the Corporation for Public Broadcasting (CivNet program), Army Corps of Engineers, USGS National Spatial Data Infrastructure Program, and ESRI, Inc. He currently serves on the Board of the Association for Community Networking, on the Steering Committee of the Global Community Networking Congress, and on Computer Professionals for Social Responsibility's DIAC program committee. Mr. Lowenberg was founding director of the Telluride Institute and its InfoZone Program, in Colorado, from 1985 to 1996. He served on the governing board of the Colorado Advanced Technology Institute's Rural Telecommunications Project from 1994 to 1997; Web authored the 1995 U.S. Economic Development Administration funded "Rural Telecommunications Investment Guide," and was a principal participant on the 1996 NTIA-TIIAP funded "Maps for People" project. He has been and continues to be a presenter, writer, and consultant on "Community Networking," "Tele-Community Development," "Networked Economics," and "Information Ecology" in the United States, Europe, Latin America, and Japan; and his telecommunications and community development projects have received federal, state and local government grants; university and corporate support; international media coverage and recognition. Richard Lowenberg's media, performance, and installation art works have pioneered in the integration of art, science, technology and ecology, with a primary focus on the social implications of the "Information Revolutions." He has received numerous grants and awards, including from the National Endowment for the Arts, and has presented exhibitions and performances internationally, including at the Whitney Museum, San Francisco Museum of Modern Arts, Kunstmuseum

Dusseldorf, Venice Biennale, and MIT List Center for Visual Arts. Most recently he has been "Artist in Bioregional Residence," University of California at Davis.

Clifford Lynch has been the director of the Coalition for Networked Information (CNI) since July 1997. CNI, jointly sponsored by the Association of Research Libraries and Educause, includes about 200-member organizations concerned with the use of information technology and networked information to enhance scholarship and intellectual productivity. Prior to joining CNI, Dr. Lynch spent 18 years at the University of California Office of the President, the last 10 as director of Library Automation. Dr. Lynch, who holds a Ph.D. in computer science from the University of California, Berkeley, is an adjunct professor at Berkeley's School of Information Management and Systems. He is a past president of the American Society for Information Science and a fellow of the American Association for the Advancement of Science and the National Information Standards Organization. Dr. Lynch currently serves on the Internet 2 Applications Council and the National Digital Preservation Strategy Advisory Board of the Library of Congress and was a member of the National Research Council committee that recently published *The Digital Dilemma: Intellectual Property in the Information Infrastructure.*

Richard Metzger is partner in the law firm Lawler, Metzger & Milkman LLC in Washington, D.C. Mr. Metzger brings direct insight into federal telecommunications regulation and policy making, having served as deputy chief and subsequently chief, of the Common Carrier Bureau of the Federal Communications Commission from 1994 to 1998. In these positions, Mr. Metzger was actively involved in the FCC's implementation of the Telecommunications Act of 1996. In particular, during his tenure in the Bureau, he supervised the preparation of recommendations to the Commission on a wide range of critical issues, including rules governing interconnection, access charge reform, and universal service. Prior to joining the Commission, Mr. Metzger was a member of the law firm of Rogers and Wells, resident in the Washington, D.C. office. His areas of emphasis in private practice included telecommunications, antitrust, and public utility regulation. Mr. Metzger is a graduate of Williams College, Phi Beta Kappa. He received a J.D. degree from Georgetown University Law Center.

Elizabeth Mynatt is an assistant professor in the College of Computing at the Georgia Institute of Technology. There she directs the research program in "Everyday Computing"—examining the implications of having computation continuously present in many aspects of everyday life. In home environments, Dr. Mynatt aims to enable older adults to continue living independently, through the use of future home technologies, as opposed to moving to institutional care settings. Dr. Mynatt is an internationally recognized expert in the areas of ubiquitous computing and assistive technologies. Prior to her current position, she worked for 3 years at Xerox PARC—the birthplace of ubiquitous computing—alongside its inventor, Mark Weiser. Her research explored how to augment everyday places and objects with computational capabilities. She has chaired multiple conferences on computer interface technologies and auditory displays, published numerous articles, and is an active leader in her field. Dr. Mynatt is a Sloan Research Fellow. Her research is supported by multiple grants from the National Science Foundation including a 5-year NSF CAREER award. Dr. Mynatt is the Associate Director of the Georgia Tech Graphics, Visualization and Usability (GVU) Center, and is responsible for research and educational objectives in human-computer interaction, including a highly regarded HCI Master's Degree Program that bridges computing, psychology, design and communication. Dr. Mynatt received her Ph.D. in computer science at Georgia Tech under the guidance of Dr. James Foley. Her dissertation work pioneered creating nonspeech auditory interfaces from graphical interfaces to enable blind computer users to work with modern computer applications.

Eli M. Noam has been a professor of economics and finance at Columbia Business School since 1976. In 1990, after having served for 3 years as Commissioner with the New York State Public Service Commission, he returned to Columbia. He is the director of the Columbia Institute for Tele-Information. CITI is an independent university-based research center focusing on strategy, management, and policy issues in telecommunications, computing, and electronic mass media. In addition to leading CITI's research activities, Dr. Noam initiated the MBA concentration in the Management of Entertainment, Communications, and Media at the Business School and the Virtual Institute of Information, an independent, Web-based research facility. He has also taught at Columbia Law School and Princeton University's Economics Department and Woodrow Wilson School. Noam has published over 19 books and 400 articles in economic journals, law reviews, and interdisciplinary journals. His books include the authored, edited, or co-authored volumes *Telecommunications in Europe; Television in Europe; Telecommunications Regulation: Today and Tomorrow; Video Media Competition; Services in Transition: The Impact of Information Technology in the Service Industry; The Law of International Telecommunications in the United States; The International Market in Film and Television Programs; Telecommunications in the Pacific Basin; Private Networks, Public Objectives; Global and Local Networks; Asymmetric Deregula-*

tion: The Dynamics of Telecommunications Policies in Europe and the United States; Telecommunications in Western Asia and the Middle East; Telecommunications in Latin America; Telecommunications in Africa; The New Investment Theory of Real Options and Its Implications for Telecommunications Economics; and *Interconnecting the Network of Networks* (Spring 2001). His forthcoming books include *Media Concentration in the United States* and *The Dark Sides of the Internet*. He has served on the editorial boards of Columbia University Press as well as of several academic journals. He was a member of the advisory boards for the federal government's FTS-2000 telecommunications network, the IRS's computer system reorganization, and the National Computer Systems Laboratory. He is a member of the Council on Foreign Relations. He received an AB (*Phi Beta Kappa*), M.A., Ph.D. (Economics), and J.D. from Harvard University.

Dipankar Raychaudhuri is currently a professor, Electrical and Computer Engineering Department, and director, WINLAB (Wireless Information Network Lab), at Rutgers University. He has previously held progressively responsible corporate R&D positions in the telecom/networking area, including chief scientist, Iospan Wireless (2000 to 2001); assistant general manager and department head, Systems Architecture, NEC USA C&C Research Laboratories (1993 to 1999); and head, Broadband Communications Research, Sarnoff Corp. (1990 to 1992). During the period from 1995 to 1999, his research group at NEC USA developed one of the world's first pre-commercial broadband wireless local area networks ("WATMnet") for use in the 5-Ghz band. His research and new technology development experience also includes VSAT networks (1984 to 1987), digital TV/HDTV (1988 to 1991), ATM/IP switching and QoS (1993 to 1997), multimedia network processor (1993 to 1995), and MIMO/OFDM system (2000 to 2001). Dr. Raychaudhuri obtained his B.Tech (Hons) from the Indian Institute of Technology, Kharagpur, in 1976 and the M.S. and Ph.D degrees from SUNY, Stony Brook, in 1978 and 1979. He is a fellow of the IEEE.

Bob Rowe has been a commissioner of the Montana Public Service Commission since 1993. His educational credentials include a B.A. from Lewis and Clark College; a J.D. from the University of Oregon; and additional graduate work in public administration and public policy at Harvard University's Kennedy School Executive Program. Mr. Rowe is a past president of the National Association of Regulatory Utility Commissioners (NARUC) and a past chair of the NARUC Telecommunications Committee. He is a member of the National Regulatory Research Institute's board of directors, the Michigan State University Institute of Public Utilities Advisory Committee, and the New Mexico State University Center for

Public Utilities Advisory Council. He is also a member of the Montana Food Bank Network's board of directors and a member of the State Bar of Montana Professionalism Committee. He is past chair of the Regional Oversight Committee for US West. Before election to the Montana Public Service Commission, he was in public interest practice; was a VISTA volunteer; and was a public interest lawyer, specializing in utility law and policy; he also worked for the Montana Legal Service Association, a private nonprofit organization, and he represented a variety of community organizations in rate cases and other utility-related proceedings. He researched and wrote on customer-oriented utility policy for the National Consumer Center, the National Center for Appropriate Technology, and other organizations.

Steven S. Wildman is director of the James H. and Mary B. Quello Center for Telecommunication Management and Law and the James H. Quello Chair of Telecommunications Studies at Michigan State University. The center, and through it his chair, is endowed, supporting broad-based and affiliation-dependent research in support of policy making. Previously, Dr. Wildman was an associate professor at Northwestern University and director of its Program in Telecommunications Science, Management, and Policy. His research interests include determinants of market structure and economic aspects of information and communication. He has served as a consultant on matters relating to broadcasting, cable television, and voice and nonvoice telecommunications. His publications include *International Trade in Films and Television Programs* (1988), *Electronic Services Networks: A Business and Public Policy Challenge* (1991), *Video Economics* (1992), and *Making Universal Service Policy: Enhancing the Process Through Multidisciplinary Evaluation* (1999). Professor Wildman received his Ph.D. from Stanford University.

E

List of Acronyms

ADSL   asymmetric digital subscriber line
ANSI   American National Standards Institute
ASIC   application specific integrated circuit
ATM   asynchronous transfer mode
BLEC   building-focused local exchange carriers
CATV   originally community antenna television; now synonymous with cable TV
CDMA   code-division multiple access
CDPD   cellular digital packet data
CLEC   competitive local exchange carrier
CO   central office
CPE   customer premises equipment
DARPA   Defense Advanced Research Projects Agency
DBS   direct broadcast satellite
DHCP   dynamic host configuration protocol
DLC   digital loop carrier
DLEC   data local exchange carrier
DMT   discrete multitone transmission
DSL   digital subscriber line
DSLAM   DSL access multiplexer
DSP   digital signal processor
ETSI   European Telecommunications Standards Institute
FCC   Federal Communications Commission
FEXT   far end cross talk
FTTC   fiber to the curb

FTTH	fiber to the home
GEOS	geo-synchronous orbit satellites
HDSL	high-speed digital subscriber line
HDTV	high definition television
HFC	hybrid fiber coax
HPNA	Home Phone Networking Alliance
IEEE	Institute of Electrical and Electronics Engineers
IETF	Internet Engineering Task Force
ILEC	incumbent local exchange carrier
IP	Internet protocol
ISDN	integrated services digital network
ISP	Internet service provider
ITU	International Telecommunication Union
LAN	local area network
LEC	local exchange carrier
LEOS	low earth orbit satellites
LMDS	local multipoint distribution services
LOS	line of sight
MAC	medium access control
MDUs	multi-dwelling units
MIMO	multiple in, multiple out
MMDS	multipoint multichannel distribution service
MSO	multiple system operator
NEXT	near end cross talk
NII	national information infrastructure
NSF	National Science Foundation
NSP	native signal processor
NTIA	National Telecommunications and Information Administration
OFDM	orthogonal frequency division multiplexing
PCS	personal communications service
PEG	public, educational, and government
PON	passive optical network
POTS	plain old telephone service
PPP	point-to-point protocol
PSD	power spectral density
QAM	quadrature amplitude modulation
QOS	quality of service
RADSL	rate adaptive digital subscriber line
RF	radio frequency
RLP	radio link protocol
SDMI	Secure Digital Music Initiative
SDSL	symmetric digital subscriber line
SDTV	standard definition television

SONET	synchronous optical network
TDM	time division multiplexing
TDMA	time division multiple access
UDP	user datagram protocol
USB	universal serial bus
VADSL	very-high data rate asymmetric DSL
VDSL	very high speed digital subscriber line
VLSI	very large scale integrated circuit
VOD	video on demand
VoDSL	voice over DSL
VoIP	voice over Internet Protocol
VPN	virtual private network
VTIP	video telephony over Internet Protocol (IP)
W3C	World Wide Web Consortium
WAN	wide area network
WDM	wavelength-division multiplexing
WLAN	wireless local area network
WLL	wireless local loop